COMMAND
PERFORMANCE

PAUL B. STARES

COMMAND PERFORMANCE

The Neglected Dimension of European Security

THE BROOKINGS INSTITUTION
Washington, D.C.

Copyright © 1991

THE BROOKINGS INSTITUTION

1775 Massachusetts Avenue, N.W., Washington, D.C. 20036

Library of Congress Cataloging-in-Publication data:

Stares, Paul B.
    Command performance : the neglected dimension of
European security / Paul B. Stares.
        p.   cm.
    Includes bibliographical references and index.
    ISBN 0-8157-8112-1—ISBN 0-8157-8111-3 (pbk.)
    1. Command and control systems—Europe.
2. Europe—National security.   3. North Atlantic Treaty
Organization.   I. Title.
    UB212.S73   1991

355.3'3041'094—dc20   91-12397
                                                          CIP

9 8 7 6 5 4 3 2 1

The paper used in this publication meets the minimum requirements of the American National Standard for Information Sciences–Permanence of paper for Printed Library
Materials, ANSI Z39.48-1984

ⒷTHE BROOKINGS INSTITUTION

The Brookings Institution is an independent organization devoted to nonpartisan research, education, and publication in economics, government, foreign policy, and the social sciences generally. Its principal purposes are to aid in the development of sound public policies and to promote public understanding of issues of national importance.

The Institution was founded on December 8, 1927, to merge the activities of the Institute for Government Research, founded in 1916, the Institute of Economics, founded in 1922, and the Robert Brookings Graduate School of Economics and Government, founded in 1924.

The Board of Trustees is responsible for the general administration of the Institution, while the immediate direction of the policies, program, and staff is vested in the President, assisted by an advisory committee of the officers and staff. The by-laws of the Institution state: "It is the function of the Trustees to make possible the conduct of scientific research, and publication, under the most favorable conditions, and to safeguard the independence of the research staff in the pursuit of their studies and in the publication of the results of such studies. It is not a part of their function to determine, control, or influence the conduct of particular investigations or the conclusions reached."

The President bears final responsibility for the decision to publish a manuscript as a Brookings book. In reaching his judgment on the competence, accuracy, and objectivity of each study, the President is advised by the director of the appropriate research program and weighs the views of a panel of expert outside readers who report to him in confidence on the quality of the work. Publication of a work signifies that it is deemed a competent treatment worthy of public consideration but does not imply endorsement of conclusions or recommendations.

The Institution maintains its position of neutrality on issues of public policy in order to safeguard the intellectual freedom of the staff. Hence interpretations or conclusions in Brookings publications should be understood to be solely those of the authors and should not be attributed to the Institution, to its trustees, officers, or other staff members, or to the organizations that support its research.

In memory of my father

Foreword

FOR MORE than four decades NATO has dedicated itself to deterring the threat of Soviet aggression. Now, the ending of the cold war and the demise of the Warsaw Pact demand a basic change in Western security arrangements. Until an effective cooperative security regime emerges in Europe, the North Atlantic Treaty Organization must adapt to the radically altered circumstances and rededicate itself to meeting new challenges to peace and security in the region. This goal entails more than reducing force levels, lowering combat readiness, and reforming military doctrine; it requires reorienting the underlying command system of the alliance.

As Paul B. Stares argues in this book, NATO's command arrangements have not received the attention they deserve. Traditionally, military analysts and defense planners have focused on manpower and weaponry rather than the adequacy of the vitally important command arrangements on which military forces depend to function and operate effectively in crisis and war. Stares explores the complex relationship between command system performance and military effectiveness and uses this analysis to assess NATO's current command arrangements. This study exposes serious deficiencies in many areas important to future European security. Accordingly, the author offers possible remedies in the conclusion of the study.

Paul B. Stares, a senior fellow in the Foreign Policy Studies program, acknowledges the assistance of many people who have helped him in this study. A great intellectual debt is owed to his colleagues Bruce G. Blair and John D. Steinbruner, whose seminal work in the field of command system performance stimulated much of the thinking behind the study. The author is grateful to Daniel Lindley III for outstanding research assistance at the outset of the project and to Drew Portocarrero for skillfully guiding it to completion. Sara Jamieson, Rebecca Rubin, Kim Motylewski, Craig A. Shelburne, and Kyle J. Ray also provided research assistance.

For making field research in Europe possible, the author gratefully acknowledges the help of the Office of the Chief of Staff, U.S. Army, particularly Colonel Don Snider; the U.S. Mission to NATO; Headquarters, the British Army of the Rhine; Headquarters, Allied Air Forces, Central Europe; Headquarters, U.S. Army Europe; and the MITRE Corporation. More than one hundred interviews were carried out in Washington, D.C., and Europe with serving or retired officials knowledgeable about the workings of NATO's command system. These interviews were conducted on the understanding that they would not be for attribution. The author thanks these individuals, without whom the study would not have been possible. The hospitality of Janet Cooper and Harry Dean, Edward and Nancy Dove, Ken Francis, Karin Kessler, Detlev Lange, Eileen E. Stares, and Glen and Anthea Vaal is also greatly appreciated.

Roger Beaumont, Richard K. Betts, Bruce G. Blair, Stephen Biddle, Colonel Alan D. Campen (retired), Joshua M. Epstein, Air Commodore Gabriel I. Ferenczy (retired), General Martin Farndale (retired), Ambassador Gordon Smith, Jeffrey T. Richelson, John D. Steinbruner, and particularly Colonel Owen Wormser (retired) made valuable comments on various drafts of the study. Paul M. Cole, C.H.U. de Frères, Christine Edmunds, Robert S. Litwak, Michael K. MccGwire, and Nancy E. Soderberg also deserve acknowledgment for their support and encouragement.

Theresa B. Walker edited the manuscript, and Annette D. Leak incorporated revisions. Adrianne Goins and Vernon Kelley verified the book's factual content, Susan Woollen prepared the manuscript for publication, and Fred Kepler prepared the index.

Funding for this study was provided by the Carnegie Corporation of New York and the John D. and Catherine T. MacArthur Foundation. The author and Brookings are grateful for that support.

The views expressed in this study are those of the author and should not be ascribed to the persons or foundations whose assistance is acknowledged above, or to the trustees, officers, or other staff members of the Brookings Institution.

Bruce K. MacLaury
President

April 1991
Washington, D.C.

Contents

Abbreviations
and Acronyms

AAFCE	Allied Air Forces Central Europe
AAWHQ	AFCENT alternate wartime headquarters
ACCHAN	Allied Command Channel
ACCIS	automated command and control information system
ACCS	Air Command and Control System
ACE	Allied Command Europe
ACE HIGH	Allied Command Europe Communications Network (NATO)
ACLANT	Allied Command Atlantic
ACO	airspace control order
ACOC	Airborne Combat Operations Center
ACU	air control unit
AD	air directive
ADOLT	Air Defense Liaison Teams
AFATDS	Advanced Field Artillery Tactical Data System
AFCENT	Allied Forces Central Europe
AFNORTH	Allied Forces Northern Europe
AFSATCOM	Air Force Satellite Communications System
AFSOUTH	Allied Forces Southern Europe
ASAS	All Source Analysis System
ASAT	antisatellite; antisatellite weapon
ASOC	Air Support Operations Center
ATACS	Army Tactical Communications System (U.S.)
ATAF	Allied Tactical Air Force
ATM	air task message
ATO	air task order
ATOC	Allied Tactical Operations Center
ATR	air tasking request
AUTODIN	Automatic Digital Network
AUTOVON	Automatic Voice Network
AWACS	Airborne Warning and Control System
AWHQ	alternate wartime headquarters

BALTAP	Baltic Approaches Command
BDE	brigade
BEF	British Expeditionary Force
BICES	Battlefield Information Collection and Exploitation System
BITS	Battlefield Information and Targeting System
BN	battalion
BRISS	British Intelligence Support System
BRITNIC	British National Intelligence Cell
CAOC	Combined Air Operations Center
CAP	combat air patrol
CBL	cross-border links
CCIRM	Collection Coordination Intelligence Requirements Management System
CCIS	Command, Control, and Information System
CENTAG	Central Army Group Central Europe
CFE	conventional forces in Europe
CH	Chain Home stations
CHL	Chain Home Low stations
CIMEX	Civil Emergency Exercise
CINCENT	commander in chief, Allied Forces, Central Europe
CINCEUR	commander in chief, Europe
CINCHAN	allied commander in chief, Channel
CINCPAC	commander in chief, Pacific
CINCSOUTH	commander in chief, Allied Forces, Southern Europe
CINCUKAIR	commander in chief, U.K. Air Forces
CINCUSAFE	commander in chief, U.S. Air Forces, Europe
CINCUSAREUR	commander in chief, U.S. Army, Europe
CINCUSNAVEUR	commander in chief, U.S. Naval Forces, Europe
CIP	Central Region Improvement Program
CMO	collection management office
COIC	Combat Operations Intelligence Center
COMAAFCE	commander, Allied Air Forces, Central Europe
COMCEN	mobile communications center
COMCENTAG	commander, Central Army Group, Central Europe
COMINT	communications intelligence
COMNORTHAG	commander, Northern Army Group
CP	command post
CRC	Conduct Reporting Center
CRINCA	Central Region Intelligence Communications Architecture
CRJCMO	Central Region Joint Collection Management Office
CRJOIC	Central Region Joint Intelligence Center
CRP	Conduct Reporting Post
CSCE	Conference on Security and Cooperation in Europe

CSMS	Counter Surprise Military System
CUSRPG	Canada-U.S. Regional Planning Group
DCINCEUR	deputy commander in chief, Europe
DCS	Defense Communications System
DOD	Department of Defense
DOO	daily operations order
DPC	Defense Planning Committee
DSCS	Defense Satellite Communications System
DTM	defense tasking message
DTO	defense tasking order
EACIC	Echelon-Above-Corps Intelligence Center
ECMO	European collection management office
ETS	European Telephone System
EUCOM	European Command
FACP	Forward Air Control Party
FAFIO	Federal Armed Forces Intelligence Office
FLTSATCOM	Fleet Satellite Communications
FOSIC	Fleet Ocean Surveillance Information Command
FOSIF	Fleet Ocean Surveillance Information Facility
GDP	General Defense Plan
GENIC	German National Intelligence Cell
GLCM	ground-launched cruise missile
HF	high frequency
HILEX	High-Level Exercise
HQ	headquarters
I&W	indications and warning
IBERLANT	Iberian Atlantic Command
INF	intermediate-range nuclear forces
IVSN	initial voice switched network
JCMO	joint collection management office
JCS	Joint Chiefs of Staff
JIC	Joint Intelligence Center
JSTARS	Joint Surveillance and Target Attack Radar System
JTIDS	Joint Tactical Information Distribution System
LANDJUT	Allied Land Forces Jutland
LERTCON	Alert Condition
LOCE	Joint Tactical Fusion-Limited Operational Capability Europe
LOS	line of sight
MC	Military Committee
MEDCENT	Mediterranean Central Area Command
MCE	modular control equipment
MIDS	Multifunction Information Distribution System
MNC	major NATO commander
MSC	major subordinate commander

MW	microwave
NAC	North Atlantic Council
NADGE	NATO Air Defense Ground Environment
NCA	National Command Authorities
NCCIS	NATO Command, Control, and Information System
NDDN	Norwegian Defence Digital Network
NICS	NATO Integrated Communications System
NICSCOA	NATO Integrated Communications System, Central Operating Authority
NORECHAN	Northeast Channel Sub-Area Command
NORLANT	North Atlantic Area Command
NOSC	NATO Operations Support Cell
NORTHAG	Northern Army Group Central Europe
NTTS	NATO Terrestrial Transmission System
OPS	operations
PSC	principal subordinate commander
PTT	postal, telephone, and telegraph
PWHQ	primary wartime headquarters
RAF	Royal Air Force
REFORGER	Return of Forces to Germany
RPV	remotely piloted vehicle
SACEUR	supreme allied commander, Europe
SACLANT	supreme allied commander, Atlantic
SAM	surface-to-air missile
SATCOM	satellite communications
SCARS	Status Control Alerting and Reporting System
SCC	SHAPE Command Center
SCEPC	Senior Civil Emergency Planning Committee
SD&IC	System Design and Integration Contract
SGT	satellite ground terminal
SHAPE	Supreme Headquarters Allied Powers, Europe
SHD	special handling detachment
SHORAD	short-range air defense
SITCEN	Situation Centre
SOC	Sector Operations Center
SQOC	Squadron Operations Center
STANAG	NATO Standardization Agreement
TACAIR	Tactical Air
TACFIRE	Tactical Fire Direction
TACP	Tactical Air Control Party
TACS	Tactical Air Control System
TARE	telegraph automatic relay equipment
TASS	Tactical Automated Switching System
TCF	technical control facility
TENCAP	tactical exploitation of national capabilities

TFC	Tactical Fusion Center
TOC	Tactical Operations Center
TREDS	Tactical Reconnaissance Demonstration System (Metro Tango)
TRI-TAC	U.S. joint tactical communications equipment
UKADGE	U.K. Air Defense Ground Equipment
UKAIR	U.K. Air Forces
USAFE	U.S. Air Force, Europe
USAREUR	U.S. Army, Europe
USCINCEUR	commander in chief, U.S. European Command
USCINCLANT	commander in chief, U.S. Atlantic Command
USEUCOM	U.S. European Command
USNAVEUR	U.S. Navy, Europe
VF	voice frequency
VHF	very high frequency
WEU	Western European Union
WHIDDS	War Headquarters Information Dissemination and Display System
WHNS	Wartime Host-Nation Support
WINTEX	Winter Exercise
WISE	Warning Indications Systems, Europe
WOC	Wing Operations Center
WWIMS	Worldwide Warning Indicator Monitoring System
WWMCCS	Worldwide Military Command and Control System

CHAPTER ONE

Introduction

FOR OVER forty years NATO has been preoccupied with the task of deterring and, if necessary, defending itself against deliberate aggression by the Warsaw Pact. With the collapse of Soviet hegemony in Eastern Europe and the demise of the Warsaw Pact as a serious military threat, that need has patently lessened if not disappeared entirely; new challenges to peace and stability now demand attention. The end of the cold war, however, offers more than a pressing reason to focus on the future. It also provides a valuable opportunity to reflect on the lessons of the past. Some may feel a critical reevaluation of NATO's military posture and policy toward the Soviet threat is unwarranted since aggression was successfully deterred and the West ultimately prevailed, while others may doubt its practical value now that the situation in Europe has radically altered. Such views, however, would be complacent and shortsighted. As this book will argue, NATO has consistently neglected a vital component of its security arrangements, which not only heightened the risk of war occurring *inadvertently* but also seriously jeopardized the alliance's hopes of defending itself in the manner planned. The relevance of this component, moreover, has not disappeared with the passing of the cold war. Indeed it remains central to the task of ensuring long-term peace and stability in Europe.

The neglected component of NATO's security arrangements concerns the adequacy of the command system that the alliance established to warn of threatening developments, harness its collective military power to deter attack, and orchestrate its defensive operations should deterrence have failed. In a fundamental sense the command system is what made NATO a true military alliance rather than just a loose collection of states faced with a common threat. Without it NATO's mutual security

1

guarantees would have had little meaning and consequently little deterrent value. Despite its critical importance to both deterrence and defense, NATO's command system has attracted little attention from those professionally concerned with European security. Although the military balance and NATO's defense requirements have been subjected to repeated and often sophisticated assessments, the adequacy of the command system that the alliance would rely on to prepare for war and, if necessary, fight one has rarely if ever been questioned let alone systematically studied.[1] For this reason NATO's command system can justifiably be called the neglected dimension of European security.

That something so important should have been overlooked for so long largely reflects the predominant focus of military planning and defense analysis, which typically concentrates on aggregate force levels and weapons system characteristics rather than on the operational dimensions of military power. Even the critics of this "bean counting" approach, as it is disparagingly called, who have endeavored to simulate the interaction of forces in combat by using prescribed mathematical models to indicate relative attrition and movement, have yet to account realistically for the role of command system performance.[2] These criticsms echo earlier ones made about the standard approach to U.S.-Soviet strategic force balance assessments that typically consist of static comparisons of each side's nuclear arsenals, or at best, cost-exchange

1. Nevertheless some useful preliminary research has been done. See Robert F. Coulam and Gregory W. Fischer, "Problems of Command and Control in a Major European War," in *Advances in Information Processing in Organizations,* vol. 2 (Greenwich, Conn.: JAI Press Inc., 1985), pp. 211–68; John G. Hines and Phillip A. Petersen, "NATO and the Changing Soviet Concept of Control for Theater War," *Signal,* vol. 41 (May 1987), pp. 125–39; John P. Crecine, "C³I across the Seams of Military Organizations," in Gen. Jack N. Merritt, Gen. Robert Reed, and Roger Weissinger-Baylon, eds., *Crisis Decision Making in the Atlantic Alliance: Perspectives on Deterrence* (Menlo Park, Calif.: Strategic Decisions Press, 1987), pp. 26-1–26-5; and Desmond Ball, "Controlling Theater Nuclear War," Working Paper 138 (Canberra: Australian National University, October 1987).

2. For the European military balance, two studies did attempt to weight the aggregated fire power scores according to numbers of personnel allocated to command and control (defined as the size of headquarters staff) on each side. Besides representing a very narrow conception of command and control, the correlation between the numbers of headquarters personnel and military effectiveness is highly questionable. See Barry R. Posen, "Is NATO Decisively Outnumbered?" *International Security,* vol. 12 (Spring 1988), pp. 196–97. Posen uses methodology borrowed from the Office of the Assistant Secretary of Defense for Program Analysis and Evaluation, NATO *Center Region Military Balance Study, 1978–1984* (Department of Defense, 1979), pp. I-22–I-25.

calculations to indicate relative vulnerabilities under different attack scenarios. The role of the supporting command, control, communications, and intelligence systems (c^3I) that these forces depend on to survive attack and execute their mission is rarely discussed.[3] To be fair, there are signs that the importance of command system performance—hereafter abbreviated to command performance—to crisis stability and wartime effectiveness is beginning to receive the attention it deserves, though this appreciation is still largely confined to the realm of nuclear operations. While it receives some perfunctory genuflection, command performance is generally ignored in the study of conventional forces. Command performance represents, therefore, the neglected dimension of conventional defense analysis.

Command Performance and Conventional Defense Analysis

The fundamental purpose of a military command system is to apply force in the right place, at the right time, and in the right amount.[4] Command systems, therefore, serve both a positive and negative control function. In the positive sense they enable the rational and purposeful use of an armed force in pursuit of desired objectives set usually but not exclusively by higher political authorities. Such objectives may require, for example, raising the operational readiness of the force in preparation for possible use whether it be for defensive or offensive purposes, deploying it from its peacetime locations, and ultimately directing its actions in battle against an enemy. In the negative sense, command systems also serve to prevent military force from being used either prematurely, illegitimately, or indiscriminately in peacetime and in war. Both positive and negative control functions entail a constant and cyclical process of monitoring the external environment and internal status of the force, processing the collected information, deciding what actions to take in accordance with desired objectives, communicating

3. The most eloquent and compelling critique of the traditional focus of analysis can be found in Bruce G. Blair, *Strategic Command and Control: Redefining the Nuclear Threat* (Brookings, 1985), pp. 1–11. See also Ashton B. Carter, John D. Steinbruner, and Charles A. Zraket, eds., *Managing Nuclear Operations* (Brookings, 1987).

4. F. M. Snyder, "Command and Control and Uncertainty," *Naval War College Review*, vol. 32 (March–April 1979), p. 109.

the resultant directives to the appropriate force components, and finally registering the results for the process to begin again.[5] It is not surprising, therefore, that some liken the functions of a military command system to the workings of the human central nervous system.

Given the critical role of command systems to the existence and operation of a military force, it is especially puzzling that command performance should be essentially ignored as a factor in military force assessments. Several reasons help explain this oversight.

First, the generally poor appreciation of the importance of command and control to military effectiveness owes much to the way historians have recorded military operations in the past. The physical task of directing and controlling forces in crisis and war is rarely if ever discussed. When command problems have arisen, sometimes with calamitous consequences, they have usually been treated as aberrations rather than as examples of a recurring phenomenon. As one historian who has examined the historical evolution of command systems observes, "Save perhaps for the occasional intercepted or misunderstood message or the broken-down radio, it is indeed possible to study military history for years and hardly notice that the problem exists."[6] Furthermore, those who have distilled military experience in search of the most critical factors contributing to defeat and victory in battle—surprise, concentration of force, speed of maneuver, and deception to name a few—forget or ignore how much they rely in one way or another on command performance.

Second, command systems are not viewed as military assets or symbols of military power in the same way manpower and weaponry are perceived. They do not inflict casualties on an enemy, incur damage, or occupy territory. Like the equally important and equally undervalued

5. There are many variations to this basic description of the command process, but they are all essentially the same. See Maj. George E. Orr, *Combat Operations C³I: Fundamentals and Interactions* (Maxwell Air Force Base, Ala.: Air University Press, 1983), pp. 23–46.

6. Martin van Creveld, *Command in War* (Harvard University Press, 1985), p. 11. Brian Bond, in his review of van Creveld's book, underlines this observation. Brian Bond, "Battlefield C³I throughout History," *International Security,* vol. 11 (Spring 1987), pp. 125–29. Soviet military history, by contrast, accords more attention to the role of "troop control," as indicated by numerous articles on this subject in the publication *Voyenno-Istoricheskiy Zhurnal* (*Military History Journal*). See also Roger A. Beaumont, "Command Method: A Gap in Military Historiography," *Naval War College Review,* vol. 31 (Winter 1979), pp. 61–74.

contribution of logistics, command systems essentially play a supporting role, though one that can make a critical difference to the outcome of a military operation. This perceptual problem, as will become clear during this study, has had larger ramifications in affecting the priority given to command and control in resource allocation decisions and military readiness in general.

Third, the nature of the subject has done little to encourage or facilitate rigorous investigation. On closer examination, it covers an enormous subject area with frustratingly indistinct boundaries. This unfortunate characteristic has led to a seemingly endless and largely fruitless episto-mological debate on what command and control is all about. As one analyst has lamented, "One of the least controversial things that can be said about command and control (c^3) is that it is controversial, poorly understood, and subject to wildly different interpretations. The term can mean almost everything from military computers to the art of generalship: whatever the user wishes it to mean."[7] Many of those who endeavor to get beyond the definitional debate also frequently end up committing the common but understandable error of focusing on the more visible and tangible elements of command performance, notably, the technical components of a command system. In fact three largely interlocking dimensions characterize command performance: technical, organizational, and human.

The *technical* dimension consists essentially of the equipment that supports the basic process of command just outlined. The technical dimension would include, therefore, the operational performance of such devices as intelligence collection sensors for monitoring the environment, computers and other equipment to help process the collected data, and communications systems for passing information to and from military commanders.

The *organizational* dimension consists of the underlying command structure with its explicit hierarchy of authority (chain of command) and division of functional responsibilities. It also encompasses the formal and informal operating procedures of the organization. To a large extent these practices reflect the guiding "command philosophy" or "command doctrine" of the organization. Such doctrine embodies not only a

7. Kenneth L. Moll quoted in Orr, *Combat Operations C^3I: Fundamentals and Interactions*, p. 23.

conception of how specific missions or operational tasks are to be executed but also the degree to which decisionmaking authority is centralized or decentralized within the organization. The military force's command doctrine is inculcated in peacetime training and exercises to facilitate reaction to common commands and likely scenarios.[8]

Finally, the *human* dimension refers to the physiological and psychological processes that affect how people assimilate information, make decisions, and respond to commands under the stressful conditions of crisis and war.[9] Generalship or leadership, which loosely refers to the skill with which commanding officers use information and direct subordinates, also belongs to this dimension.[10]

The amorphous nature of the subject renders precise accounting for command performance an illusive if not wholly impossible task. Clearly it is much easier to assess the more obvious variables of military effectiveness, such as firepower, than it is to determine how the multifarious and intangible dimensions of a particular force's command system might affect overall performance and ultimately the likely outcome of a military engagement. Last but by no means least, the secrecy that typically surrounds the command arrangements of a military force adds to the difficulties of conducting research in this area.

Difficult though it may be to study, the contribution of command performance to military effectiveness is too important to be ignored or glossed over. After all, no serious student of human anatomy would overlook the vital functions of the central nervous system to the welfare of the body as a whole. Chapter 2, therefore, examines first in the abstract and then, with the assistance of several historical cases of well-known battles, the role and importance of command system performance to military effectiveness. These case studies illustrate implicitly how the growth in the size and complexity of armed forces, their increasing mobility and greater geographical reach, and the heightened

8. See Raanan Gissin, "Command, Control, and Communications Technology: Changing Patterns of Leadership in Combat Organizations," Ph.D. dissertation, Syracuse University, 1979, p. 48; Dan Horowitz, "Flexible Responsiveness and Military Strategy: The Case of the Israeli Army," *Policy Sciences*, vol. 1 (Summer 1970), pp. 194–96; Orr, *Combat Operations C³I*, pp. 87–90; and Snyder,"Command and Control and Uncertainty," pp. 110–11.

9. See Norman Dixon, *On the Psychology of Military Incompetence* (London: Futura, 1976); van Creveld, *Command in War*, pp. 262–63, 265, 273; and Roger A. Beaumont, *The Nerves of War: Emerging Issues in and References to Command and Control* (Washington: AFCEA International Press, 1986), pp. 28–33.

10. See John Keegan, *The Mask of Command* (Penguin, 1987).

tempo of combat operations have together increased the reliance on, and the challenges to, effective command performance. Chapter 3 focuses on these trends and, in particular, identifies the problems that have persistently undermined the operation of command systems in the past. Although this chapter concentrates predominantly on wartime operations, it also examines the challenges to command performance in crisis situations that contain the heightened risk of war.

To complement the discussion of the problems that typically degrade command performance, chapter 3 concludes by identifying the general factors that can enhance it. Both can be of help when assessing the likely adequacy of contemporary command systems under the duress of crisis and war. The analysis, however, represents a guide to inquiry rather than an explicit methodology for research that can produce precise quantifiable results. As will become clear, there are serious barriers and limitations to analysis of this kind. Nevertheless, when armed with an understanding of the key components of a command system, their operational charateristics, and the factors that typically affect performance, it is possible to reach some conclusions about the adequacy of the system to perform its intended functions. The in-depth study of NATO's command system that follows in the second half of the book demonstrates this approach.

Command Performance and NATO Crisis Management

NATO's command system, as described earlier, represents the organizational mechanism by which the alliance would fulfill its collective commitment to defend individual members from attack. At its apex stands the political consultative bodies to which the nations each send a permanent diplomatic representative. These bodies are responsible not only for overseeing and coordinating the daily activities of the alliance but also for authorizing increases in the military readiness of its forces should the threat of war suddenly loom large. This task would include alerting NATO's active military forces, mobilizing national reserves, and, if necessary, dispatching them to forward defense positions as laid out in NATO's General Defense Plan. Such measures would be implemented through NATO's military command organization, which overlays the national command systems of each member and, in theory, binds them together. This organization has been established on a regional basis, with each area having designated military commanders, peacetime and wartime headquarters with permanent staff, and supporting communications networks.

It is a fact of alliance life, however, that NATO's command system has no supranational authority. Sovereignty rests unequivocally with the national governments. As a result, NATO's political bodies must decide on what actions to take with the unanimous consent—or at least passive acquiescence—of every member nation. NATO is also entirely dependent on warning intelligence provided by the national representatives; it has no independent means to collect information or power to demand it. Furthermore, NATO's military forces remain firmly under national control in peacetime. Operational control is only relinquished and transferred to NATO ("chopped over" in the jargon) after explicit governmental approval has been given. Thus, except for some small, special-purpose multinational units, NATO's military commanders have no operational control over the forces they nominally command.

Given the nature of alliance decisionmaking and command arrangements, many military planners and independent defense experts have for a long time doubted NATO's capacity to respond quickly and effectively to sudden indications of warlike preparations by the Warsaw Pact. Their skepticism is also based in part on numerous historical studies that have shown that it is not the absence of warning but a failure of response that has caused so many states to succumb to surprise attack.[11] In all but the most unambiguously and universally threatening cases, it is anticipated that NATO would face serious difficulties in reaching consensus and unanimity on what actions to take. Depending on circumstances, a crisis might engender quite different reactions from alliance members. The relative proximity to events and different national perspectives could produce radically divergent appreciations of the situation and consequently differing policy prescriptions. Debilitating schisms might develop as a consequence between those states proposing precautionary military measures and those believing such actions either unnecessary

---

11. The seminal work on this topic is Richard K. Betts, *Surprise Attack: Lessons for Defense Planning* (Brookings, 1982). See also Air Chief Marshal Michael Armitage, "Identifying Crises," in Gen. John T. Chain, Jr., Gen. Robert Dixon, and Roger Weissinger-Baylon, eds., *Decision Making in the Atlantic Alliance: The Management of Political-Military Crises* (Menlo Park, Calif.: Strategic Decisions Press, 1986), pp. 12–19.

or potentially provocative. Given the difficulty of distinguishing purely defensive from offensive preparatory military acts, many leaders might hesitate before authorizing such actions in the belief that they might be misconstrued and make war more likely.[12]

The internal governmental debates could prove equally divisive for the same reasons. This problem seems particularly likely in coalition governments, of which there are usually several in NATO. Such cleavages would almost certainly become more difficult to reconcile as the risk of war intensifies. In particular, the immensely sensitive and, for NATO, unprecedented decision about whether to mobilize forces represents the greatest challenge to the cohesion of the alliance. Many are certain to view such a decision as tantamount to accepting the inevitability of war. Faced with these challenges it is not surprising that so many have feared the alliance would procrastinate or unravel completely in a serious crisis, with fateful consequences for deterrence and defense.

Until fairly recently, the difficulties facing alliance decisionmaking in war-threatening situations were widely considered to have grown even more formidable. The expansion of the Warsaw Pact's offensive military potential during the 1970s caused NATO to reappraise the amount of warning time that it could expect to receive before an invasion of Western Europe. What had previously been estimated at thirty days of warning time, which gave the alliance approximately a week to consult on what actions to take, was reduced in 1978 to fourteen days, leaving only four days for consultation.[13] What subsequently became known as the "short-warning" or "standing-start" attack scenario raised further doubts about whether the alliance could respond and authorize the necessary defensive countermeasures in time for them to be effective. It became clear from estimating the required lead time to implement certain precautionary measures, such as calling up reserves, chopping command authority over national forces to NATO, and activating the necessary logistical mechanisms to smooth the way for reinforcement and full-scale mobilization, that some extremely sensitive political decisions

12. This problem is commonly characterized as the "preparation-provocation" dilemma. For a useful discussion of this and other dilemmas facing NATO decisionmakers in a crisis, see Phil Williams, "NATO Crisis Management: Dilemmas and Trade-Offs," *Washington Quarterly*, vol. 12 (Spring 1989), pp. 29–39.

13. Patrick E. Tyler and R. Jeffrey Smith, "Study Finds NATO War Plans Outdated," *Washington Post*, November 29, 1989, pp. A1, A22.

would have to be made very quickly and most probably before their absolute necessity had been clearly established.[14]

NATO responded to this new challenge by implementing certain measures to shorten its reaction time to sudden military threats and speed up the planned transition process from peace to war. The system for gathering and disseminating intelligence was upgraded to provide decisionmakers with more timely and coherent evidence to make unpalatable decisions; new procedures and communications systems were introduced to facilitate alliance consultation; and the alerting and mobilization mechanisms were reviewed, refined, and exercised more regularly to help NATO leaders grapple with threatening situations in a militarily prudent but nonprovocative manner. NATO's senior military commanders were also given greater autonomy to order precautionary defensive measures in the event a dangerous military situation suddenly arose that effectively precluded higher political authorization. At more or less the same time, individual members of NATO, either independently or in concert with others, made their own arrangements to respond to sudden military threats. Though these measures were taken in the context of enhancing NATO's overall military readiness, they were symptomatic of a desire to ensure that members' security interests did not become hostage to the fortunes of alliance decisionmaking in a crisis and, in particular, to the possible hesitations or obstructions of others. Needless to say, this motive was never publicly acknowledged.

Though carried out for understandable reasons, NATO's efforts to improve the responsiveness of its command system to the threat of a "short-warning" attack unwittingly exacerbated the managerial problem facing the alliance in a crisis. With the actions of so many centers of decision and different national command systems to coordinate, the task of maintaining coherence and ensuring control was already formidable. By diffusing military alerting and mobilization authority still further in the alliance and by creating ways to bypass potential institutional bottlenecks, the latitude for independent and uncoordinated action expanded. The danger of unauthorized and other unwanted military

14. See Jeffrey Simon, "An Overview of NATO-Warsaw Pact Mobilization Issues," in Simon, ed., *NATO-Warsaw Pact Force Mobilization* (Washington: National Defense University Press, 1988), pp. 1–27; and Project on a Resources Strategy for the United States and Its Allies, *NATO: Meeting the Coming Challenge: An Alliance Action Plan for Conventional Improvements and Armaments Cooperation* (Washington: Center for Strategic and International Studies, 1987), pp. 15–18.

activities occurring in a crisis, with their potential for unwelcome consequences, also increased. At the very least such actions advanced the possibility that NATO's efforts to project a benign image of its intentions in a crisis would be contradicted and misunderstood. At worst they heightened the risk of a chain reaction of escalatory military behavior starting through ostensibly defensive actions being misconstrued as intentionally offensive, prompting further precautionary military activities in response. Once started the chain reaction might gather uncontrollable momentum, making war if not inevitable then certainly more likely.

The probability of such unintended interactions occurring in a crisis and leading to war might have been negligible had the military postures of both alliances not also become more offensively oriented by the 1980s. Although the policy of NATO and the Warsaw Pact remained avowedly defensive, both sides developed the means to carry out rapid, deep, and potentially devastating strikes against each other's forces at the outset of war. This potential increased not only the pressure to take precautionary and possibly ambiguous military measures to reduce the impact of such attacks before they occurred but also, as some have argued, the incentives to strike preemptively if war were considered inevitable and imminent.[15] With such an inflammable mixture, the possibility of inadvertent escalation leading to a spontaneous combustion between two well-primed and heavily armed adversaries grew very real.

As a result of its preoccupation with deterring calculated aggression by the Warsaw Pact, NATO paid little attention to the danger of war occurring inadvertently. In fact the traditional fear that NATO would respond too slowly to warlike indicators dominated expert opinion and obscured the distinct possibility that the alliance—or at least parts of it—might react too rapidly. As indicated earlier, there has been little public scrutiny of the mechanisms and procedures that NATO developed to manage a crisis and, if necessary, prepare for war. Few people discussed, let alone evaluated, the technical means and organizational arrangements used to develop and coordinate alliance actions. Similarly, except for some brief descriptions of NATO's alerting procedures, details

15. See John D. Steinbruner, "Revolution in Foreign Policy," in Henry J. Aaron, ed., *Setting National Priorities: Policy for the Nineties* (Brookings, 1990), p. 70; and statement of Phillip Karber in *Defining Conventional Stability in the European Theatre,* Hearings before the Defense Policy Panel of the House Committee on Armed Services, 100 Cong. 2d sess. (Government Printing Office, 1989), pp. 134–37.

of the measures that the alliance planned to take to raise the combat readiness of its military forces remained pitifully scarce.[16] Chapter 4, therefore, examines NATO's crisis management apparatus and the plans and procedures that it developed for making the transition to war.

Command Performance and the Conventional Defense of NATO

From the 1960s onward NATO's efforts to deter and defend against the threat of Warsaw Pact aggression were guided by its declared strategy of flexible response and forward defense. NATO, in short, vowed to meet aggression at any level, escalate to higher levels if necessary, and defend its territory as close to its borders as possible. Though forward defense was accepted for the whole of the alliance, it was conceived primarily with NATO's central front—essentially West Germany's border with East Germany and Czechoslovakia—in mind. It was here that the specter of a Soviet-led Warsaw Pact invasion was most apparent and also where NATO's geographical room to maneuver or trade space for time was the most constricted. There were also strong West German sentiments against a defensive strategy that implied NATO was willing to relinquish, however temporarily, parts of the Federal Republic to an enemy, and for a strategy that aimed to spare as much territory as possible from the inevitable devastation of war. Forward defense satisfied both desiderata.

By adopting a defensive posture, however, NATO ceded to the Warsaw Pact the advantage of being able to choose the time and place to mount an attack and mass its forces in a way to gain a heavy, perhaps overwhelming, preponderance. NATO's ability to offset that advantage rested not only on how well it reacted to warning and implemented mobilization plans but also, as many defense experts argued, on the adaptability and flexibility of its own military forces in countering emerging threats.[17] This capability in turn greatly hinged on the perfor-

---

16. For the best account to date see Bruce Blair, "Alerting in Crisis and Conventional War," in Carter, Steinbruner, and Zraket, *Managing Nuclear Operations,* pp. 77, 83.

17. See, for example, Joshua M. Epstein, *Conventional Force Reductions: A Dynamic Assessment* (Brookings, 1990); Paul K. Davis, *The Role of Uncertainty in Assessing the NATO-Pact Central Region Balance,* N-2839-RC (Santa Monica, Calif.: Rand Corp., 1988); and Crecine, "c³I across the Seams of Military Organizations," pp. 26-1–26-20.

mance of NATO's wartime command system in being able, first, to promptly detect and accurately identify the main axes of attack; second, to convey this intelligence to the relevant commanders so they could decide the appropriate defensive response and marshal the necessary resources; and third, to orchestrate the appropriate forces to ensure that their latent firepower could be used to maximum effect.

Important operational challenges confronted NATO's command system and its capacity to support the needs of forward defense. By being on the defensive, the physical components of the system—intelligence-gathering assets, headquarters, communications and so on—all had to be able to survive a potentially massive attack designed purposely to deceive, destroy, and paralyze it. By also being an alliance of sovereign states, the command system had to be able to support the demanding needs of coalition warfare. Thus, simultaneous operations involving the land, air, and naval forces of many different nations, speaking many different languages and using many different types of equipment, had to be coordinated and synchronized to realize their full combat potential or to at least prevent dangerous schisms that could be exploited by the enemy from arising.[18]

Added to these demands were also the more general challenges to fighting a high-intensity conventional war in Europe. The speed and greater reach of modern weaponry have increased the tempo of warfare and shortened the time that commanders and their staffs are likely to have to respond to events. Similarly, the lethality of today's weapons has added to the problem of managing forces by making a virtue out of dispersion and mobility. Combat along relatively static and well-delineated fronts is likely to be replaced by extremely fluid and convoluted engagements that make accurate assessments of the situation extremely difficult. Furthermore, the capacity to see and operate at night and in all types of weather has robbed combatants of what were traditionally sanctuaries for rest and recuperation, causing further physical exhaustion and stress to military commanders.[19]

18. Since Russian is the common operational language and the bulk of equipment is of Soviet design, the Warsaw Pact faced less of a problem. Other questions, however, have been raised about its wartime cohesion. See Jeffrey Simon, *The Warsaw Pact: Problems of Command and Control* (Westview, 1985).

19. See David R. Segal, "Cohesion, Leadership, and Stress in Airland Battle 2000," in Gerald W. Hopple, Stephen J. Andriole, and Amos Freedy, eds., *National Security Crisis Forecasting and Management* (Westview, 1984), pp. 178–85; and Beaumont, *Nerves of War*.

Despite the importance of NATO's command system to the conventional defense of Western Europe, serious deficiencies were allowed to exist that raise, in retrospect, serious questions about its adequacy in wartime. Key elements of the system lay vulnerable to attack, while the technical facilities and organizational arrangements for sharing intelligence and coordinating operations fell well short of what was clearly required. These shortcomings in NATO's wartime command arrangements stemmed from several interrelated sources. The difficulty alluded to earlier of assigning value to command performance, compared with assessing the more obvious attributes of military power, undoubtedly caused NATO to devote much less attention and consequently allocate far fewer resources to ensuring the adequacy of its command system. What typically suffered in the competition for scarce resources at the national level faced even greater obstacles at the alliance level. The neglect is also a legacy of the widespread expectation that a large-scale war in Europe would escalate quickly into a nuclear conflagration. For a long time, therefore, the need for a robust command system capable of supporting prolonged conventional operations was not considered a pressing requirement. In fact NATO only began to develop something like a true conventional warfighting command system after the adoption of the doctrine of flexible response in 1967 that put more emphasis on non-nuclear defense preparedness. Even so it was not until the late 1970s and early 1980s that this doctrinal shift began to be reflected in hardware and infrastructure. The vagaries and sluggishness of NATO's procurement system did much to delay the implementation of the modernization effort as well as to encourage haphazard and uncoordinated development, which still manifests itself today.

Chapter 5 describes in greater detail the deficiencies of NATO's wartime command arrangements, using a massive Warsaw Pact attack against the central front as the base case. It is important to acknowledge some limitations of this assessment. First, the study focuses predominantly on the technical and organizational elements of NATO's command system, with the all-important human dimension unavoidably absent.[20]

20. Even identifying the more salient components of NATO's command system presented major analytical challenges, as Joshua Epstein has observed: "While the phrase 'NATO's C^3' seems clear enough at first blush, depending on what one means by it, 'NATO's C^3' could encompass everything from the West German Postal Service to the British Parliament. The physical objects that might reasonably be included in NATO's C^3 are terribly wide-ranging. Divisional, corps, army group, and theater command

Second, as indicated earlier, the command arrangements and procedures that drive a military organization in crisis and war are traditionally among its most closely held secrets. NATO is no different in this respect. An unclassified study, therefore, cannot pretend to be definitive. Even so, as the case study attests, a tremendous amount of information is available in the public domain. With the further use of material gathered in confidential interviews, one can make a reasonably informed and independent assessment of NATO's command system.[21] Third, no attempt was made to conduct a parallel assessment of the Warsaw Pact's command system to ascertain NATO's relative adequacy. Although a strong case can be made for a comparative analysis, the paucity of publicly available information on the Pact's command system would almost certainly have made the study extremely unbalanced and its final conclusions of questionable value.

Now that the military threat to NATO has virtually evaporated, it would be easy to dismiss the continuing relevance of the analysis contained in both chapters 4 and 5. This conclusion would be shortsighted for several reasons. As argued at the outset, there are important lessons to be drawn from the military confrontation between NATO and the Warsaw Pact, particularly concerning the largely unappreciated danger of inadvertent war. The exposure of NATO's command deficiencies also serves as a sobering testament of the alliance's neglect of a vital area worthy of further reflection. Finally and most importantly, NATO's command system remains essentially unchanged despite the radically different circumstances in Europe. If the alliance is to serve a useful role in preserving peace and stability in Europe, then it must also reconfigure its command arrangements, many of which remain relevant, to meet the

---

headquarters would be natural candidates. The inclusion of thousands upon thousands of NATO electronic telecommunications, warning, target acquisition, and data processing systems would be no less reasonable. . . . Which, from among the enormous array of components, is one to choose? To what set of targetable objects does the analyst think he is referring when he says 'NATO c^3'?'' Joshua M. Epstein, *Measuring Military Power: The Soviet Air Threat to Europe* (Princeton University Press, 1984), pp. 134–35.

21. The breadth of knowledge of those interviewed with access to classified information was almost always limited to their immediate area of interest. Expertise within NATO is typically compartmentalized according to a specific region, a certain level of command, or a functional area such as intelligence dissemination or air defense. Given the size of the system, this fragmentation is hardly surprising. At the same time it indicates the difficulties that even analysts with privileged access to information face in reaching an overall assessment of NATO's command system.

most likely security challenges of the future. The command system as it stands today represents, therefore, the baseline for such changes.

Command Performance and Future European Security

Paradoxically, the end of the cold war and its associated constrictures has made many people nervous about the consequences for peace and stability in Europe. More specifically, without Moscow's stifling presence in Eastern Europe long-suppressed nationalist aspirations and ethnic animosities could come to the fore, creating a highly volatile situation. The same apphrehensions apply equally if not more so to the Soviet Union, with its many diverse and restless republics yearning for greater independence. With the distinct possibility that social and economic conditions in these countries could deteriorate precipitously as they adjust to democracy and free market mechanisms, the prospect of widespread domestic unrest and even civil strife becomes very real. More ominous is the danger of such agitation fomenting international conflict in an area where high levels of armaments will remain for the foreseeable future and where Soviet influence no longer exists. Such conflict may seem highly improbable, but recent events in the Persian Gulf have been a rude reminder that interstate violence is still a fact of life in the international system.

Although NATO was established and nurtured for entirely different reasons, the alliance can continue to serve its members' interests. Until the international situation becomes more settled and confidence grows in the efficacy of newly emerging pan-European institutions, notably the Conference on Security and Cooperation in Europe, NATO's security guarantees will be viewed as the best insurance policy against the uncertainty of the future. For the same reason, NATO's well-established intelligence-sharing and diplomatic consultative mechanisms will be valued as the primary means to discuss and coordinate the West's response to potential crises. NATO, with its technical facilities and expertise, can also help support the emerging arms control regime in Europe. NATO, nevertheless, must fundamentally transform the command arrangements that grew up in response to the fear of Soviet aggression. Accordingly, the final chapter of this book presents a list of recommendations for achieving this goal.

CHAPTER TWO

Command Performance and Military Effectiveness

THE METHODOLOGY typically employed to assess military balances is not unlike the approach taken to predict the outcome of a boxing match. The salient features of the opposing forces—their size, structure, and firepower—are compared in the same way that the height, weight, and general physique of two boxers are judged for relative advantage. Thus one side may be considered to have more powerful weapons at its disposal, just as one of the fighters is deemed to have better knockout potential. The other side, however, might be more mobile and able to deliver firepower at greater range, making it more difficult to strike, just as one fighter may be more nimble and possess a longer reach. From what is known about the availability of reinforcements and weapons stocks, the relative endurance of the forces in wartime is also estimated in much the same way that the boxer's stamina to go the distance is judged by past performance and by observing his training regimen. And finally the strategy and doctrine that guide the employment of military force are dissected for their reasoning and practicality, just as each boxer's approach to fighting might be debated.

These analytical judgments are necessary but clearly insufficient to a complete and more realistic assessment of the potential effectiveness of a military force. Vital information that could significantly affect the conclusions of the analysis is missing. To use the boxing match analogy once again, the calculation of who is the better fighter and therefore the likely winner would change dramatically if it were known that one of them had better eye-to-hand coordination, allowing him to parry punches and strike his opponent more consistently and effectively. The same would be true if it were also known that one of the boxers found it difficult to discriminate between feints and real punches, leaving him vulnerable to being struck. And the final appreciation would doubtless change if one of the boxers were believed to be more susceptible than the other to blows to the head (a "glass jaw" in the vernacular) that might leave him temporarily stunned and unable to function. So the same reasoning applies to the use of military forces. The final assessment of a military balance would surely change if it were discovered that one side was better able to detect military threats, marshal forces in response, and coordinate their use in battle. Presumably, it would also be altered if it were known that the information-gathering and -processing system of one of them could be easily confused, its command staff deceived, and its communications system for transmitting orders easily disrupted or destroyed, leaving the fighting elements bereft of direction and beyond control.

As the introduction to this study has argued, the relationship between command performance and military effectiveness is neither widely understood nor widely appreciated. To help remedy this deficiency, the first part of this chapter examines the role and importance of command performance in relatively abstract terms. The factors and processes at work are then illustrated with the help of three case studies of famous Second World War battles. Although the three battles chosen have received considerable attention from historians, the analytical approach taken here is a novel one that sheds new light on their outcome. These case studies, however, also illustrate the limits to the assessment of command performance, as the final section discusses in greater detail.

The Military Value of Command Performance

In a fundamental way the relationship between command performance and military effectiveness is blindingly simple: command systems enable purposeful military activity or, put differently, the matching of means to desired ends. Without some way to direct, coordinate, and control military operations, the achievement of objectives—which is the ultimate measure of effectiveness—simply would not be possible. Though effectiveness can be judged by the ability to achieve a desired outcome, more often it is equated with the ability to do so efficiently, that is, with the minimum expenditure of time, effort, and resources.[1] Military effectiveness, therefore, is frequently represented as a cost-exchange ratio, for example, the damage inflicted on an enemy against that suffered in return, or the price paid in lives lost or munitions expended to gain or hold a given piece of territory. It is important not to forget, however, that military power does not have to be exercised to be effective. The deterrence of external attack or internal disorder by the threat of military retribution is an obvious case in point.

The contribution of command and control to military effectiveness derives from the use made of its basic commodity—information. With accurate information, uncertainty about the surrounding environment can be reduced and decisions affecting the readiness, movement, and application of military force can be taken with a clearer understanding of the likely costs and benefits. If processed and delivered promptly, information can also provide more time for these decisions to be taken and, moreover, implemented with successful results. Overall it permits a clearer assessment of a situation, generates policy choices to achieve a specific outcome, and allows those choices to be weighed for their relative payoff.[2] Not surprisingly, information has been called the "most vital of all combat commodities" and the "soul of morale in combat and the balancing force in successful tactics."[3]

Information can only be used productively, however, if the *authority* to do so exists. That authority is invested in the command hierarchy or chain of command that assigns specific roles and responsibilities to designated decisionmakers for the purpose of directing the actions of their subordinates and the fighting elements of the force. Ultimately, though, command authority can only be received and information conveyed to and from decisionmakers in the military force if the *communications* also exist to do so. Communications channels, therefore, are not just conduits for information but, are also in effect, the reins

1. See Allan R. Millett, Williamson Murray, and Kenneth H. Watman, "The Effectiveness of Military Organizations," in Allan R. Millett and Williamson Murray, eds., *Military Effectiveness: Vol. 1: The First World War* (Allen and Unwin, 1988), pp. 2–4.

2. See D. S. Alberts, "C²I Assessment: A Proposed Methodology," in *Proceedings for Quantitative Assessment of the Utility of Command and Control Systems*, MTR-80W00025 (McLean, Va.: Mitre Corp., 1980), pp. 72–74; and Marvin S. Cohen and Anthony N. S. Freeling, *The Impact of Information on Decisions: Command and Control System Evaluation*, Technical Report 81-1 (Falls Church, Va.: Decision Science Consortium, February 1981).

3. S. L. A. Marshall, *Men against Fire: The Problem of Battle Command in Future War* (Gloucester, Mass.: Peter Smith, 1978), p. 92.

of power that bind the force together and maintain its cohesion. As a result, communications links typically parallel the lines of hierarchy in the force.

The use made of information, authority, and communications, which make up the three vital ingredients of command and control, influences the efficiency with which military inputs (manpower, weapons systems, logistics, and so on) are converted into military outputs (relative attrition, damage inflicted, territory occupied, or space controlled) by affecting the readiness, density, motion (direction and speed), and application of military force. The relationship can be illustrated abstractly by examining the behavior of a military force before, during, and after a battle.[4]

If military action is considered likely, either because it is to be self-initiated or expected from an adversary, the quantitative and qualitative readiness of a force can be improved in preparation. Thus the proportion of total military assets available for combat can be increased. The level of preparedness of equipment and personnel can similarly be raised to withstand the extra demands of war. The force, furthermore, can be moved and concentrated to increase the amount of usable military power at a specific time and place, either to help offset similar activities by an adversary or to overwhelm him numerically. Alternatively elements of the force might be dispersed to reduce their exposure and vulnerability to attack. The net result is that the pre-battle balance of ready forces—ready in the sense of being prepared to fight in the right place, at the right time, and in the right amount—can be favorably influenced. This capability in turn might deter a potential attacker by changing his calculation of the probable costs and expected gains, or, conversely, it might intimidate an opposing force into retreat and even peaceful submission. Finally, the command system is also used to prevent the unauthorized or premature discharge of firepower.

If and when battle is joined, the command system would help the force maneuver on the battlefield for relative advantage and engage the opponent with numerically superior forces and firepower or on terms that are not grossly inferior. This action might entail exploiting environmental features such as hills, rivers, valleys, clouds, rain, and so forth that can offer tactical benefits for defensive or offensive military action. While

4. The following section draws on the work of Daniel M. Schutzer, "c^2 Theory and Measures of Effectiveness," in John Hwang and others, eds., *Selected Analytical Concepts in Command and Control* (Gordon and Breach Science Publishers, 1982), pp. 119–44; and Alberts, "c^2I Assessment," pp. 67–91.

such combat maneuvers may contribute to a favorable cost-exchange ratio, however measured, this benefit will depend on how efficiently and effectively the available firepower is employed. Here command and performance can improve the lethality of the engaged combatants and the weapons they operate. For obvious reasons, knowledge of the whereabouts of a target increases the chances that it can be successfully attacked, assuming of course that the military capability to do so also exists. Such knowledge makes the difference between directed and undirected fire. Fewer attempts have to be made or munitions expended, therefore, to destroy a given target. Coordination and synchronization of effort among different force elements can also enhance their destructive effect when used together. Conversely, poor cooperation and timing can dissipate lethal energy and negate whatever potential synergisms may be realizable. Coordination, furthermore, can improve the economy of military effort by reducing duplication and the likelihood of self-inflicted losses from accidents.

In the aftermath of battle the command system can help exploit the fruits of victory or diminish the cost of defeat. A timely and correct appreciation of the opportunities presented by success in battle is an obvious prerequisite to their full exploitation, whether it be the acquisition of territory or the complete destruction of the opposing force and its eventual capitulation. From the other side, a functioning command system can help determine when defeat is inevitable but not yet irredeemable, thus allowing an orderly disengagement and the preservation of the force's overall cohesion to fight another day.

Command performance can be seen to rest, therefore, on three factors. The first is the quality of the information reaching the military decisionmakers, which can be gauged according to its accuracy, timeliness, relevance, completeness, and ease of use. The second is the quality of the decisionmaking that is made in response to the information. While this attribute is normally judged by how rationally available means are employed in pursuit of desired ends, the coherence and promptness of the decisionmaking are other important variables. And the third is the quality of the communications used for passing information to and from the decisionmakers. Here the main criteria are speed, capacity, reliability, and survivability of the links. These three variables are dependent on the performance of the three basic components of every command system: the technical support systems for gathering, processing, and relaying information, or intelligence, as it is usually referred to;

the organizational structure that delineates the hierarchy of authority and division of responsibilities within the military force; and last but not least, the individuals who operate the system.

Command Performance in Three Battles

Three well-known battles from the Second World War illustrate the relationship between command performance and military effectiveness: the Battle of France in 1940, the Battle of Britain in the same year, and the Battle of Midway in 1942. Besides exemplifying land, air, and sea engagements, respectively, these cases are of particular interest since the victors either were outnumbered at the outset or, as in the first case, were not favored by a numerical advantage.[5] It is not the intention here to give a detailed account of each battle; rather the purpose is to focus on the performance of each side's command system, especially the adequacy of its intelligence-gathering and -processing arrangements, command organization for decisionmaking, and communications facilities.

The Battle of France

On May 10, 1940, Germany surprised France by attacking through the hilly and heavily forested Ardennes area. Though an offensive had been expected for some time, this area was not considered a likely avenue of attack and thus was only lightly defended. By May 13, German mechanized forces with dive bombers in support had brushed aside the French covering force and crossed the river Meuse close to Sedan. Hastily improvised and piecemeal defensive efforts by the French failed to stem the German advance. Germany's armored spearheads gathered momentum and sped westward to the English Channel, eventually encircling the bulk of the Allied forces that had obligingly moved northeastward into Belgium at the beginning of the campaign. Although France did not capitulate until June 21, the first and decisive phase of the campaign ended with the evacuation of the British Expeditionary

5. For details of the prebattle balance of forces for the first two cases see Barry R. Posen, *The Sources of Military Doctrine: France, Britain, and Germany between the World Wars* (Cornell University Press, 1984), pp. 83, 95. For Midway see Gordon W. Prange, *Miracle at Midway* (Penguin, 1982), pp. 128–29.

Force from Dunkirk on June 4. Despite rough parity in the opening balance of forces and, in certain notable areas, a qualitative advantage, the Allied armies had been routed after little more than three weeks of fighting.

INTELLIGENCE. Although the German offensive effectively caught the Allies by surprise, it was not because the Allies had failed to detect preparations for the attack. In fact, by the beginning of May British and French intelligence had collected considerable evidence indicating that the main blow would fall in the Ardennes, but since this conclusion did not conform to their expectations of Germany's operational intentions, they essentially ignored the information.[6] In fairness, other factors, such as bad flying weather for reconnaissance missions and the great care that the Germans took to disguise the timing and location of the attack, helped prevent the collection of further and, perhaps decisive, evidence that might have overcome the cognitive bias of Allied intelligence.[7]

Once the campaign had started, the thick foliage of the Ardennes and the attention of German fighter aircraft further prevented French reconnaissance planes from gaining a fuller picture of the offensive.[8] Yet even when the German offensive gained momentum in the open countryside of northern France, French military intelligence proved increasingly incapable of monitoring the unfolding catastrophe on anything like an accurate and timely basis. The whereabouts of friendly forces became almost as great a mystery as the movements of the enemy. In part ignorance resulted from inadequate reconnaissance resources that were progressively decimated by enemy action.[9] More reconnaissance assets would probably not have made that much difference,

6. See Richard K. Betts, *Surprise Attack: Lessons for Defense Planning* (Brookings, 1982), pp. 32–33; and Norman F. Dixon, *Our Own Worst Enemy* (London: Jonathan Cape, 1987), p. 40.

7. See F. H. Hinsley, *British Intelligence in the Second World War: Its Influence on Strategy and Operations,* vol. 1 (London: Her Majesty's Stationery Office, 1979), pp. 127–36; Brian Bond, "The Calm before the Storm: Britain and the 'Phoney War' 1939–40, *RUSI Journal,* vol. 135 (Spring 1990), pp. 66–67; and Martin S. Alexander, "The Fall of France, 1940," *Journal of Strategic Studies,* vol. 13 (March 1990), p. 30.

8. Alistair Horne, *To Lose a Battle: France 1940* (Middlesex, U.K.: Penguin, 1984), pp. 280–81.

9. According to the famous writer Antoine de Saint-Exupéry, who was a reconnaissance pilot at the time, there were only fifty crews for the whole of the French army and these would soon be decimated by enemy fire. Antoine de Saint-Exupéry, *Flight to Arras,* trans. Lewis Galantière (Middlesex, U.K.: Penguin, 1972), p. 7. See also André Geraud, *The Gravediggers of France: Gamelin, Daladier, Reynaud, Pétain, and Laval* (Doubleday, Doran and Co., 1944), pp. 55–56.

however, as the system for reporting and disseminating intelligence was patently inadequate for the task and the abysmal state of communications only made the situation worse. As one observer recorded afterward, "The passing on of information [was] extremely inefficient, whether it emanated from lower or higher formations."[10]

British intelligence, with few exceptions, fared no better than its French counterpart. Such was the ignorance of German movements into France that for two weeks after the invasion the records of the discussions of the British cabinet and chiefs of staff on the fighting continued to be headed "The Netherlands and Belgium."[11] The British Expeditionary Force (BEF) likewise lacked sufficient reconnaissance aircraft to support its operations while an Anglo-French plan drawn up before the attack to coordinate intelligence collection proved inadequate.[12] British intelligence, however, did have some success in intercepting and decrypting German military radio communications. The system for interpreting and disseminating what would become known as Ultra intelligence was still in its infancy, however. Thus, while considerable quantities of decrypted messages were passed to the BEF, they more often than not arrived too late to be of immediate operational value. At the same time, the volume of signals intelligence collected locally by British forces swamped their capacity to process and make fruitful use of it.[13]

The experience of the First World War, which had encouraged the Allies to form a wholly static conception of future warfare, left the BEF's intelligence organization utterly unprepared for the demands of fighting a high-tempo, mobile campaign. As the Allied forces reeled back in disarray, so their intelligence arrangements, particularly the liaison links between them, broke down. The unplanned decision by the commander of the BEF, General John Standish Gort, to move to a command post fifty miles away from his main headquarters where most of his intelligence staff resided, and then at a critical juncture in the fighting to send the director of military intelligence and most of his staff to command an ad hoc field force with just one intelligence officer left behind at the main headquarters, was particularly disastrous.[14] As the official historian

10. Marc Bloch, *Strange Defeat: A Statement of Evidence Written in 1940*, trans. Gerard Hopkins (Octagon Books, 1968), pp. 44–47. See also Horne, *To Lose a Battle*, p. 154; and Saint-Exupéry, *Flight to Arras*, pp. 11–12.
11. Hinsley, *British Intelligence*, p. 143.
12. Hinsley, *British Intelligence*, p. 148.
13. Hinsley, *British Intelligence*, pp. 144, 146.
14. See Dixon, *Our Own Worst Enemy*, p. 43.

records, "As a result of these unrehearsed measures, and of poor communications between GHQ [general headquarters] and the command post, information collated at GHQ often failed to pass from the command post to the lower formations in time to be of use to them, while much of the information which divisions at the front sent into the command post was never passed back to the GHQ."[15] The one success story for British intelligence during the campaign was the lucky capture of German documents indicating that an attack was imminent in a sector of the front that had just been vacated by Belgian forces. Gort's timely transfer of two British divisions to cover the gap, according to one historian, "saved the British Expeditionary Force."[16]

With surprise and initiative on its side, German intelligence did have some initial advantages over the Allies. From captured British documents and information gained by penetrating French military communications, the intelligence branch of the German General Staff was able to put together an accurate assessment of Allied dispositions, including their weaknesses before the invasion of France. As the official British historian notes, "This influenced the selection of the precise point of the German break-through on 9 May; established that on the eve of the campaign German forces exceeded the French by two to one; helped the Germans to appreciate that the Allied armies would advance to the Dyle [River] when the attack began; and reduced German anxiety by strengthening the assessment that the French would be unable to launch an effective counter-attack on the flank of the main German thrust."[17] Once the attack began, German intelligence continued to play a vital role. Since blitzkrieg tactics put great emphasis on identifying lines of least resistance and then rapidly exploiting them, the armored columns were usually preceded by reconnaissance units that operated well in advance and fed information back to their commanders. Arrangements could also be made to have photos taken by reconnaissance

---

15. Hinsley, *British Intelligence,* p. 147. See also Brian Bond, *France and Belgium, 1939–1940* (University of Delaware Press, 1975), p. 104. Some modest success was achieved, however, with the introduction of roving intelligence officers known as Phantom units that operated independently at the front. Their reports on what they saw and heard deliberately bypassed the normal channels to speed up the reporting and provide some independent source of information. Though this system was still in its infancy, it proved effective in later campaigns. See R. J. T. Hills, *Phantom Was There* (London: Edward Arnold and Co., 1951), pp. 27–32.

16. L. F. Ellis is quoted in Hinsley, *British Intelligence,* p. 143.

17. Hinsley, *British Intelligence,* p. 164.

aircraft dropped to the mobile headquarters so that they would be aware of the opposition that lay up ahead and plan their movements accordingly.[18] Supplied by such good intelligence from these and other sources, notably Sigint (signals intelligence), German forces "could move with almost faultless assurance towards their objectives."[19]

COMMAND ORGANIZATION. After the war Field Marshal Montgomery, who commanded one of the British divisions during the campaign, would describe, somewhat colorfully, the Allied command arrangements for the defense of France as a "complete dog's breakfast."[20] Certainly it is hard to imagine a more cumbersome and confusing chain of command to manage a campaign. At its pinnacle stood General Maurice Gamelin (later replaced by General Maxime Weygand) as the supreme commander of all French land forces, with his headquarters at Vincennes on the outskirts of Paris. Operational control of the forces in the crucial northeastern sector of France, however, was the responsibility of his deputy, General Alphonse Georges, who had his main headquarters at La Ferté, approximately thirty-five miles to the east. Unfortunately the two officers were barely on speaking terms, which may explain why Georges spent most of his time at a separate command post twelve miles away in Bondons. To complicate matters further, yet another headquarters under the command of Georges' chief of staff, General Joseph Doumenc, was established at Montry midway between them. (Doumenc ended up spending his mornings at Montry and his afternoons at La Ferté whether Georges was there or not.) Besides the dissipation of authority inherent in this fragmented command arrangement, Georges' staff, which had built up a good working relationship before the hostilities, was at a crucial moment divided up and sent to several different locations.[21]

France's air forces, to make matters worse, operated under a separate chain of command with General Joseph Vuillemin in overall charge at yet another headquarters in Coulommiers, outside of Paris. Coordination between the air force and the ground forces under General Georges was the responsibility of General Marcel Têtu, the "Officer Commanding

18. Len Deighton, *Blitzkrieg: From the Rise of Hitler to the Fall of Dunkirk* (St. Albans, Herts., U.K.: Triad/Granada, 1981), pp. 213–15.

19. Kenneth Macksey, *Military Errors of World War Two* (Poole, Dorset, U.K.: Arms and Armour Press, 1987), pp. 34–35.

20. Montgomery is quoted in Dixon, *Our Own Worst Enemy*, p. 43.

21. See Horne, *To Lose a Battle*, pp. 152–55; Deighton, *Blitzkrieg*, pp. 138–40; and Bond, *France and Belgium*, p. 81.

the Air Cooperation Forces." However, the decision to apportion available aircraft before the campaign to individual "Zones of Air Operations," which roughly corresponded with the army groups' areas of responsibility, meant that "individual army commanders found it impossible to obtain a sufficient concentration of air power at the right moment."[22]

The BEF's command arrangements were no less confusing. Although deployed in the sector controlled by General Gaston Billotte's First Army Group, General Gort received his orders from Gamelin through Georges. He retained the right, moreover, to appeal directly to the British government if he felt that the BEF's interests were jeopardized by French orders.[23] What links the BEF had with the French high command began to grow more tenuous as the situation deteriorated, particularly after the senior French commanders began to unload their responsibilities onto their subordinates; Gamelin passed the buck to Georges who in turn gave it to Billotte. Already overwhelmed by his enormous responsibilities, the hapless Billotte gave less and less attention to overseeing the movements of the BEF. Later he suffered a mental breakdown. Gort, as a consequence, began operating as a virtual free agent with minimum coordination with the French. The liaison arrangements, which had never been very strong in the first place, eventually collapsed completely as the BEF increasingly acted independently to extricate itself from the continent.[24]

By comparison there was little division of authority in the German command arrangements for the invasion of France. While senior commanders disagreed over how far and how fast to exploit their success, cooperation and coordination among the different arms of the German forces were, on the whole, exemplary. The Wehrmacht's command system, moreover, was more decentralized and less rigid than that of the French and therefore better suited to blitzkrieg-type operations. As Robert A. Doughty concludes,

22. Horne, *To Lose a Battle*, p. 153.

23. See Bloch, *Strange Defeat*, p. 74; and Horne, *To Lose a Battle*, p. 153.

24. During its retreat toward Dunkirk, the BEF not only began blowing up bridges in its wake, with little or no consideration of France's needs, but also prematurely destroyed the telephone exchange at Lille, depriving the First French Army of most of its communications. See Bloch, *Strange Defeat*, p. 75. Relations between the two Allies would steadily deteriorate for the rest of the campaign to the point where France's forces would later deliberately obstruct Britain's air operations in the south of France. See Noel Barber, *The Week France Fell* (Stein and Day, 1976), p. 94.

The [French] army's doctrinal and organizational system stressed the power and authority of army-group, army, and corps commanders and left little flexibility or room for initiative to lower level commanders. Each lower level had less room for maneuver than the level immediately above it. The entire system was designed to be propelled forward by pressure from above, rather than by being pulled from below. In contrast to a decentralized battle in which officers were expected to show intiative and flexibility, the French preferred rigid centralization and strict obedience. Unfortunately, this resulted in a fatal flaw; the French military establishment could not respond flexibly to unanticipated demands and could hardly capitalize upon an important gain made by a lower level unit.[25]

COMMUNICATIONS. The disunity in the French high command was compounded by the lamentable state of communications. None of the main headquarters was interconnected by teletype or linked in the same manner to its armies in the field. The telephone system was also unreliable, and the telegram service was chronically late in delivery. Gamelin, having seen no reason to acquire a radio transmitter, didn't even have one at his headquarters at Vincennes. He relied instead on motorcycle dispatch riders, who frequently met with accidents on the congested roads, or he undertook tiring and time-consuming personal visits to the other command posts. Not surprisingly, as one historian notes, "It was impossible for the Commander in Chief to receive direct and instantaneous reports from other headquarters or to intercept radio messages from the armies in action or from aircraft so as to get a better idea of the situation immediately."[26]

Communications were no better at the tactical level. Having spent no more than a tiny fraction of its military budget on communications equipment between 1923 and 1939 and very little on research and development of more advanced systems, it is not suprising that serious deficiencies were exposed once the campaign began.[27] Thus, for instance, there was little if any provision for communications between air and ground forces to coordinate operations. Three quarters of France's tanks, furthermore, were fitted without radios (signal flags being the

25. Robert A. Doughty, "The French Armed Forces, 1918–40," in Allan R. Millett and Williamson Murray, eds., *Military Effectiveness: Vol. II: The Interwar Period* (Allen and Unwin, 1988), p. 57.

26. William L. Shirer, *The Collapse of the Third Republic: An Inquiry into the Fall of France in 1940* (Simon and Schuster, 1969), p. 621. As Gamelin's aide would later remark, Vincennes was like "a submarine without a periscope."

27. The amount has been put at 0.15 percent. See Doughty, "French Armed Forces," p. 58. See also Shirer, *The Collapse,* pp. 619–20.

principal form of communication). When tanks did have radios, they frequently proved unreliable.[28] Many French accounts of the battle mention the general ineffectiveness of radio equipment.[29] Paradoxically, communications, even when functioning properly, often contributed to the general panic that beset French forces at key moments in the battle.[30]

The BEF's communications also suffered from serious deficiencies. Again the belief, based on the experience of the First World War, that the pace of operations would be relatively static left the British forces with a preponderance of wire communications equipment that soon became useless once the campaign entered its mobile phase. Radios with trained personnel were also in short supply, and what sets there were could operate only at limited ranges. Furthermore, the unexpected increase in signals traffic (especially encrypted messages) soon outstripped the capacity of the system to handle it, creating intolerable communications delays in the process.[31]

The German forces, by contrast, had a thoroughly modern communications system at their disposal, and one that was fully adaptable to the fluid conditions of the modern battlefield. Although the Allies' success at breaking the German code would eventually expose its fatal weakness, the German signal organization was extremely effective in maintaining contact with its forces even during their rapid advance across France. In particular, many believe that the use made of radio for controlling armored units and for coordinating air support gave the German forces a decisive advantage.

The importance of communications to blitzkrieg-style operations had been recognized well before it was proven in battle. During a visit by a British official to prewar Germany, General Erhard Milch, Germany's state secretary for air, had confided that the "real secret [of armored warfare] is speed—speed of attack through speed of communications."[32] The innovator behind the introduction of radios to armored forces was

28. Macksey, *Military Errors of World War Two*, p. 32. Horne states that the proportion was even larger. Horne, *To Lose a Battle*, p. 218.

29. Jeffrey A. Gunsburg, *Divided and Conquered: The French High Command and the Defeat of the West, 1940* (Greenwood Press, 1979), p. 268; and Doughty, "French Armed Forces," p. 58.

30. The panic that set in at Sedan is one example. See John A. English, *A Perspective on Infantry* (Praeger, 1981), pp. 101–02.

31. See Maj. Gen. R. F. H. Nalder, *The History of British Army Signals in the Second World War* (London: Royal Signals Institution, 1953), pp. 33–35.

32. Quoted in Gordon Welchman, *The Hut Six Story* (McGraw-Hill, 1982), p. 20.

undoubtedly General Heinz Guderian who as a signals officer in the First World War had witnessed the disastrous breakdown of communications in the opening German offensive against France in 1914. With the aid of Fritz Fellgiebel, the inspector of the Signal Corps, Guderian formulated the requirements and design specifications for equipping the panzers with radios.[33] As General Hermann Balck, one of Guderian's disciples, observed after the war,

> Guderian made two very important contributions in the area of panzer warfare communications. The first contribution was to add a fifth man, a radio operator, and a radio to each tank in the tank division. This allowed both small and large tank units to be commanded and maneuvered with a swiftness and flexibility that no other army was able to match. As a result, our tanks were able to defeat tanks that were quite superior in firepower and armor.
>
> Guderian's second contribution was to give the panzer division a signal organization that allowed the division commander to command from any point within the division.[34]

Though Guderian's innovations were met with some skepticism at the time, the success of the operations into Poland and France, some of which he personally led, later vindicated him. His basic system for controlling armored forces was subsequently adopted by every other country and is still in evidence today.

OVERVIEW. Many factors contributed to the fall of France in 1940; the relative quality of military doctrine, training, morale, and equipment of the two sides undoubtedly played their part. As important, if not more so, was the comparative performance of the Allied command system and its German counterpart. The Allies' failure at the outset to act on the indications that German forces were about to attack in the Ardennes left France's two weakest armies—the Ninth and Second—to defend

33. See Kenneth Macksey, *Guderian: Panzer General* (London: MacDonald and Jane's, 1975), pp. 66–67.

34. Quoted in James Fallows, *National Defense* (Random House, 1981), pp. 28–29. Another German general, F. W. von Mellenthin, attested to the benefits of radio when he stated in his memoirs that "the up-to-date wireless equipment of our armored units gave them a clear advantage in maneuver" over the French. See Maj. Gen. F. W. von Mellenthin, *Panzer Battles: A Study of the Employment of Armor in the Second World War,* trans. H. Betzler (University of Oklahoma Press, 1971), p. 15. French tanks also suffered the disadvantage that their commanders "laid and fired the gun: in German models the commander just commanded while another crew member aimed and fired the gun." See Macksey, *Guderian,* p. 104.

against a massive concentration of German armor without an organized reserve in support. The initiative might still have been regained and the attack repulsed had the French high command grasped the significance of events and marshaled the available forces to mount a serious counterattack. By the time headquarters realized what was happening, it was too late; German forces had already broken out and were streaming across France at a pace that Allied responses were never able to match. Poor intelligence and communications progressively divorced the high command from the reality of the situation. Its capacity to influence the campaign was wholly inadequate for the tempo at which it was being fought. As an illustration, General Gamelin admitted after the war that it took an average of forty-eight hours for orders issued by the commander in chief to be executed at the front.[35] It is no wonder that the French high command reminded one observer of a "laboratory guinea pig whose cerebellum has been severed."[36] The situation was no better at the tactical level. Deficiencies in communications, interservice coordination, and Allied liaison arrangements resulted in unsynchronized actions that dissipated the effectiveness of the Allies' military power whenever it was applied. Their fragmented counterattacks posed no serious threat to the German advance.[37]

The German command system, however, allowed its forces to concentrate to gain local numerical superiority, to outmaneuver their opponents on the battlefield, and to exploit rapidly whatever tactical opportunities arose during an engagement. The forward location of headquarters kept the commanders in direct touch with the course of the battle and better able, as a result of a greater decentralization of authority, to react more quickly than their opponents to the fluid situation. Coordination among the different arms also permitted the German forces to direct devastating fire at the *Schwerpunkt*—place of main effort—when it was most needed. Whereas it would commonly take five hours for the French command system to process requests for close air support, such aid was virtually on call for the German ground forces.[38] Overall, as Barry Posen has

---

35. Shirer, *The Collapse*, pp. 621–23.
36. Geraud, *Gravediggers of France*, p. 75.
37. See Deighton, *Blitzkrieg*, pp. 330–31; and Horne, *To Lose a Battle*, p. 528.
38. Geraud, *Gravediggers of France*, pp. 55–56; and Shirer, *The Collapse*, pp. 621–62. For more details on the organization of German close air support see Riley Sunderland, *Evolution of Command and Control Doctrine for Close Air Support* (Washington: Office of Air Force History, 1973), pp. 3–6.

observed, the combination of battlefield tactics that fostered the collapse of the enemy's command system with the possession of one that was optimized to exploit the collapse proved decisive.[39]

The Battle of Britain

Following its triumph in the battle of France, the German Luftwaffe set about securing air superiority over the Royal Air Force (RAF) in preparation for the invasion of Great Britain. Historians commonly group the ensuing air battles into three phases: the first, between July 1 and approximately August 12, consisted mainly of attacks on shipping in the channel and against ports along the south coast of England; the second, and most crucial, lasted to September 7, with the German bombers directing their attacks against RAF airfields and supporting infrastructure; and the third, signaled by the fateful switch of the main German effort to London, ended in October. Over this entire period, the Luftwaffe lost 1,733 aircraft of all types and the RAF about half that figure.[40] The failure of the German air force to break the back of the RAF is usually considered one of the most important turning points of the war, an outcome owing in no small part to the relative performance of each side's command systems.

INTELLIGENCE. The importance of radar as a source of vital early warning information to Britain is now well recognized. Although some may disagree with classifying the chain of radar sites along the coastline of England as intelligence assets, they were undeniably the RAF's principal source of information to fight the air battle. By the middle of 1940, the RAF Fighter Command had operational two types of radar (or radio direction-finding (RDF) devices, as they were then called) to warn of approaching aircraft. The main system, known as the Chain Home (CH) stations, could detect aircraft below 15,000 feet. This capability was augmented in key places with the relatively sophisticated Chain Home Low (CHL) stations, which were able to give more precise readings of aircraft traveling at lower altitudes. Though rudimentary, the system was nevertheless effective in giving the approximate height, location,

39. Posen, *Sources of Military Doctrine*, p. 206.

40. R. Ernest Dupuy and Trevor N. Dupuy, *The Encyclopedia of Military History from 3500 B.C. to the Present*, 2d rev. ed. (Harper and Row, 1986), p. 1066.

direction, and strength of attacking aircraft.[41] More important, it could provide this information far enough in advance for Fighter Command to react and allocate its forces to meet the attack.

Since the radar stations were positioned on the coast and directed outward, Fighter Command was also dependent on a network of observers to keep track of the attacking forces once they had passed inland. Armed with nothing more than a pair of binoculars and an aircraft recognition handbook, the spotters of the Royal Observer Corps played a valuable and underrated role in the battle of Britain. Besides radar and visual observers, the RAF made increasing use of signals intelligence gathered in advance of a raid. While the Ultra intelligence was often too fragmentary or decrypted too late to be of operational value, intercepts of the low-grade Luftwaffe traffic—principally the radio communications among the aircraft preparing to attack—became a valuable additional source of early warning information to Fighter Command.[42]

In contrast, as one historian has argued, "A constant German handicap throughout the battle was poor Intelligence."[43] Even though it was known before the war that the British were working on radar, a July 1940 Luftwaffe assessment of the RAF by the head of the Luftwaffe's intelligence branch, Major Beppo Schmid (his rank betraying the lowly status given to his job), inexplicably failed to make any reference to radar or Fighter Command's system of air defense. Eventually the Luftwaffe's signal intelligence service and German Post Office engineers would monitor the RAF's radar transmissions and fighter communications, but they erroneously concluded that the fighters were tied to their ground stations and were unable, as a consequence, to assemble at short notice wherever they might be needed.[44] Nevertherless, before the big offensive of August 13, the Luftwaffe did try to disable the chain of radar stations in what is perhaps the first case of a deliberate and preemptive command suppression attack. The strike proved quite successful in

41. For a discussion of the genesis and operation of the Chain Home system see Len Deighton, *Fighter: The True Story of the Battle of Britain* (St. Albans, Herts., U.K.: Triad/Panther, 1979), pp. 109–21.

42. See Deighton, *Fighter*, pp. 202–03; Hinsley, *British Intelligence*, pp. 179–82; and Sebastian Cox, "Battle of Britain," conference paper to Colloque International, in *Histoire de la Guerre Aerienne*, Paris, Ecole Nationale Superieure de Techniques Avancées, September 1987.

43. B. H. Liddell Hart, *History of the Second World War* (G. P. Putnam's Sons, 1971), p. 94.

44. Deighton, *Fighter*, p. 201.

tearing a 100-mile-wide gap in the radar chain, which German bombers were subsequently able to exploit. But the results of this attack went unappreciated, and the tactic was never seriously repeated. In what has been called "one of the greatest errors of the war," Hermann Goering, the head of the Luftwaffe, called off all further attacks against the radar stations, and, with the exception of some later attempts to jam the radar system, the RAF's early warning system was allowed to function without any real interference.[45]

German intelligence also failed in other important ways. Through poor photoreconnaissance it consistently underestimated Fighter Command's strength throughout the battle, and, most critically, the grievous damage it had inflicted on the RAF's sector airfields by the end of August. It is generally accepted that had the Luftwaffe continued with these attacks instead of switching to London the outcome of the battle could well have been very different.[46]

COMMAND ORGANIZATION. The attention given to the role of radar has largely eclipsed the importance of the organization that made use of the information that it and other sources collected. The RAF's air defense system was divided geographically into four groups, with 11 Group responsible for London and southeast England where most of the fighting would occur. Each group was further divided into sectors organized around a major RAF airfield that typically hosted two or three fighter squadrons. An engagement usually began with the radar plots being phoned through to the filter room at Fighter Command's headquarters at Bentley Priory in northwest London. Here the plots were compared with other radar reports and also checked against the known location of friendly aircraft.[47] The filtered information—estimated height, strength, and direction of the raid—along with a specific designation was then passed simultaneously to the operations rooms at the sector, group, and main Fighter Command headquarters where it was displayed on large tabletop maps. While Fighter Command headquarters monitored events, the group operations rooms were responsible for assigning specific

45. Deighton, *Fighter,* pp. 205–09, 223. The British were also successful in deceiving German intelligence by broadcasting false signals saying that at least one of the radar stations had escaped destruction.

46. Hart, *History of the Second World War,* p. 95.

47. The RAF, besides fitting Special Identification Friend or Foe (IFF) radio broadcasting devices to every aircraft, also established a network of high-frequency direction-finding stations in each sector to take bearings on the communications of its fighters.

squadrons to meet the attack and also for coordinating antiaircraft fire in their area and warning the civil defense forces. The controllers at the sector operations rooms in turn alerted their squadrons, "scrambled" them at the appropriate moment, and finally guided or "vectored" them by radio to intercept the attacking forces.[48]

There was little margin for error. Twenty minutes' warning was about the best that the radar along the Kent coast could give, although Sigint would sometimes provide some advance notice to prepare the defenses. Once the attacking aircraft had been detected, it then took approximately four minutes for the plot to be filtered and passed to the various operations rooms. Since attacking aircraft would take only five to six minutes to cross the channel at its narrowest point while, on average, the fighters needed thirteen to seventeen minutes (depending on the aircraft) to get off the ground to an altitude of 20,000 feet, the group controllers did not have much time to assign forces to meet the attack.[49] The performance of the system was undeniably helped by the RAF's prewar exercises, which helped iron out some initial problems. As the battle progressed, Fighter Command constantly refined the system on the basis of operational experience.[50] Despite the inherent fragility of the system—the radar stations, operations rooms, and communications were all highly susceptible to bomb damage—Fighter Command also showed great resilience and adaptability in keeping it in service.

In contrast to Fighter Command's highly integrated air defense organization, the attacking German air forces suffered from a divided command arrangement. Responsibility for the air offensive against England fell predominantly to the Second and Third Air Fleets, the former operating from northeastern France and the Low Countries and the latter from northwest France. The self-contained nature of each air fleet had proved effective for supporting the ground war in France, but

48. For further details see Deighton, *Fighter*, pp. 118–26.
49. These figures are taken from Cox, "Battle of Britain," p. 4.
50. See John M. Ziman, *The Force of Knowledge: The Scientific Dimension of Society* (Cambridge University Press, 1976), p. 314. Fighter Command also established a small study group to assess the performance of its air defenses. Known as the Stanmore Research Section, its work is usually considered to represent the beginning of what became known as operations research. See in particular Stanmore Research Section, *The Capacity of the R.D.F. System,* Report 110 (London: Royal Air Force, November 1940). This and other reports can be found in the Air Historical Branch Archives of the U.K. Ministry of Defence, London. I am grateful to its staff, especially Sebastian Cox, for helping me locate historical material about the battle as well as for much useful guidance.

it was not well suited to the demands of an all-air campaign against Britain. Each fleet formulated its own plans and submitted them independently for Goering's approval.[51] As a consequence many of the attacks were neither regularly synchronized to apply maximum pressure on the RAF's defenses nor specially designed to exploit its weaknesses. When this happened—whether by design or accident—the results were significantly better.

COMMUNICATIONS. Without communications, Britain's air defense system simply could not have functioned. As two U.S. Army observers reported at the time

> The secret of the success of the operations is rapid, reliable and accurate channels of communications. The British have installed a very elaborate system of communications, consisting of the telephone, the teletypewriter and the radio. This . . . must have been extremely expensive and required years, but it is the framework upon which the defenses of Britain are built. If England successfully resists an invasion it will be because of this. . . . The fact that an airplane can be picked up by a radio watchman and its position, direction of flight, and so forth reported to a fighter station in a matter of seconds is illustrative of the care with which this system has been designed and of its value.[52]

Although the high-frequency radios used by Fighter Command had a limited range and sometimes suffered from mutual interference, they were at least minimally effective. The same was evidently not true for the German fighters. Their "greatest handicap," according to one historian, "was the primitiveness of their radio equipment. Although they had radio-telephony for intercommunications during flight, theirs was poor compared with the British—and they could not be controlled from the ground."[53] Neither, incredibly, could the German fighters communicate with the bombers they were escorting.[54]

OVERVIEW. Again, numerous factors contributed to the outcome of the Battle of Britain. The combat qualities of the RAF fighters, the skill and motivation of their pilots (the immortalized "few"), the British aircraft manufacturing base that kept up with their losses, and the limited

51. Hart, *History of the Second World War*, pp. 90–91; and Deighton, *Fighter*, p. 193.

52. Quoted in David L. Woods, *A History of Tactical Communication Techniques* (Orlando, Fla.: Martin-Marietta Corp., 1965), p. 202.

53. Hart, *History of the Second World War*, p. 92.

54. Deighton, *Fighter*, p. 232.

range of the German fighters, which reduced their flying time over England, are some of the more significant ones. So too was the performance of Fighter Command's air defense system. As Winston Churchill observed after the war, "All the ascendency of the Hurricanes and Spitfires would have been fruitless but for this system of underground control centres and telephone cables."[55] The integrated nature of the system in which the information gathered by forwardly positioned warning sensors was quickly processed and passed to fighter controllers, who in turn directed their aircraft to meet the threat, was unprecedented in warfare. Churchill caught the essence of the system when he remarked that "it had been shaped and refined in constant action, and all was now fused together into a most elaborate instrument of war, the like of which existed nowhere in the world."[56]

The RAF's air defense command and control system contributed to its military effectiveness in three fundamental ways. First, by allowing aircraft to be scrambled on warning, the system reduced Fighter Command's vulnerability to attack on the ground. Second, by avoiding the need for standing patrols of British airspace, the system dramatically improved Fighter Command's economy of effort. Its limited resources could be used when and where they were most needed, thereby reducing the demands on men and machines. This benefit alone has been calculated as practically doubling the effective strength of Fighter Command.[57] The system also allowed the architects of the RAF victory—the head of Fighter Command, Air Chief Marshal Sir Hugh Dowding and the commander of 11 Group, Air Vice Marshal Keith R. Park—to husband their scarce resources by committing only single squadrons to meet each attack. They also rotated those units exhausted from the battle with fresh ones from other groups.[58] Third, the system improved the probability that the enemy could be successfully engaged. It has been estimated that the

55. Winston S. Churchill, *Their Finest Hour* (Houghton Mifflin Company, 1949), p. 333.

56. Churchill, *Their Finest Hour*, p. 334.

57. Ziman, *Force of Knowledge*, p. 315. The value of this system was demonstrated at a later date when the RAF was forced to adopt standing patrols to meet the threats from low-flying aircraft that were not detectable by radar. See Research Branch, *An Analysis of the Effectiveness of the Measures Used against Low Flying Raids by German Fighters and Fighter-Bombers from December 1941 to June 1943*, Fighter Command Report 697 (London: Fighter Command, 1950), p. 5.

58. RAF Air Historical Branch, *Air Defence of Great Britain*, vol. 2, AIR 41/15 (London: Public Records Office, n.d.), pp. 568–70.

possession of radar increased the probability of interception by a factor of about ten.[59] Given sufficient warning by radar, the RAF fighters could also climb to a superior altitude and make use of the position of the sun to gain tactical advantage over their prey. Together these operational benefits helped Fighter Command prevail over an enemy who failed to appreciate the workings of the system and who suffered command shortcomings of its own.

The Battle of Midway

Just as the Battle of Britain is viewed as a watershed in the course of the European war, so the encounter between Japanese and American naval forces at Midway in June 1942 is widely seen as one of the turning points of the Pacific war. What began as an attempt to lure the U.S. Pacific fleet into a decisive battle by invading the Midway Islands ended with the Japanese Combined Fleet under the command of Admiral Isoroku Yamamoto losing four aircraft carriers and one heavy cruiser. The U.S. Navy lost one carrier and one escort destroyer in return. As a consequence, Japanese naval forces would never again foray offensively so deep into the Pacific. In the words of Admiral Chester W. Nimitz, the commander in chief of the U.S. Pacific fleet, the battle of Midway "made everything else possible."[60] Relative command performance again made a critical contribution to the outcome of the battle.

INTELLIGENCE. The foundation of the American victory at Midway was undoubtedly laid with its success in breaking the Japanese naval communications code. Well before the battle had started, the U.S Navy Combat Intelligence Office at Pearl Harbor furnished Nimitz with accurate details of Japan's operational intentions and order of battle from decoded communication intercepts. So accurate was this advance warning that a U.S. intelligence officer's prediction of when and where the first contact would be made with the Japanese fleet was off by only five minutes, five degrees, and five miles.[61] This information robbed the

59. This increase was then reportedly doubled through the efforts of a small team of operational researchers working for Fighter Command. Charles Goodeve, "Operational Research," *Nature,* vol. 161 (March 1948), p. 377. I am grateful to Professor Ronnie Shepherd of the Royal Ordnance Systems Group for bringing this article to my attention.

60. Quoted in Prange, *Miracle at Midway,* p. 395.

61. Prange, *Miracle at Midway,* p. 102. For background information on U.S intelligence before Midway see David Kahn, *The Codebreakers: The Story of Secret Writing* (Signet, 1973), pp. 300–11.

Japanese of strategic surprise and allowed Nimitz to bolster the forces on Midway, concentrate his carrier forces, and position them advantageously to meet the impending attack.

Vital though this information was, it should not obscure the fact that on the eve of the battle, the U.S fleet was still in the dark over the precise movements of the Japanese fleet.[62] In order to strike the first and potentially decisive blow, it was essential that U.S. reconnaissance aircraft pinpoint the whereabouts of the Japanese fleet before it discovered the presence of the waiting U.S. carriers. To achieve this aim, Nimitz cleverly positioned his naval forces beyond the range of Japanese carrier-based reconnaissance aircraft while leaving the search mission to the longer-range land-based surveillance aircraft on Midway. The plan worked: in what Nimitz would later call "the most important contact of the battle," Midway's aircraft were able to radio back the location of the approaching Japanese fleet without compromising the presence of the U.S. carrier force.[63]

The importance of intelligence to the U.S. victory at Midway should not hide how much poor Japanese intelligence contributed to Japan's defeat. From the beginning of the operation, the Japanese were plagued with a series of intelligence failures. Having lost the use of its spies at Pearl Harbor, the Japanese navy developed a plan for long-range aircraft and submarines to patrol close to Hawaii and report on the movements of U.S. naval forces. One of these submarines, however, was sunk en route, while the others arrived after the U.S. fleet had left for their positions off Midway. The air reconnaissance mission, meanwhile, had to be abandoned after it was discovered that the prearranged rendezvous point for refueling the aircraft was unexpectedly occupied by American forces.[64] Ironically, the Japanese navy had also put great faith in being able to track the whereabouts of the U.S fleet by intercepting its radio communications. While the U.S. ships already at sea evidently escaped detection by this method, Yamamoto's headquarters ship did pick up unusual and, to some, suspicious radio activity emanating from Hawaii.[65] Such was the paranoia over breaking radio silence, however, that this intelligence was never shared with Admiral Chuichi Nagumo, the commander of the Japanese carrier force spearheading the attack on

62. Prange, *Miracle at Midway*, pp. 125–26.
63. Quoted in Prange, *Miracle at Midway*, pp. 99, 190.
64. Prange, *Miracle at Midway*, pp. 31–32, 54, 122–23, 145.
65. See Walter Lord, *Incredible Victory* (Pocket Books, 1968), pp. 38–39.

Midway. Furthermore, the radio receiver on his flagship was less powerful than Yamamoto's, which effectively cut him off from Tokyo's intelligence as well.[66] Thus in their effort to deny intelligence to the enemy, the Japanese ended up denying to themselves what they had collected.

These shortcomings might still have been rectified had the Japanese fleet's scouting aircraft not performed so abysmally at the outset of the battle. The origins of this failure can be traced back to well before the war. The predominantly offensive orientation of the Imperial Navy meant that fleet reconnaissance—considered essentially defensive in nature—received little emphasis in planning, training, or equipment priorities. Consequently, the Japanese navy never developed dedicated carrier-borne search aircraft. Instead it relied on modified bombers; nor did the navy train its aviators in specialized surveillance techniques. Also, in order not to deplete the fleet's offensive potential, no more than 10 percent of its aircraft could be used for aerial reconnaissance. As one historian has remarked, "Failure to appreciate and utilize aerial reconnaissance handicapped the Nagumo force in every action from Pearl Harbor onward."[67]

At Midway, the Japanese also suffered from a flawed search plan that failed to maximize the chances of detecting enemy forces in its vicinity. As a result, large, and what proved to be important, gaps occurred in reconnaissance coverage of the area.[68] Still, even at this late stage, the ignorance of the Japanese commanders might have been rectified had it not been for the horrendous quality of the reporting from the scouting aircraft that eventually discovered the presence of the U.S. carriers. At what in hindsight appear as crucial moments in the battle, Admiral Nagumo received a succession of frustratingly incomplete, ambiguous, or conflicting reports from his scout planes. Had these messages been more accurate and timely, they might have changed the whole course of the engagement and its eventual outcome. As Nagumo lamented afterward, "We had practically no intelligence concerning the enemy. We never knew to the end where and how many enemy carriers there

66. Prange, *Miracle at Midway*, pp. 145–46. Ironically the role played by U.S. radio intelligence during the battle appears to have been negligible. Japan also changed its naval code just before the battle.

67. Prange, *Miracle at Midway*, p. 182.

68. Prange, *Miracle at Midway*, pp. 185–86, 380. Though it is hard to determine its impact on the course of the battle, the Japanese carriers, unlike their American counterparts, had no radar.

were."[69] As he was to discover, "fighting blind" can be a fatal handicap.

COMMAND ORGANIZATION. The Japanese naval force was also hampered by a divided command arrangement for the operation. Despite being in overall command, Admiral Yamamoto located his headquarters on the battleship *Yamato,* which sailed 300 miles behind Nagumo's main carrier strike force. This separation, as just indicated, not only deprived Nagumo of the latest intelligence reports on U.S. naval activity but also divorced Yamamoto from control of the battle once it had commenced. Nothing illustrates this handicap more clearly than the bizarre directive that Nagumo received from Yamamoto toward the end of the battle. With two of his carriers already sunk, another in the process of being abandoned, and a fourth irretrievably aflame, Nagumo was urged to continue the invasion plan of Midway and engage the enemy fleet.[70]

Nimitz, in contrast, kept in touch with events throughout the battle but rarely intervened to influence its course.[71] Instead he delegated tactical control of U.S. operations to his two task force commanders— Admirals Frank Jack Fletcher and Raymond A. Spruance. The U.S. tactical command arrangements also proved flexible in adversity. After the loss of his flagship, the carrier *Yorktown,* Fletcher selflessly transferred tactical control of the battle to Spruance rather than go through the lengthy procedure of reconstituting his command on another carrier.[72]

COMMUNICATIONS. Both sides suffered from poor communications at Midway. In many respects the United States had a definite advantage in operating close to its main base. The undersea cable between Hawaii and Midway was also helpful as a reliable and secure link, something that radio could not provide. Communications between Midway and the naval task forces, in contrast, were never good, causing uncoordinated actions on several occasions. In fact the after-action reports by officers aboard the U.S. carriers complained bitterly of the failure of Midway to pass potentially vital information to the task forces, information that might have cost the United States dearly or, alternatively, been used to exact an even higher toll on the enemy.[73]

69. See Prange, *Miracle at Midway,* pp. 223–25, 278–79, 296–97, quotation on p. 94.

70. Prange, *Miracle at Midway,* p. 304.

71. Nimitz intervened, for instance, at the outset of the battle when he believed that Fletcher might mistake the Japanese landing force for the main carrier group. Prange, *Miracle at Midway,* p. 170.

72. Prange, *Miracle at Midway,* pp. 288–89.

73. Prange, *Miracle at Midway,* pp. 105, 230, 242–43, 301, 389.

Japanese communications, as just discussed, were hampered by the self-imposed restrictions on the use of radio and by the distance between Tokyo and the ships at sea. "How to get in touch with his ships without betraying his whereabouts plagued Yamamoto all through the cruise and during the sea fight that followed."[74] One Japanese report on naval communications during the war argues, furthermore, that a malfunctioning radio transmitter prevented one of the reconnaissance aircraft from alerting Nagumo to the presence of the U.S. carriers, thereby contributing to the catastrophe that befell his force.[75] The subsequent U.S. attacks on the Japanese carriers also dealt a serious blow to Japanese communications. As the same Japanese report states, "Communications became impossible, and even when the emergency communications plan was undertaken, communications remained temporarily in a state of considerable confusion. The fleet headquarters was then transferred . . . to the CL *Nagara,* which took command and placed communications under control. However, signal communications and radio communications were not efficiently executed due to shortage of equipment and personnel."[76] Control of aircraft operations was also shifted to the remaining carrier, the *Hiryu,* but its communications capacity was insufficient to handle the extra load. Although further attacks were launched from this carrier, "Considerable confusion resulted due to maladjustment of the transmitters and poor tuning."[77] What effect this had on Japanese combat performance at this late stage in the battle is hard to judge, however.

OVERVIEW. Doubtless the forewarning provided by U.S. naval intelligence gave Nimitz an important advantage in planning and preparing for the battle of Midway. As General George C. Marshall later declared, "We were able to concentrate our limited forces to meet their naval advance on Midway when otherwise we almost certainly would have been some 3,000 miles out of place."[78] Beyond allowing U.S. forces to be readied in position at the right place and at the right time, the intelligence, as indicated earlier, enabled Midway's defenses to be

74. Prange, *Miracle at Midway,* p. 129.
75. Military History Section, Headquarters, Army Forces Far East, *Operational History of Naval Communications: December 1941–August 1945,* Japanese monograph 118 (Washington: Department of the Army, Office of the Chief of Military History, 1953), pp. 259–60.
76. Military History Section, *Operational History,* p. 260.
77. Military History Section, *Operational History,* p. 261.
78. Kahn, *Codebreakers,* p. 314.

upgraded and its reconnaissance aircraft readied to provide advance warning on the whereabouts of the Japanese fleet. Intelligence failures contributed almost as much to Japan's defeat as U.S. intelligence did to its victory. The poor performance of Japan's reconnaissance aircraft was especially grievous and conceded a serious, arguably decisive, advantage to the Americans.

The Limits of Analysis

These three case studies illustrate the importance of command performance to the outcome of battle. What they do not show, though, is how important it was. In other words, what difference did relative command performance really make in each battle? Could a fully functioning and effective Allied command system in 1940, for example, have compensated for the other deficiencies in the Allied military posture? Would all the benefits that the RAF's air defense system gave its fighters have been for nought had the German Luftwaffe not made the fateful switch from attacking RAF airfields to bombing London? And finally, despite the advance warning, the battle of Midway was still a very close call for the Americans. As Gordon W. Prange is careful to emphasize, "The final debacle was due to a stroke of good luck on the United States side—the uncoordinated coordination of the [U.S.] dive bombers hitting three carriers at once while the torpedo strikes were still in progress. Except for those six short minutes, Nagumo would have been the victor, and all his decisions would have been accounted to him for righteousness. Timidity would have become prudence, vacillation due deliberation, rigidity attention to the voice of experience."[79] Collectively these questions beg the larger question of whether command performance can be measured or accounted for in a precise and meaningful way. More important, can a command system be evaluated in advance of being put to the test to determine likely performance and adequacy?

In an effort to bring some clarity and rigor to the task of answering these questions, some analysts make the distinction between measures of performance, measures of effectiveness, and measures of force

79. Prange, *Miracle at Midway*, pp. 374–75.

effectiveness.[80] The distinction between each of these measures can best be described with reference to the operation of a specific command system, such as the one employed by the RAF during the Battle of Britain. Here the technical characteristics of the air defense radars, their detection capabilities and reliability, as well as the speed and capacity of the communications links among the different command centers would constitute measures of performance. How the different components of the command system collectively functioned to improve overall military performance exemplifies measures of effectiveness. These measures would include, therefore, Fighter Command's reaction time to raid warnings and the probability that attacking aircraft could be intercepted and destroyed with or without the benefit of early warning (standing patrols versus scrambled intercepts). Finally, measures of force effectiveness would determine the extent to which the command system contributed to the final outcome of an engagement—in this case the ratio of attrition between the RAF and the Luftwaffe. Other variables—the pilot's skill, aircraft performance, relative quality of the weapons— would have to be considered to make such a judgment.

Although some limited success has been achieved in quantifying measures of effectiveness, it has generally been in narrowly defined cases. For example, the marginal value of a new surveillance sensor for detecting and tracking certain military targets, or a data processing system for managing inflowing information can be evaluated by holding other variables constant. Even the more complex task of assessing different configurations of headquarters to determine optimum performance levels for specific tasks can to some extent be measured. Similarly, for well-defined command systems with fairly circumscribed mission responsibilities, such as air defense or strategic nuclear retaliation, some measures of effectiveness are possible.[81] These studies have value but only with the knowledge that other factors, which may influence the performance of a command system, are excluded or held constant. To endeavor to account for everything seems a hopeless task, however. Since the underlying process of command and control is about gathering, evaluating, and communicating information, so much of what is impor-

---

80. This section draws on the work of Alberts, "C²I Assessment." See also Schutzer, "C² Theory"; and Alexander H. Levis, "Modeling and Measuring Effectiveness of C³ Systems," in *Integration and Cooperation,* proceedings of the 1986 AFCEA European Symposium (Washington: AFCEA International Press, 1987), pp. 107–11.

81. See Alberts, "C²I Assessment."

tant is beyond practicable quantification. Some qualities of information—accuracy, completeness, and promptness—can be recorded and measured, but what about the tacit and informal types of information that often make such a difference in command interactions?[82] And what about the human factors that affect how information is received, processed, and utilized by decisionmakers under stressful conditions?

Even the more limited and what seems by comparison straightforward exercise of determining the vulnerability of a command system to attack is fraught with uncertainty. The physical hardness of a command center or communications facility to certain forms of attack can be computed with reasonable precision, as can the susceptibility of a radio link to electronic jamming, but how does one assess the consequences of their loss or disruption? There may be back-up systems available to take their place either permanently or temporarily, but are they equally capable and are they available immediately? If not, what effect does the difference in capability and the time taken to activate the alternative make to overall effectiveness? And finally how does one evaluate the capacity of personnel to improvise, show initiative, and pick up the reins of leadership if elements of a command system are damaged or destroyed?[83] In narrowly defined contexts the analytical uncertainty can be bounded in a way that permits conclusions to be reached with some confidence, but in much larger cases it seems too great to allow any precise or definitive assessment.

Although command performance cannot be meaningfully measured, it is too important to be ignored or classified as just another intangible factor, like morale, that influences military effectiveness. Knowledge of the discernible components of a command system, what functions they are designed to perform, and the nature of the challenges and problems they could encounter when put under stress does permit some qualified judgments about their likely performance. It is also possible to reach some conclusions about whether the command system in any way prevents or limits a commander's freedom of action to perform a given mission, for example, by depriving a commander of essential information or connectivity to his subordinate units.

82. See Martin van Creveld, *Command in War* (Harvard University Press, 1985), p. 262.

83. Some of these questions have been raised in the context of a NATO–Warsaw Pact war by Joshua M. Epstein, *Measuring Military Power: The Soviet Air Threat to Europe* (Princeton University Press, 1984), p. 195.

CHAPTER THREE

Command Challenges: Friction and Fluency

FEW HAVE MANAGED to convey so evocatively how a military commander can lose control over his forces with such disastrous consequences as Leo Tolstoy in his classic account in *War and Peace* of the Battle of Borodino in 1812. As he records, Napoleon was too far from the scene of action to sense what was happening and directly influence the course of the battle. In short, he lost control of his forces and, in the confusion and uncertainty that prevailed, thousands of men perished.[1] While the Napoleonic wars "mark[ed] the end of an epoch in which it was possible for a commander in chief to overlook a field *and* take a direct part in the conduct of the engagement," subsequent technical and managerial innovations to help keep decisionmakers in touch with events and in control of operations have not succeeded in turning the clock back to an earlier era.[2] Just over a century later, despite the advent of elaborate staff systems, reconnaissance aircraft, and field telephones, the British high command was just as ignorant, perhaps more so, of what was transpiring during the Battle of the Somme as Napoleon had been at Borodino.[3] More than eighty years after that, with all the technological

---

1. Leo Tolstoy, *War and Peace* (Modern Library, 1983), pp. 733–34, 747–48.
2. Martin van Creveld, *Command in War* (Harvard University Press, 1985), p. 95 (emphasis in original).
3. John Keegan, *The Face of Battle* (London: Jonathan Cape, 1977), pp. 259–60.

marvels at the disposal of modern military commanders, the task of command is no easier and in many respects has grown much harder than it was in Napoleon's day.

Military command systems have become increasingly complex organisms and, as a result, more prone to what has been called "command friction."[4] As will become evident, this phenomenon is remarkably common, causing on many occasions a significant degradation of military effectiveness. Awareness and understanding of the most common sources of command friction can serve as a general frame of reference for evaluating the susceptibility of contemporary command systems, such as NATO's, to this phenomenon. Understanding and knowing how to reduce this friction and enhance its converse—"command fluency"— are equally important and are discussed, therefore, in the concluding part of this chapter.

Command Challenges

Although the basic purpose of command and control has remained constant, the challenges to effective management of military forces in periods of crisis and war have undoubtedly grown despite and sometimes paradoxically because of the technical and organizational efforts to make it easier. While technology has striven to keep up with the added demands, it has in some respects become part of the problem. The most significant challenges are as follows.[5]

—Force size. For some states, the sheer size of the forces that they must maintain control over has grown. Millions of men and women are now under arms in some countries, with still greater numbers ready to be mobilized at short notice. Coalition groupings add further to the size of military forces and with it the burden on the mechanisms of control.

4. This term, as far as it is known, was first coined by Edward Luttwak who was no doubt inspired by Carl von Clausewitz and his general concept of "friction" in war. See Edward N. Luttwak, *Strategy: The Logic of War and Peace* (Belknap Harvard, 1987), pp. 13–15.

5. This section draws in part on van Creveld, *Command in War*, pp. 1–5; and Air Vice Marshal P. R. Mallorie, "Electronic Warfare: Command, Control, Communications, and Intelligence," in Maj. Gen. K. Perkins, ed., *Weapons and Warfare: Conventional Weapons and Their Roles in Battle* (London: Brassey's Defence Publishers, 1987), pp. 232–34.

The capacity of a single person or group of individuals to oversee and directly influence their actions has inevitably declined as a consequence.

—Spatial dispersion. For many of the same countries, management of forces has become a global undertaking. The two world wars and the extension of the superpower confrontation beyond Europe have widened the geographical span of control that certain states must now exercise over their dispersed forces.[6] Military forces also long ago ceased being confined to the earth's surface and now operate in many different dimensions—ground, air, sea, undersea, and most recently outer space. Each medium has distinctive operational characteristics and environmental constraints that pose added challenges to command and control. The growth in the size of forces, their increasing mobility, and the need to disperse forces to minimize their exposure to the growing lethality of modern weaponry have furthermore enlarged the area over which battles are now frequently fought.

—Force complexity. The multidimensional nature of military operations as well as the growing sophistication and diversity of modern weaponry has inevitably created a greater specialization of personnel skills and, with it, the further organizational partition of armed forces. Mutual cooperation and coordination, as a consequence of these trends, have become more necessary and more difficult to achieve.

—Operational tempo. The increasing reach of armed forces and the speed at which they and their weaponry travel have raised the tempo of military operations, reducing in the process the time for political and military decisionmakers to respond to events. Command systems, therefore, have to function more quickly if they are to stay apace of fast-breaking developments.

—Operational span. At the same time as reaction times have contracted, the normal span of military operations has expanded. What was typically confined to daylight and benign weather is now frequently practiced twenty-four hours a day and in all seasons. The respite, therefore, that commanders and their staffs might have enjoyed during an imposed lull in the fighting has been progressively eroded, placing on them still greater physical stress and mental strain than before. Differences between time zones of the centers of decision and the locus of operations have a similar effect.

6. Whether the demands placed on today's superpowers are significantly different in relative terms from those facing, for example, ancient Rome at the height of its empire is debatable.

—Escalatory danger. The danger of escalation in the nuclear age has reduced what latitude there was for accidental or unauthorized uses of force. Much tighter controls and safety precautions are necessary to ensure that military operations are fully responsive to political authority.

As a consequence of the growing challenges to command and control, three principal trends are discernible in the evolution of command systems. The first is a greater dependency on technical support systems. Electro-mechanical devices have become virtually indispensable to the collection, processing, and dissemination of information. In some cases the command response times have become so short that they preclude useful human involvement in decisionmaking, leaving this function to automated devices. The second trend is greater organizational complexity. As the size and diversity of modern military forces have grown, command organizations have become more elaborate and complex. The increasing specialization of military functions, as just indicated, has caused greater bureaucratic division within a military force. As a result, more force components have to be supervised, coordinated, and directed to effect the smooth running of the organization. This necessity in turn has led to a growth in the size of the command components of military force. The number of personnel with command functions—intelligence analysts, headquarters staff, signals units—has proliferated along with the operating rules and procedures that are required to run the system.[7]

The third and related trend is a greater devolution of authority. The growth in the size of forces as well as the contraction of decision response times has inevitably required commanders to delegate more of their authority to subordinates to take decisions affecting military operations. More centers of decisionmaking have to be coordinated and managed as a consequence. This trend has not gone unresisted, however. Over the same period political and military decisionmakers have endeavored to centralize control, partly out of fear of escalation in the nuclear age and partly because communications technology has opened up opportunities that permit it. The trade-off between centralization and decentralization has become an enduring dilemma to military commanders.

With these three trends—greater technical dependency, organizational complexity, and devolution of authority—command systems have become more exposed to the vagaries of command friction.

7. See Richard E. Simpkin, *Race to the Swift: Thoughts on Twenty-First Century Warfare* (London: Brassey's Defence Publishers, 1985), pp. 261–63.

Command Friction

Human beings and machines rarely operate at peak performance. Something usually subtracts from their full working potential. The loss of efficiency may be minor with negligible results, but it can also be serious with important consequences. Military command systems, like any other complex social organism that relies on electromechanical devices, are subject to operational problems that degrade performance. Under normal circumstances "command friction" may be little more than a nuisance. At other times, such as during periods of extraordinary demand and stress, the effect on command performance and with it military effectiveness can be considerable and sometimes even catastrophic. The sources of command friction are manifold, but they fall into two categories: those that are externally generated and those that are internally generated. Such friction can affect every part of the command process from the collection of information to how it is used and transmitted.

Command friction is most likely to manifest itself when the normal pattern of operations is interrupted or when sudden and unexpected demands are placed on the command system. Wartime, obviously, is the most stressful time and for this reason the following examples, which illustrate the multifarious sources of command friction, have been drawn from wartime experience.[8] Command friction, however, is by no means confined to conditions of combat. Similar problems have affected command performance during international crises as will be illustrated later.

External Sources

There are two basic sources of external friction: those induced by the enemy and those induced by the environment.

ENEMY FRICTION. By far the most serious external source of command friction derives from the deliberate interference of an adversary. Military commanders have always tried to gain advantage on the battlefield

---

8. Although command friction has been evident since war became an organized human activity, the following examples are drawn from the Second World War onward.

by manipulating the information that the enemy collects about their strength, disposition, and, ultimately, their intentions. Such deception has traditionally entailed either hiding information from the other side or presenting it with false information. Combatants have also often exploited weaknesses in their opponent's command arrangements, such as disunity in their leadership or poor cohesion and coordination among their military forces. Although these measures might today be called command suppression tactics, the idea of deliberately undermining or disabling an enemy's command system as a coherent objective in military strategy is relatively new. Only since the expansion of command organizations in the late nineteenth and early twentieth centuries and, moreover, with their increasing dependence on electromechanical devices for collecting and transmitting information, have they become a target for deliberate attack.

One of the first to articulate the potential benefits of directing attacks on an opponent's command system was J. F. C. Fuller. In a book written in 1925 he wrote,

> The brains of an army are its staff—army, corps, and divisional headquarters; could we suddenly remove these from an extensive sector of the enemy's front the total collapse of the fighting personnel would be but a matter of hours, even if only slight pressure is exerted against it. . . . [O]ur present theory of offensive action is based on the idea of destroying personnel, new means of war, so I am convinced, will force us to substitute a theory based on the idea of destroying command—not after the enemy's personnel has been disorganized, but, when it is possible, *before it has been attacked,* so that it may be found in a state of disorganization when attacked. I am convinced that this will take place, because in this form of attack I see the highest application of the principle of surprise—surprise by novelty of action—or the impossibility of counter-action even when the unexpected has become the commonplace.[9]

This is the general approach that was practiced with devastating effect by the Wehrmacht. Yet while blitzkrieg had the effect of confusing and paralyzing the enemy's command system, it was not so much the result of deliberate attack or interference with the instruments of command as the indirect effect of rapid and deep maneuver.[10] In fact there seems to be little evidence that the technical components of the Polish, French,

---

9. Col. John Frederick Charles Fuller, *The Foundations of the Science of War* (London: Hutchinson and Co., Ltd., 1926), p. 292 (emphasis added).

10. See Barry R. Posen, *The Sources of Military Doctrine: France, Britain, and Germany between the World Wars* (Cornell University Press, 1984), p. 206.

or Soviet command systems were singled out for attack as part of a premeditated plan before the German offensives of 1940–41.[11]

It was also well into the war before the Allies began to practice deliberate countercommand and control tactics. The preparation for the Normandy landings and the Allied bomber offensive are probably the two main cases where a concerted effort was made to deceive and degrade the enemy command system.[12] Localized and sporadic communications jamming and command post targeting were the norm.[13]

With the exception of the air campaigns, there was little opportunity for the United States to practice electronic jamming or other countermeasures during its two principal postwar military engagements in Korea and Vietnam.[14] In fact it was not until the Arab-Israeli conflicts of 1967, 1973, and 1982 that countercommand and control warfare really came into its own.

The preemptive Israeli strike at the beginning of the Six-Day War in 1967 singled out the antiquated and exposed Egyptian military communications system for attack. Some have even argued that its vulnerability may have added to the Israeli incentives for preemption.[15] The strike

11. In the latter case, at least, there is some disagreement over how much the collapse of the Soviet command system was preplanned. See Amnon Sella, "'Barbarossa': Surprise Attack and Communication," *Journal of Contemporary History,* vol. 13 (July 1978), pp. 555–83; and Russel H. S. Stolfi, Lonnie O. Ratley III, and John F. O'Neill, Jr., *German Disruption of Soviet Command, Control, and Communications in Barbarossa, 1941,* prepared for the Department of Defense (Monterey, Calif.: Naval Postgraduate School, 1983), pp. 107–08.

12. See Alfred Price, *Instruments of Darkness: The History of Electronic Warfare* (London: Macdonald and Jane's, 1977), pp. 97–250. Price claims that bomber command's jamming of German air defenses probably saved around a thousand aircraft. See also Gordon Welchman, *The Hut Six Story* (McGraw-Hill, 1982), pp. 238–41.

13. For example, the U.S. Army employed an airborne jamming system to disrupt German tank communications during the Battle of the Bulge. See George Raynor Thompson and Dixie R. Harris, *The Signal Corps: The Outcome (Mid-1943 through 1951)* (Washington: U.S. Army, Office of the Chief of Military History, 1966), pp. 163–64. The Allies on a number of occasions also used their code-breaking success to ambush enemy commanders (for example, Admiral Isoroku Yamamoto) and attack their headquarters (for example, Panzer Group West Headquarters during the Normandy campaign). See David Kahn, *The Codebreakers: The Story of Secret Writing* (New American Library, 1973), pp. 330–38; and David Eisenhower, *Eisenhower: At War 1943–45* (Vintage Books, 1987), p. 289.

14. Price, *Instruments of Darkness,* pp. 251–53, 259–73; John D. Bergen, *Military Communications: A Test for Technology,* U.S. Army in Vietnam Series (Washington: U.S. Army, Center of Military History, 1986), pp. 393–94.

15. Robert D. Glasser, "Preemption in the Nuclear Age," Ph.D. dissertation, Australian National University, Canberra, Australia, 1988, pp. 56–57.

plan was also a subtle one: parts of the Egyptian communications system were selectively spared to allow their commanders to feed back self-serving and deceptively optimistic reports during the initial stages of the war. Once this had occurred the remaining links were severed to keep the Egyptian high command ignorant of the true situation at the front.[16]

The Egyptians evidently learned from this experience as they took great care to target the Israeli command system in the first days of the Yom Kippur War in 1973. Command posts, communications facilities, radar and signals intelligence (Sigint) sites were systematically and successfully attacked, causing great confusion for the Israelis.[17]

Arguably the most successful example of a well-planned and -executed countercommand and control operation in recent years was carried out by the Israeli air force in Lebanon in 1982, when in the space of ten minutes it virtually wiped out the entire network of Syrian surface-to-air batteries in the Bekaa Valley at little or no cost to itself. The Israelis carefully orchestrated the use of remotely piloted vehicles designed to deceive the Syrian air defense radars and collect valuable signals intelligence on their characteristics. They also used converted Boeing 707 ECM aircraft that could jam Syria's radars. Finally, Israel's airborne surveillance aircraft directed and coordinated subsequent attacks. In the air battles that took place, the Israelis gained a massive advantage over their Syrian opponents by jamming the communications links with Syria's ground controllers, thereby depriving them of early warning information. These countermeasures undoubtedly contributed to the heavily lopsided exchange ratio of more than eighty-five Syrian aircraft destroyed to Israel's two.[18]

ENVIRONMENTAL FRICTION. The other principal source of external

16. See Richard K. Betts, *Surprise Attack: Lessons for Defense Planning* (Brookings, 1982), p. 68.

17. See Peter Allen, *The Yom Kippur War* (Charles Scribner's Sons, 1982), pp. 62–63; Lt. Gen. Saad el Shazly, *The Crossing of the Suez* (San Francisco, Calif.: American Mideast Research, 1980), pp. 226, 235; and Col. R. M. Portugalskiy, "The Disruption of Enemy Troop Control," *Voyenno-Istoricheskiy Zhurnal*, no. 1 (January 1988), pp. 74–79, reprinted in *Joint Publications Research Service (JPRS) Report: Soviet Union Military History Journal* (June 15, 1988), pp. 34–37.

18. There has been some disagreement about these numbers. See Benjamin Lambeth, *Moscow's Lessons from the 1982 Lebanon Air War*, R-3000-AF (Santa Monica, Calif.: Rand Corp., 1984), pp. 4–11; and Mario de Arcangelis, *Electronic Warfare: From the Battle of Tsushima to the Falklands and Lebanon Conflicts* (Poole, Dorset, U.K.: Blanford Press, 1985), pp. 265–72.

command friction is the environment. There are numerous cases of the environment interfering with the performance of intelligence sensors and communications equipment at key moments during a war. The foliage of the Ardennes impeded French photoreconnaissance of the German offensive in 1940. Intelligence collection by the British in the jungles of Malaya and the Americans in Vietnam came up against the same problem. Mist, rain, fog, and cloud cover have all had the same effect at some time or another. Bad weather, for example, helped obscure the German buildup before the Battle of the Bulge in 1944 and the Japanese fortifications on the island of Iwo Jima, which in both cases had costly consequences.[19] Even with the impressive technical advances since then, intelligence collection is still in many respects at the mercy of the weather. Cloud cover over the Falklands, for instance, made reconnaissance difficult for the British during the Anglo-Argentinian conflict.[20]

The quality of communications also can vary with environmental conditions. The hills of Italy and Korea, the built-up areas of Germany, and the dense jungle foliage of Burma and the Pacific islands all helped to reduce the range of radios or interfere with reception during combat in those theaters.[21] The problem with jungle foliage in Vietnam prompted the use of helicopter-mounted radio relays, but although this use helped extend the range of tactical radios, it added to the congestion of the usable frequencies.[22] Atmospheric disturbances caused by sunspot activity, tropical storms, and the northern lights (aurora borealis) have also affected radio propagation in wartime.[23]

19. Charles B. MacDonald, *A Time for Trumpets: The Untold Story of the Battle of the Bulge* (William Morrow and Company, 1985), p. 56; Ronald H. Spector, *Eagle against the Sun: The American War with Japan* (Free Press, 1985), p. 498; and Dwight D. Eisenhower, *Crusade in Europe* (DaCapo Press, 1983), p. 346.

20. Drew Middleton, "Falkland Blockade: Gaps Still to Plug," *New York Times,* May 12, 1982, p. 12. See also Max Hastings and Simon Jenkins, *The Battle for the Falklands* (W. W. Norton and Company, 1983), p. 322.

21. See David L. Woods, *A History of Tactical Communication Techniques* (Orlando, Fla.: Martin-Marietta Corp., 1965), p. 232; Thompson and Harris, *Signal Corps: The Outcome,* pp. 219–20; and Maj. Gen. R. F. H. Nalder, *The History of British Army Signals in the Second World War* (London: Royal Signals Institution, 1953), pp. 95–96.

22. Bergen, *Military Communications,* pp. 155–56.

23. Woods, *History of Tactical Communication Techniques,* pp. 231–32; and Maj. Gen. Thomas Matthew Rienzi, *Communications-Electronics, 1962–1970,* Vietnam Studies (Washington: Department of the Army, 1972), p. 18.

Internal Sources

External sources of command friction can help expose and exacerbate problems that are essentially self-induced or internally generated. These can be categorized according to whether they are primarily technical, organizational, or human.

TECHNICAL FRICTION. Armed forces have often found their command and control equipment to be inadequate under the duress of wartime use. Sometimes this failure results from faulty design and insufficient testing or because unanticipated demands are made of the equipment. Several cases illustrate this problem. The harsh conditions of the North African desert evidently rendered British tank radios notoriously unreliable during the campaign there in the Second World War.[24] Similarly, Allied communications during the early amphibious operations of the war suffered because very little of the signaling equipment had been waterproofed against the possibility of water immersion or even the effects of sea spray.[25] These operations taught other lessons about the fragility of equipment. During the landings in North Africa (Operation Torch) the headquarters of the Western task force was located aboard the cruiser *Augusta*. No one had foreseen, however, that when the ship's guns opened fire as part of the preparatory bombardment, the ensuing recoil would knock out virtually all of the communications equipment aboard. Though in this instance the consequences were minor because the assault was largely unopposed, the identical mistake during the more difficult landings at Tarawa in the Pacific proved extremely costly to the U.S. Marines.[26]

Perhaps the most calamitous breakdown of communications from unreliable equipment occurred during the British airborne assault at Arnhem in 1944. Many of the radios dropped by air were too fragile to withstand the shock of the landing, and most of those that did, failed either to operate reliably or with the expected range. The scattered

24. Welchman, *The Hut Six Story*, p. 226.
25. Woods, *History of Tactical Communication Techniques*, p. 234; and Thompson and Harris, *Signal Corps: The Outcome*, p. 33.
26. See George Raynor Thompson and others, *The Signal Corps: The Test (December 1941 to July 1943)* (Washington: Department of the Army, Office of the Chief of Military History, 1957), p. 359; William B. Breuer, *Operation Torch: The Allied Gamble to Invade North Africa* (St. Martin's Press, 1985), pp. 202–03; and Spector, *Eagle against the Sun*, pp. 261–63. After the Tarawa operation the U.S. Navy used specially configured headquarters ships to direct amphibious landings.

elements of the British First Airborne Division, as a result, were never able to combine or coordinate their operations against the unexpectedly heavy opposition in the area. Meanwhile the Allied high command remained ignorant of the division's precarious situation until it was too late to do anything about it. Only on the last day of the operation, for instance, was close air support made available.[27]

U.S. forces also suffered from unreliable or inappropriate equipment in military operations after the war. Much of the U.S. communications equipment fielded, at least initially, in Korea and Vietnam, for example, had not been properly designed to operate in those relatively harsh environments.[28]

Next to fragile and unreliable equipment as a source of technically related command and control failure is the simple problem of not having enough working equipment to satisfy operational needs. Insufficient reconnaissance assets cost the French and Japanese forces in the two battles described earlier. German military intelligence on the eastern front in the Second World War also labored under the same handicap.[29] The lack of interpreters, air crews trained for photoreconnaissance, and intelligence analysts reportedly also contributed to the U.S. failure to predict the Chinese intervention in the Korean War.[30] A more recent case is the Falklands conflict in which the absence of airborne early warning aircraft cost the Royal Navy dearly when defending against Argentinian air attacks.[31]

Insufficient communications can be just as debilitating to military effectiveness. The collapse of Soviet communications at the outset of the Barbarossa offensive, for example, can be attributed as much to the paucity of signaling equipment as to the indirect effect of the German

27. See Christopher Hibbert, *The Battle of Arnhem* (Macmillan, 1962), pp. 71–73, 94–97, 204–05; Cornelius Ryan, *A Bridge Too Far* (Pocket Books, 1984), pp. 149–50, 200–01, 210–11; and Kenneth Macksey, *Military Errors of World War Two* (Poole, Dorset, U.K.: Arms and Armour Press, 1987), pp. 198–99.

28. See Robert Frank Futrell, Brig. Gen. Lawson S. Moseley, and Albert F. Simpson, *The United States Air Force in Korea, 1950–53* (Duell, Sloan, and Pearce, 1961), pp. 77–78, 429; and Bergen, *Military Communications*, pp. 258–59.

29. See Gen. Paul Deichnamm, *German Air Force Operations in Support of the Army,* U.S. Air Force Historical Studies, no. 163 (Arno Press, 1968), pp. 19–22, 60–66, 69–72.

30. See Richard Ned Lebow, *Between Peace and War: The Nature of International Crisis* (Johns Hopkins University Press, 1984), pp. 157–58.

31. John Nott, "The Falklands Campaign," *Proceeding/Naval Review,* vol. 109 (May 1983), pp. 129–30.

attacks.[32] The fall of Crete in 1941 is another example. The loss of Allied command and control from a shortage of communications equipment was so critical that one New Zealand staff officer reported after the war that "a hundred extra wireless sets could have saved Crete."[33] Much the same fate befell the American forces during the initial stages of North Korea's invasion of the South in 1950. As the official historian records, "The lack of information of the true state of affairs caused by the almost complete breakdown in all forms of communication was the major factor leading to the disaster."[34]

The frequency of such cases can be explained largely by the consistently low priority given to the acquisition of command and control equipment in comparison to the weapons they support. This bias is particularly evident when the mission also suffers from a low priority. Communications equipment for enabling close air support is a prime example. Even after the benefits of such support to Allied ground operations had been proven in North Africa, the resources devoted to making coordination possible were still pitifully small by the time the Normandy invasion was launched. During the British Goodwood offensive, for instance, only one forward air control unit was provided to direct air support for the entire central axis of the attack, and when this detachment was destroyed, no other means were available.[35] Similarly the British airborne forces at Arnhem at the last moment were given only two jeep-mounted radios to call in air strikes, and these turned out to be ineffective because they had not been modified to operate on the appropriate frequencies.[36]

A variation on the same theme of technical insufficiency is the common problem of information overload. This problem occurs when the volume of communications traffic exceeds the capacity of the available channels to handle it, causing lengthy and potentially critical delays. Command centers can also become so inundated with information that they can no

32. See Stolfi, Ratley, and O'Neill, *German Disruption of Soviet Command, Control, and Communications in Barbarossa, 1941*, pp. 21–23; John Erickson, *The Road to Stalingrad: Stalin's War with Germany*, vol. 1 (Harper and Row, 1975), pp. 116–20.

33. I. McD. G. Stewart, *The Struggle for Crete: 20 May–1 June 1941: A Story of Lost Opportunity* (Oxford University Press, 1966), p. 481.

34. Roy E. Appleman, *United States Army in the Korean War: South to the Naktong, North to the Yalu (June–November 1950)* (Washington: Department of the Army, Office of the Chief of Military History, 1961), p. 179.

35. Max Hastings, *Overlord: D-Day and the Battle for Normandy* (Simon and Schuster, 1984), p. 270.

36. Hibbert, *Battle of Arnhem*, pp. 96–97.

longer process and assimilate it in the time necessary to make useful decisions. During the critical first few hours of the Normandy invasion, for instance, the Allied headquarters in England was so overwhelmed with incoming traffic that the switchboard operators fell twelve hours behind in transcribing the radio messages. General Dwight D. Eisenhower, as a result, remained largely ignorant of events throughout the day. Even after his advanced headquarters had been established on French soil, the situation if anything got worse. High-priority messages would take twenty-four hours and sometimes longer to reach their destination.[37]

Not surprisingly the problem of information overload becomes particularly acute when the normal pattern of operations is unexpectedly disrupted, such as during a crisis or surprise attack. Emergency situations not only cause a sudden surge of demand for communications, but typically the character of the message traffic also changes. In particular, high-precedence communications requiring encryption or special handling dramatically increase, placing an added burden on the system. This state of events was evident at the Battle of the Bulge in 1944, during the opening attacks of the Korean War, and at the beginning of the Tet offensive in Vietnam.[38]

The Vietnam War provides a classic illustration of the problem of information overload. Here the demand for information and with it communications among the U.S. forces became virtually insatiable, outstripping the capacity of the system to satisfy their needs.[39] The increasing specialization of modern armies described earlier is largely to blame for the growth in demand. Whereas, for example, a U.S. division in the field during the Second World War was typically provided with four communications channels from its corps headquarters, and then with eight in Korea, combat brigades often had thirty-two in Vietnam.[40] The overly centralized nature of the U.S. command decision-making process in Vietnam, with Washington frequently intervening

37. Eisenhower, *Eisenhower: At War,* p. 267; and Macksey, *Military Errors,* p. 184.

38. Thompson and Harris, *Signal Corps: The Outcome,* p. 158; James A. Field, Jr., *History of United States Naval Operations: Korea* (Government Printing Office, 1962), pp. 56–57; and Bergen, *Military Communications,* p. 265.

39. The U.S. commander Gen. Creighton W. Abrams described the demand for communications as "almost a bottomless pit. No matter how big you make the system, there are more people going to want to talk over it and more people going to want to send things over it." Quoted in Rienzi, *Communications-Electronics,* p. 157.

40. Rienzi, *Communications-Electronics,* p. 57.

directly in operational matters, added to the strain on the communications system. This was reflected in the tremendous message traffic in and out of Vietnam during certain periods of the war.[41] The situation was no different for communications within Vietnam as messages were commonly held up by delays in the system. The tactics used to bypass clogged channels and speed up communications usually only made matters worse. The proliferation of "sole user" circuits reserved for certain individuals or units, for example, crowded the already congested airwaves. Troops would also raise the priority status of their messages to gain quicker service. The devaluation of the message-precedence system not only guaranteed that messages sent with the lowest classification would be hopelessly delayed, but its widespread abuse eventually became self-defeating. The situation became so bad that the Joint Chiefs of Staff were forced to instigate a separate category for their own high-priority communications.[42]

Incompatible equipment and procedures is another kind of self-inflicted technical command problem. The much-publicized difficulties that U.S. forces experienced in communicating with one another during the invasion of Grenada in 1983 may have been viewed by some as an aberration, but this problem has a long history.[43] The effectiveness of U.S. antisubmarine warfare operations in the Atlantic during the early part of the Second World War, for example, was diminished by incompatible communications between surface ships and surveillance aircraft.[44]

41. For example, the U.S. Army's main communications facility at Phu Lam, which had been handling more than 250,000 messages a month at the beginning of 1965, became so overwhelmed by September that a backlog of more than 1,000 messages often awaited processing. While the addition of another relay center eased matters initially, by the end of the same year both centers were creaking under the strain of processing a half-million messages a month. Rienzi, *Communications-Electronics,* pp. 27–28.

42. See Rienzi, *Communications-Electronics,* p. 91; and Bergen, *Military Communications,* pp. 257–58.

43. A Defense Department report on the lessons of the Grenada operation admitted that "poor communications was the single most glaring deficiency of the entire operations." See *Department of Defense Appropriations for 1987,* Hearings before the Subcommittee on the Department of Defense of the House Committee on Appropriations, 99 Cong. 2 sess. (GPO, 1986), pt. 1, p. 159. See also *Defense Organization: The Need for Change,* Committee Print, Senate Committee on Armed Services, 99 Cong. 1 sess. (GPO, October 1985).

44. See Samuel Eliot Morison, *History of United States Naval Operations in World War II, Vol. 1: The Battle of the Atlantic: September 1939–May 1943* (Little, Brown and Company, 1947), pp. 106, 307.

Differences in communications equipment and operational techniques also hampered close air support among the U.S. Army, Air Force, and Navy in Korea, and again in Vietnam.[45] The interoperability problem is by no means solely an American affliction, however. Direct communication between the aircraft of Japan's navy and army, for example, was virtually impossible until the latter stages of the war because their two systems had not been standardized.[46]

The problems that Allied national forces have experienced in communicating with one another in wartime are more understandable. Such afflictions are especially evident in the early days of a coalition or in hastily planned operations. A good illustration is the Battle of the Java Sea in 1942 when the absence of a common code for tactical signaling among the combined task force of British, Dutch, and U.S. ships played a major part in its defeat at the hands of the Japanese.[47]

The proliferation of communications systems and other electronic devices on the battlefield has created a compatibility problem of a different kind, namely, mutual transmitter interference. Bad experiences with congested frequencies and inadvertent jamming on the beachheads of North Africa and Sicily did much to convince the Allies of the seriousness of this problem. Consequently, elaborate preparations were made to minimize such occurrences during the Normandy invasion when an estimated 90,000 transmitters were expected to operate in close proximity to one another.[48] With the growth in radio users since the Second World War, mutual interference has grown steadily worse. It was experienced on many occasions during the Vietnam War and Middle East conflicts. A more specific example can be cited from the Falklands conflict when the sinking of HMS *Sheffield* was attributed to the fact that its main search radar, used to warn the ship of impending attack, had been

45. Field, *History of United States Naval Operations: Korea,* pp. 387–90; Arthur T. Hadley, *The Straw Giant: Triumph and Failure: America's Armed Forces* (Random House, 1986), p. 112; and General Accounting Office, *Interoperability: DOD's Efforts to Achieve Interoperability among C^3 Systems,* GAO/NSIAD-87-124 (Washington, 1987), pp. 8–9.

46. The army relied on numerical code while the navy used Japanese characters. See Military History Section, Headquarters, Army Forces Far East, *Operational History of Naval Communications,* Japanese monograph 118 (Washington: Department of the Army, Office of the Chief of Military History, 1953), p. 201.

47. Samuel Eliot Morison, *History of United States Naval Operations in World War II, Vol. 3: The Rising Sun in the Pacific: 1931–April 1942* (Little, Brown and Company, 1948), pp. 342–43.

48. Thompson and Harris, *Signal Corps: The Outcome,* pp. 33, 89.

switched off because it was interfering with satellite communications to London.[49]

ORGANIZATIONAL FRICTION. Unity of command is generally considered a cardinal principle for every military organization. Command unity in the military context demands a single and unambiguous source of authority—a commander in chief—with executive power over all the forces assigned to an area of operations. A fragmented command obviously increases the likelihood that the organization will be pushed in different and contradictory directions, dissipating its latent power in the process. Command unity also requires that the authority divested in subordinate commanders to carry out the component tasks or mission of the organization be clearly defined and understood. An ambiguous or overlapping division of responsibility can result in some tasks being duplicated while others are performed poorly or not at all. When certain tasks or missions require the involvement of more than one organizational unit, then obviously the appropriate coordinating mechanisms must also be in place to facilitate cooperation. Overall, the command organization has to be integrated vertically so that it is fully responsive to the will of the supreme commander and integrated laterally so that its actions are properly coordinated and synchronized. Unity of command, however, is a principle that is more often extolled than practiced, as the following examples illustrate.

The unpreparedness of U.S. forces at Pearl Harbor for meeting the Japanese attack in 1941 owed much to the absence of an integrated army and navy command organization with an overall commander in chief to coordinate the defenses. The army and navy commanders—Lieutenant General Walter C. Short and Admiral Husband E. Kimmel respectively—were unaware, for example, of each other's access to intelligence material, of the alert procedures of each service, and the reconnaissance patrols and radar coverage that the forces under their two commands provided to warn of attack. As the congressional investigating committee concluded, "There was a complete failure in Hawaii of effective Army-Navy liaison during the critical period November 27–December 7. There was but little coordination and no integration of Army and Navy facilities and efforts for defense. Neither of the responsible commanders knew what the other was doing with respect to essential military activities."

49. Julian S. Lake, "The South Atlantic War: A Review of the Lessons Learned," *Defense Electronics*, vol. 15 (November 1983), p. 94.

Despite this same committee's recommendation that "unity of command [be] imposed at all military and naval outposts," the subsequent U.S organizational arrangements for the Pacific campaign were anything but unified.[50] Admiral Chester W. Nimitz was made commander in chief of the Pacific theater with his headquarters in Hawaii, while General Douglas MacArthur took charge of the Southwest Pacific theater with his headquarters in Brisbane, Australia. Not surprisingly both men filled the main staff positions at their headquarters with officers from their own service. As a result there were frequent accusations from the other service that it was excluded from the decisionmaking process or that its forces were inappropriately employed. Since both commands eventually pursued two separate offensive campaigns against the Japanese, the competition for scarce resources was considerable. On more than one occasion, the division of effort weakened the U.S. forces and unnecessarily exposed them to the possibility of defeat.[51]

The U.S. antisubmarine campaign in the Atlantic theater suffered—at least initially—from similar organizational problems. While the navy was responsible for securing the sea-lanes, the U.S. Army Air Force had control over all land-based aircraft, including those used for antisubmarine surveillance. The different command arrangements, operational procedures, and communications systems of the two services ensured that the U.S. effort was less than fully effective. Only in 1943 did the navy finally secure all the aerial aspects of antisubmarine warfare.[52]

German command arrangements in the latter part of the Second World War were probably the most chaotic among the principal combatants. Four separate military staffs—Hitler's own, the army's, the air force's, and the navy's—supervised operations in their own spheres of influence. Only Hitler's overarching involvement ensured any kind of coordination among them.[53] German command arrangements before the Normandy campaign give some indication of how tangled they could get. While responsibility for the defense of France and the Low Countries had been given to Field Marshal Gerd von Rundstedt, his nominal subordinate,

50. Information and quotations taken from Peter P. Wallace, *Military Command Authority: Constitutional, Statutory, and Regulatory Bases,* Harvard University, Program on Information Resources Policy (1983), pp. 41–46.

51. See D. Clayton James, with Anne Sharp Wells, *A Time for Giants: Politics of the American High Command in World War II* (Franklin Watts, 1987), pp. 112–13, 244; and Spector, *Eagle against the Sun,* pp. 144–46; 224–25, 245–46.

52. See Morison, *Battle of the Atlantic,* pp. 237–47.

53. John Keegan, *The Mask of Command* (Penguin, 1988), p. 273.

Field Marshal Erwin Rommel (who commanded army group B, consisting of the Fifteenth and Seventh Armies), nevertheless possessed the right to bypass von Rundstedt and appeal directly to Hitler's own staff on matters of strategy. Meanwhile Hitler's staff maintained under its direct operational control a separate three-division panzer reserve force with headquarters in the Paris area. To make matters worse for von Rundstedt, the Luftwaffe controlled all coastal antiaircraft units and parachute troops while the navy controlled all naval units, shore installations, and coastal artillery. Furthermore, the ss retained administrative and disciplinary powers over its own forces in the area.[54] Although it is hard to gauge what impact this incredibly confused command setup had on German effectiveness, it cannot have helped matters.

American employment of air power in the two principal conflicts involving U.S. forces since the Second World War was also hampered by a fragmented command organization. In Korea, General MacArthur again eschewed the principles of a true joint command in establishing the U.S. Far East command. With its predominantly army bias, the headquarters Far East command effectively abdicated responsibility for overseeing the air campaign to its air force and navy subordinate commands. Since neither would relinquish control of its air assets to another service, the United States essentially operated two air campaigns in Korea with, initially at least, a minimum of centralized direction and coordination.[55] As the official Air Force history states, "At the outset of the Korean war, the defective theater command system prevented the fullest employment of airpower, delayed the beginning of a comprehensive air-interdiction program for more than a month, and. . . caused confusion and loss of effectiveness at the very time that every single aircraft sortie was vital to the survival of the Eighth Army in Korea."[56]

In Vietnam, a unified command was established (known as Military Assistance Command Vietnam) under General William C. Westmoreland, but its jurisdiction extended only to the borders of that country. The extensive carrier-based air campaign conducted by Task Force 77 was under the control of the commander in chief, Pacific (CINCPAC), to whom Westmoreland also reported. CINCPAC, moreover, had nominal charge through Strategic Air Command of B-52 bomber operations against Vietnam. Finally, the U.S. Marine Corps aircraft operated

54. Eisenhower, *Eisenhower: At War*, p. 170.
55. See Futrell, Moseley, and Simpson, *United States Air Force*, pp. 43–55.
56. Futrell, Moseley, and Simpson, *United States Air Force*, p. 55.

virtually independently of U.S. Air Force tactical aviation until 1968 when it was placed under the control of the air deputy to Westmoreland.[57]

More recent examples of command disunity can be found in the U.S. rescue attempt in 1980 of hostages held in Iran, among Argentinian forces during the Falklands War, in the U.S. Marine expeditionary force to Lebanon in 1983, in the U.S. invasion of Grenada in the same year, and among the Iranian forces fighting the war against Iraq.

Maintaining unity of command over coalition forces poses even greater organizational challenges. This is certainly true for tightly coupled alliances that set out to integrate military planning and operations. Here national as well as service interests have to be accommodated within the chain of command. In wartime, national control of forces may also have to be relinquished to a commander of a foreign, albeit friendly, power, which can become yet another source of friction. Even without the added burden of interallied politics, the coordination of alliance forces is much harder because of differences in operational procedures, command philosophies, and, in some cases, the native languages of members. Moreover, the barriers to sharing information, especially sensitive intelligence, are for obvious reasons much higher among nations than within them. The acrimony and divisiveness that can erode alliance cohesion have provided, as a consequence, ample opportunities for adversaries to exploit the weak links and schisms among them. It is no wonder, therefore, that coalitions, at least until fairly recently, have not fared well in battle. As General Eisenhower once observed, "History testifies to the ineptitude of coalitions in waging war."[58]

The Anglo-American alliance in the Second World War is rightly held up as a model of effective coalition management, but it evolved only after the Allies learned some painful lessons. The debacle of Allied cooperation in 1940 has already been described. In the Far East the ill-fated ABDACOM (American, British, Dutch, and Australian Command), hurriedly established in 1942, fared no better against the Japanese and

57. See Wallace, *Military Command Authority*, pp. 47–51; and William W. Momyer, *Airpower in Three Wars* (Arno Press, 1980), pp. 65–110. Gen. William Westmoreland complained bitterly during and after the Vietnam War about the command arrangements. He argued for a separate southeast Asia command with control over U.S. forces in Laos and Thailand as well as all air assets in the region. Besides the virtue of a unified command, this arrangement, he believes, would have provided a counterweight to Washington's interference in operational matters. See Gen. William C. Westmoreland, *A Soldier Reports* (Dell, 1980), pp. 94–97, 543.

58. Eisenhower, *Crusade in Europe*, p. 4.

quickly collapsed.[59] Even after the tide of the war had turned in the Allies' favor and the foundations of the Anglo-American alliance had been laid with the creation of a joint planning organization and a unified command structure, the Allied setbacks suffered during the Tunisian campaign in 1943 drove home the need for more effective liaison arrangements and common operational procedures.[60] Subsequent operations in Italy and northwestern Europe, though ultimately successful, also proved that there were definite limits to Allied integration. For example, national forces were rarely combined below the corps level. When a combination of lower formations was tried during the Anzio landing, for example, the results were not encouraging.[61] Inter-Allied friction over matters of theater strategy, logistical priorities, and command prerogatives was also never far from the surface and often erupted into the open. During the Battle of the Bulge, to cite a notable case, Allied command relations were severely strained by the transfer of the U.S. First and Ninth Armies, over the objections of General Omar Bradley, to Field Marshal Bernard L. Montgomery's control.[62]

The Axis experience with coalition warfare, though limited in comparison, also deserves some comment, not least for the lessons that NATO can derive from it. Unlike the Allies, the Axis powers never established any comparable combined command organization for planning and supervising military operations. Instead, the Germans relied on a set of ad hoc command arrangements for coordinating operations with their allies.[63] On the eastern front, the Romanian, Hungarian, and Italian armies operated under the overall direction of a German army group commander, but the individual armies had considerable discretion for day-to-day decisions. The generally low caliber of these allied forces and their inferior equipment, training, and logistical support did not matter so much during the early advance into Russia, but as the front

59. See Spector, *Eagle against the Sun,* pp. 127–34; and Morison, *Rising Sun in the Pacific,* p. 336.

60. Lt. Col. John Hixson and B. Franklin Cooling, *Allied Interoperability in Peace and War* (Carlisle Barracks, Pa.: U.S. Army Military History Institute, 1978), pp. 52–80.

61. See Lt. Col. John A. Hixson, "Operation Shingle: Combined Planning and Preparation," *Military Review,* vol. 69 (March 1989), pp. 63–76.

62. See Eisenhower, *Eisenhower: At War,* pp. 562–63, 570–77, 592–93.

63. This section draws on chap. 6 of Hixson and Cooling, *Allied Interoperability,* pp. 156–77; Gen. G. Blumentritt, "Wartime Alliances," MS B-661 (Washington: Department of the Army, 1947); and Maj. Gen. B. Mueller-Hillebrand, "Germany and Her Allies in World War II: A Record of Axis Collaboration Problems," MS P-108 (Washington: Department of the Army, 1954, 1955).

expanded, the Germans became more dependent on their allies to defend what they had gained. Recognizing that their weaker Axis partners could become a military liability, the Germans initially bolstered the allied sectors with German units held in reserve at key locations—commonly known as "corset stays"—and with stronger liaison arrangements. As the demands of the war in the East grew, however, the ability to spare German forces for this role diminished, leaving the allies increasingly alone and exposed, a condition that would have fatal consequences.

At Stalingrad, the Romanian Third and Fourth Armies were left holding the flanks of the German salient. With all their attention on the siege of the city, the German commanders had neglected to establish appropriate liaison arrangements with the Romanians to share intelligence and coordinate reconnaissance activities. They also ignored the periodic warnings sent in by the Romanians of intensified Russian activity along their sectors of the front. Not surprisingly the Russian forces had deliberately singled out these underequipped and relatively isolated forces to receive the main blow in their counteroffensive of 1942. The results were predictable: the front quickly disintegrated under the carefully orchestrated Russian assault. Moreover, the subsequent breakdown in communications with the Romanians left the German commanders initially in the dark about the extent of the disaster. Later they had little means to organize new defensive positions to stem the rout. As a result, the German Sixth Army in Stalingrad was left surrounded to await its slow and painful demise.[64]

Germany's weak allies would be singled out repeatedly for subsequent Russian attacks on the eastern front with again predictable consequences. The Italian Eighth Army was so badly mauled by the fighting on the lower Don that it returned home. The remnants of the Romanian and Hungarian armies also took further punishment and eventually withdrew from any further role in the war effort.[65]

Postwar experiences in managing coalition operations confirmed many of the lessons learned in the Second World War. The Korean conflict, for example, drove home how poor command links among different national units of varying quality—notably U.S. and Republic

64. For further details see Alan Clark, *Barbarossa: The Russian-German Conflict, 1941–45* (Quill, 1985), pp. 240–41; Alexander Werth, *Russia at War 1941–1945* (Avon, 1964), p. 463; and Erickson, *The Road to Stalingrad*, pp. 465–66.

65. See Werth, *Russia at War*, pp. 471–72.; and Clark, *Barbarossa*, pp. 269, 370.

of Korea forces—could prove an operational liability in conflict.[66] With more than twenty countries sending contingents to fight under the U.N. banner in Korea, language differences also became more of a command problem than usual.[67] While language was not a concern for the Arab coalition in the Yom Kippur War of 1973, poor coordination between the Syrian and Egyptian attacks undoubtedly helped Israel's predicament in fighting a two-front campaign. Despite the ostensible creation of a unified Arab command, the "conduct of the war did not indicate that one ally knew what the other was doing. Such lack of communication allowed the Israelis to determine where they could commit their overtaxed forces without encountering two winner-take-all efforts simultaneously."[68]

The standard method to improve coordination among and control over subordinate forces is to centralize information gathering and decisionmaking within the organization. Centralizing decision authority, however, poses some significant trade-offs to command performance and, with it, military effectiveness. On the one hand, decisions can be taken on the basis of more complete information from multiple sources than would be available to lower levels in the command hierarchy. Greater supervision can also be exerted on operations to ensure that they conform to the original intentions and directives of the commander. Highly centralized systems, however, impose greater demands on communications and data processing since more information has to be passed up and down the chain of command. This flow increases the risk, as noted earlier, of overloaded communications channels in periods of peak demand. Similarly, unless the information reaching the top has been filtered in some way to extract the relevant from the irrelevant, the higher echelons of command could be deluged with more information than they can usefully assimilate. Yet the process of filtering information through successive layers of command risks slowing down the system's response to events and increases the likelihood that the information will become corrupted or distorted by the time it reaches the top. The net result is a sluggish, inflexible command system where decisions are taken on the

66. B. Franklin Cooling, "Allied Interoperability in the Korean War," *Military Review*, vol. 63 (June 1983), pp. 40–41.

67. See Cooling, "Allied Interoperabilty in the Korean War," pp. 26–52. Sometimes this problem occurred even between U.S. and British forces. See Max Hastings, *The Korean War* (Simon and Schuster, 1987), p. 218.

68. Frank Aker, *October 1973: The Arab-Israeli War* (Archon Books, 1985), p. 77.

basis of information that no longer faithfully reflects unfolding events. Centralized command systems, for similar reasons, are also more vulnerable to decapitating-type attacks that leave lower command echelons without the direction they have become accustomed to. Since discretion and initiative are not encouraged at these levels, the ability of the lower echelons to adapt to conditions of command disruption is limited. Conversely, their ability to exploit the fleeting opportunities of the battlefield is also constrained by rigid adherence to established plans and operational procedures.

The Soviet command arrangements in the Second World War are an obvious case that illustrates both the costs and benefits of highly centralized systems.[69] During the early stages of the German invasion, the impact of the widespread breakdown in Soviet communications was made worse by the centralization of authority. Officers at the front were left directionless and too intimidated by Stalin's authority to take the initiative. Moscow, meanwhile, remained in ignorance of the rapidly unfolding disaster and, if anything, contributed to the growing confusion by issuing orders that bore little relation to what was patently called for at the time.[70] Once the tide had irrevocably turned on the eastern front, Stalin's unchallenged ability to pick and choose where the main effort was to be applied, and if necessary switch direction to maintain momentum, proved an operational asset. Even so, this opportunity was not without drawbacks at the tactical level. As one German general observed, "The foolish repetition of attacks on the same spot, the rigidity of Russian artillery fire, and the selection of the terrain for the attack, betrayed a total lack of imagination and mental mobility. Our Wireless Intercept Service heard many a time the frantic question: 'What are we to do now?' Only a few commanders of lower formations showed independent judgement when faced with unforeseen situations. On many occasions a successful attack, a breakthrough, or an accomplished encirclement was not exploited, simply because nobody saw it."[71]

69. The centralized direction of the war effort by Hitler is another example, but other factors helped compensate for some of centralization's shortcomings. See Keegan, *Mask of Command*, pp. 301–04.

70. See Erickson, *The Road to Stalingrad*, pp. 123–27.

71. Maj. Gen. F. W. von Mellenthin, *Panzer Battles: A Study of the Employment of Armor in the Second World War*, trans. H. Betzler (University of Oklahoma Press, 1971), p. 186. See also pp. 296–98. Compare with Marshal M. N. Tukhachevskii's comments in Richard Simpkin, in association with John Erickson, *Deep Battle: The Brainchild of Marshal Tukhachevskii* (London: Brassey's Defence Publishers, 1987), p. 150.

The Soviet command style was later exported to the Egyptian and Syrian armed forces, which elicited similar statements of contempt from the Israeli commanders who observed it firsthand.[72] The American prosecution of the war in Vietnam has also been criticized for being overly centralized. Fear of superpower nuclear escalation, combined with the advent of near-instantaneous global communications systems, ensured much greater—some believe excessive—involvement by Washington in the day-to-day running of the war.[73] Besides infringing on what were viewed as traditional military prerogatives, Washington's involvement, as noted earlier, added to the burden on the supporting communications and information processing systems. The helicopter also came into its own as a tool for command in Vietnam, although with mixed results. The speed and flexibility of the helicopter were a definite boon in the inaccessible countryside of Vietnam but at the same time the use of helicopters frequently resulted in tactical actions being oversupervised by senior commanders literally from above.[74]

Decentralizing command authority poses the reverse set of operational trade-offs. On the one hand, the burden and dependency on communications can be reduced with greater delegation of decisionmaking authority. The reaction time to events may also be shortened if the advice and consent of higher authorities are not always required. Should the communications links in the chain of command be broken as a result of technical failures or the deliberate interference of an enemy, lower levels, for the same reason, are also better prepared to function without specific and continuous guidance from above. On the other hand, however, lower decision thresholds and more diffuse centers of authority make coordination harder and increase the risk of loss of control over the conduct of operations.

The doctrine known as *Auftragstaktik* used by the German army in the Second World War is frequently cited as an example of a decentralized command system. Although there is some debate over how best to translate *Auftragstaktik*—"mission-oriented tactics" being the most common—there is general agreement that the Wehrmacht gave great

---

72. See Edward N. Luttwak and Daniel Horowitz, *The Israeli Army 1948–1973* (Abt Books, 1983), pp. 174, 286–89.

73. See chap. 7 of van Creveld, *Command in War*, pp. 232–60.

74. van Creveld, *Command in War*, pp. 255–56; and Gen. Bruce Palmer, Jr., *The 25-Year War: America's Military Role in Vietnam* (Simon and Schuster, 1985), pp. 62–63.

latitude and discretion to junior commanders to achieve generally stated objectives prescribed in advance. The brevity and simplicity of commands not only reduced the burden on communications but also made for greater responsiveness at the tactical level. The Wehrmacht's flexibility in attack and tenacity in defense have been widely attributed to this underlying command philosophy.[75]

The modern-day exponent of a decentralized command style is undoubtedly the Israeli Defense Force.[76] Its success in battle against the Arabs has also been credited, at least partially, to its more flexible and responsive command system. But as the Israelis experienced on numerous occasions, the greater latitude for local initiative can lead to some costly mistakes from uncontrolled and uncoordinated actions. This problem was particularly evident in the 1956 Sinai campaign, and, although the Israelis subsequently introduced the practice of optional control whereby senior commanders could intervene at critical moments in the battle to reimpose central direction and coordination, there were recurrences of costly errors in 1967 and 1973.[77]

HUMAN FRICTION. Command systems, however well constructed and organized, can function only as well as the people who use them. Human-related friction, therefore, is just as important a factor in command performance as the others already described. Unfortunately it is the most difficult to study and the least predictable.

In some respects the phenomena are the same. People, like equipment and organizations, are subject to the extraordinary stress of combat. Fear, excitement, the burden of command responsibilities, personal losses, information overload, and lack of sleep can exact their toll on the performance of individuals. In some cases performance may improve, but this effect can rarely be sustained over time. Efforts to deal with stress, notably with drugs and alcohol, can also be deleterious. The decline in performance can manifest itself in various ways: loss of concentration, selective use of information, errors of judgment, operating mistakes, and ultimately physical and emotional collapse.

75. See Lt. Col. R. J. Kershaw Para, "Lessons to Be Derived from the Wehrmacht's Experience in the East, 1943–45," RUSI Journal for Defence Studies, vol. 132 (September 1987), pp. 61–62.

76. See van Creveld, Command in War, pp. 194–95; and Dan Horowitz, "Flexible Responsiveness and Military Strategy: The Case of the Israeli Army," Policy Sciences, vol. 1 (Summer 1970), pp. 191–205.

77. See van Creveld, Command in War, pp. 197–231; and Luttwak and Horowitz, Israeli Army, pp. 118, 148, 160–63.

Numerous cases can be cited to illustrate this phenomema. The case of General Gaston Billotte during the fall of France has already been mentioned. His compatriot General Alphonse Georges also suffered a mental breakdown at the height of the battle.[78] Stalin is believed to have experienced the same thing at the outset of Germany's suprise attack on the Soviet Union. The same fate and the lesser problem of battle weariness would befall many other commanding officers during the Second World War, resulting in their removal. Other examples can be found in more recent conflicts. During the Yom Kippur War, for instance, Lieutenant General Saad el Shazly, Egypt's chief of staff, was relieved of his command after suffering a "psychological breakdown" during the climax of the battle.[79] Not long before this incident, General Saad Mamoun, the Egyptian Second Army commander, was stricken by a heart attack.[80]

Personal rivalries and animosities among senior commanders can also affect decisionmaking and coordination. Generals Maurice Gamelin and Georges were barely on speaking terms during the early phase of the German invasion of France. Personal friction was also evident among the senior German commanders during Operation Barbarossa, among Allied commanders of the ill-fated ABDACOM, among U.S commanders during the Japanese invasion of the Aleutians and at the Battle of Leyte Gulf, and between U.S. and British officers in Italy and northwestern Europe, as well as more recently between Egyptian Generals Ahmed Ismail and Shazly and Israeli Generals Ariel Sharon and Shmuel Gonen during the Yom Kippur War.[81]

Command Friction between Peace and War

Though wartime represents the harshest test for a command system, the threat of hostilities can also be extremely stressful for many of the

78. Brian Bond, *France and Belgium, 1939–1940* (University of Delaware Press, 1975), p. 102.

79. Nadav Safran, *Israel: The Embattled Ally* (Belknap Harvard, 1978), p. 310. His removal, however, may have had more to do with a personal clash with General Ahmed Ishmail. See Col. Trevor N. Dupuy, *Elusive Victory: The Arab-Israeli Wars, 1947–1974* (Harper and Row, 1978), pp. 518–19.

80. Aker, *October 1973*, p. 100.

81. See Clark, *Barbarossa*, pp. 70–71, 91–92; Spector, *Eagle against the Sun*, pp. 179, 181; E. B. Potter, *Nimitz* (Annapolis: Naval Institute Press, 1976), pp. 340–41; Dupuy, *Elusive Victory*, pp. 475–76, 481–83, 518–19, 585–86; and James, with Wells, *Time for Giants*, pp. 112–13.

same reasons. The tempo of military operations typically picks up, the demand for information increases, new command and communications channels are activated, and unfamiliar emergency procedures take effect. The system may also have to labor under great uncertainty about the intentions of a potential adversary and even who the adversary may be. If war is not yet considered, inevitable major tensions could develop within the command system between those wanting to be prepared for the worst and those wanting to ensure that nothing happens that might exacerbate the situation and provoke hostilities. In large and complex military organizations where multiple centers of decision exist and where considerable latitude for initiative resides (and which might expand in emergencies), the appropriate balance is not only difficult to reach but also arduous to maintain. As past crises indicate, command friction of the types just discussed can complicate and undermine control, with adverse consequences.

Although the command system remains more or less sacrosanct from direct military attack until the outbreak of hostilities, it is not immune to other forms of external influence and interference. In crises, states try to manipulate the information that the other side collects by broadcasting what they want to be received and hiding what they don't. A common tactic to mask combat preparations and make the interpretation of intentions more difficult is to use military exercises as a cover. This form of deception was used successfully by Soviet and Warsaw Pact forces before the invasion of Czechoslovakia in 1968, by Egyptian forces before their attack on Israel in 1973, and again by the Soviets during the Polish crises of 1980–81.[82] Similarly the electromagnetic signals, communications, and radar emissions normally emitted by military forces can also be curtailed or modulated in misleading ways in the knowledge that the other side will be monitoring them. Deceptive broadcasting and the use of radio silence are common techniques that were also employed in the cases just listed. Furthermore, the absence of hostilities does not preclude jamming and other forms of nondestructive electronic interference with intelligence sensors and communications systems.

As discussed, environmental factors have also been known to impede

---

82. See Betts, *Surprise Attack,* pp. 72, 82–83; and Thomas M. Cynkin, *Soviet and American Signalling in the Polish Crisis* (St. Martin's Press, 1987), pp. 20–21; and Alexander M. Haig, Jr., *Caveat: Realism, Reagan, and Foreign Policy* (Macmillan, 1984), pp. 243–44.

intelligence collection at key moments in a crisis. During the imposition of martial law in Poland in December 1981, for example, cloud cover evidently obscured the movement of troops and militia from U.S. reconnaissance satellites, leaving the United States literally blind to what was going on. As U.S. Secretary of State Alexander M. Haig later recalled, "We were handicapped by the absence of information. Our allies seemed to have no better data than we, and the press had so far been effectively muffled by the cutoff in telephone and telegraph traffic to and from Poland. Though we made many attempts to establish contact with our embassy in Warsaw over a secure satellite link, we were unsuccessful."[83] His predecessor Henry Kissinger had found himself in a similar predicament during a visit to Moscow at the height of the Yom Kippur War in 1973. Communications between Moscow and Washington proved impossible for several extremely sensitive hours because of atmospheric disturbances.[84] On a more localized but no less important scale, atmospheric disturbances played havoc with U.S. shipboard radars in the Tonkin Gulf in 1964, creating false images of attacking North Vietnamese torpedo boats that resulted in U.S. retaliatory raids and a serious escalation of the war.[85] The fact that it was nighttime also meant that visual sightings could not be made to confirm the ambiguous radar reports. Darkness and poor visibility would later contribute to the mistaken identification and subsequent destruction of the Korean airliner KAL 007 by a Soviet air defense interceptor near Sakhalin Island, sparking a serious crisis in September 1983.[86]

Internally induced friction has also played a role on many similar occasions. Technical inadequacies and malfunctions affected NATO's intelligence collection effort and diplomatic communications during the

83. Haig, *Caveat*, p. 248. Just before the imposition of martial law the United States had been relying on extremely good intelligence from a spy in the Polish General Staff, but this advantage abruptly ended when this source came under suspicion and fled Poland. See Bob Woodward, *Veil: The Secret Wars of the CIA, 1981–1987* (Simon and Schuster, 1987), pp. 33, 66, 177–78.

84. Kissinger suspected other causes at the time. See Henry Kissinger, *Years of Upheaval* (Little, Brown and Company, 1982), pp. 556–57.

85. See Office of the Director of Defense Research and Engineering Weapons Systems Evaluation Group, *Command and Control of the Tonkin Gulf Incident 4–5 August 1964*, Critical Incident Report 7, Top Secret, declassified (Washington, 1965), pp. 15–16. Sunspot activity also hampered communications between Saigon and Washington in the wake of the incidents. See Rienzi, *Communications-Electronics*, p. 18.

86. See Seymour M. Hersh, *"The Target is Destroyed": What Really Happened to Flight 007 and What America Knew about It* (Random House, 1986), pp. 85–86.

1968 Czech crisis, the 1973 Yom Kippur War, and the 1981 Polish crisis.[87] The processing, analysis, and sharing of intelligence in at least the first two of these cases also suffered from organizational forms of command friction.[88] In part these problems stemmed from the fragmentation of responsibility for intelligence collection and analysis that, as others have demonstrated, is not an uncommon problem in crises.[89]

The greater decentralization of command authority brought about by the growth and geographical dispersion of military forces may have improved responsiveness to local fast-breaking events but at the expense of rendering coordination and control over military operations more difficult in crises. Incidents from several past crises illustrate this problem.

In 1961, for instance, East Germany banned Western personnel from coming closer than one hundred meters to the newly constructed Berlin Wall. In response Allied commandants, without referring to their governments, ordered a full alert of Western forces in the city and dispatched a thousand troops with tanks to move within the forbidden distance of the wall. Fearful that this action would cause an incident that might escalate the crisis, the United States later ordered its troops to pull back.[90] Although President John F. Kennedy tightened his supervision and control of activities in Berlin to ensure that a nuclear war was not started by, in his words, "a trigger-happy sergeant on a truck convoy at a checkpoint in East Germany," subsequent incidents raised apprehensions in Washington.[91]

87. See Betts, *Surprise Attack*, pp. 83–84; Jeffrey T. Richelson, "From Corona to Lacrosse: A Short History of Satellites," *Washington Post*, February 25, 1990, pp. B1, B4; Marvin Kalb and Bernard Kalb, *Kissinger* (Little, Brown and Company, 1974), p. 493; Haig, *Caveat*, p. 248; and interviews. Other factors also complicated matters. For instance, in the first case, local NATO commanders were told to desist from certain intelligence-gathering activities because of their potentially provocative nature. See Gen. James H. Polk, "Reflections on the Czechoslovakian Invasion, 1968," *Strategic Review*, vol. 5 (Winter 1977), pp. 32–33.

88. See Betts, *Surprise Attack*, pp. 84, 110; "The Report on the CIA that President Ford Doesn't Want You to Read," *Village Voice*, February 16, 1976, p. 78; and William E. Colby and Peter Forbath, *Honorable Men: My Life in the CIA* (Simon and Schuster, 1978), pp. 367–68.

89. See Betts, *Surprise Attack*, pp. 92–95; and Ephraim Kam, *Surprise Attack: The Victim's Perspective* (Harvard University Press, 1988), pp. 179–86.

90. Richard K. Betts, *Soldiers, Statesmen, and Cold War Crises* (Harvard University Press, 1977), pp. 144–45.

91. Quoted in Norman Gelb, *The Berlin Wall: Kennedy, Khrushchev, and a Showdown in the Heart of Europe* (Times Books, 1986), p. 84.

Soon after retired General Lucius D. Clay became Kennedy's personal representative in Berlin, he circumvented normal military command channels and ordered the U.S. military garrison to carry out several highly provocative actions to demonstrate Allied legal rights. Some were countermanded at the last moment while the others resulted in some of the most tense confrontations of the cold war, including the famous incident at Checkpoint Charlie in which U.S. and Soviet tanks faced each other for sixteen nerve-wracking hours.[92] These incidents alarmed not only Washington but also its NATO allies. A furious General Lauris Norstad, then supreme allied commander in Europe, demanded to know why he had been excluded from prior knowledge and planning of the confrontation in Berlin, especially after NATO had drawn up detailed plans on how Allied military forces would be deployed and used in the city. Clay was reined in further and later resigned in frustration at the constraints placed on his freedom of action.

President Kennedy and his senior advisers would learn more about the limits of their control over military operations during the Cuban missile crisis in October 1962. The unauthorized decision by the commander in chief of Strategic Air Command to broadcast the nuclear alert order to his forces *en clair* so as to intimidate the Soviets, the overzealous prosecution by the U.S. Navy of antisubmarine warfare operations against Soviet submarines, and the accidental penetration of Soviet air space by a U-2 reconnaissance plane at the height of the crisis illustrate the problem of controlling large military organizations gearing up for possible combat. Similarly, under time constraints, local Soviet commanders in Cuba shot down an American U-2 plane without seeking higher-level approval, much to Nikita Khrushchev's reported horror.[93]

Throughout the Czech crisis of 1968, the overriding U.S. and NATO concern was to avoid any actions that might be considered provocative or indicate a desire to intervene in the invasion. As a result a large-scale Bundeswehr exercise planned for the area close to the Czech-West German border was pulled back well within the frontier, additional and

92. See Betts, *Soldiers, Statesmen, and Cold War Crises*, pp. 145–46; and Gelb, *Berlin Wall*, pp. 254–57.

93. The following information is drawn from John D. Steinbruner, "An Assessment of Nuclear Crises," in Franklyn Griffiths and John C. Polanyi, eds., *The Dangers of Nuclear War* (Toronto University Press, 1979), pp. 37–40; Scott D. Sagan, "Nuclear Alerts and Crisis Management," *International Security*, vol. 9 (Spring 1985), pp. 112–22; and Raymond L. Garthoff, *Reflections on the Cuban Missile Crisis*, rev. ed. (Brookings, 1989), pp. 61–62, 84–85.

even normal border reconnaissance operations were canceled, and requests to alert and move U.S. mechanized forces to cover the border were denied. Nevertheless local NATO commanders still used and, at times, exceeded their discretionary authority to raise the military readiness of their forces. A British air force commander, for example, apparently ordered the dispersal of his aircraft against attack although this order was later countermanded; four U.S. cavalry units primed themselves for combat "without official instructions from anyone and despite the orders forbidding their alert"; and West German armored units began loading their tanks and trucks with ammunition on the informal recommendation of General James H. Polk, the U.S. Seventh Army commander, "without checking with any higher German authority."[94] By far the most troubling incident occurred when a West German divisional commander based in the Nuremberg area evidently ordered his forces to load up with ammunition, leave their barracks, and move to their assigned defense positions close to the Czechoslovakian frontier. According to unpublished reports the Bundeswehr officer in question believed that the Soviet Union might use the invasion of Czechoslovakia as a staging ground for an attack on the West and therefore decided that his units should be prepared for such an eventuality. The deployed units were later recalled, though not until after much concern had been generated in NATO circles.[95] In contrast, NATO would eventually declare its lowest level of heightened readiness, only to have it barely implemented.[96]

To cite another example, soon after the shootdown of KAL 007, a local U.S. commander reportedly ordered six F-15 interceptors and an Airborne Warning and Control System surveillance aircraft based in Japan to fly close to where the incident occurred, with veiled instructions to provoke, in effect, a reaction from Soviet air defenses and "take advantage of the situation." Apparently no one in Washington had cleared this operation or even knew about it. While the headquarters of the Fifth U.S. Air Force in Japan eventually intervened to prevent a

---

94. Betts, *Surprise Attack,* p. 86.; and Polk, "Reflections on the Czechoslovakian Invasion," p. 35.

95. Though the details of this previously unpublicized incident are still hazy, the central elements of the event have been corroborated in several interviews with serving and retired Bundeswehr officers.

96. Betts, *Surprise Attack,* pp. 84–85; and Philip Windsor, "Yugoslavia, 1951, and Czechoslovakia, 1968," in Barry M. Blechman and Stephen S. Kaplan, eds., *Force without War: U.S. Armed Forces as a Political Instrument* (Brookings, 1978), p. 480.

dangerous confrontation, the Soviets nevertheless put their forces on heightened alert and sent some of their most advanced fighters to the area.[97]

Finally, there are numerous examples of how human shortcomings have affected command performance under stressful conditions. Information can be erroneously transmitted or misunderstood, as occurred with the attack on the U.S.S. *Liberty* in 1967 and the more recent *Vincennes* incident in 1988.[98] Sometimes preconceived notions override the clear transmission and receipt of information, as apparently happened in 1978 when a Soviet air defense ground controller, ignoring the visual confirmation that a Korean airliner had strayed into Soviet air space near Murmansk, authorized its destruction.[99]

Command Fluency

It would be simple and convenient to believe that achieving command fluency is just a matter of reducing command friction. To a certain extent this proposition is true. It is clearly desirable to reduce the vulnerability of the physical components of a command system to external interference and direct attack. The survivability of the system can be improved by a variety of passive and active techniques, including camouflage, deception, mobility, physical hardening, antijamming methods, active defenses, and ultimately redundancy, that is, duplication. The techniques chosen are not mutually exclusive and in fact they can be highly complementary. The mix and relative emphasis will depend on the nature of the threat, cost considerations, and performance trade-offs. It is also important that the personnel that use and operate the system be trained to function under stressful conditions. They must be able to act when parts of the system have been degraded by enemy action that necessitates the use of unfamiliar equipment and processes. This capability, as indicated earlier, will depend to a great extent on how decentralized the system is and the level of initiative that personnel are encouraged to take.

It is likewise desirable to minimize the incidence of internally derived

97. Hersh, *"The Target Is Destroyed,"* pp. 74, 114.
98. See Molly Moore, "Human Errors Blamed in U.S. Downing of Iranian Jet," *Washington Post,* August 4, 1988, pp. A1, A28.
99. Hersh, *"The Target Is Destroyed,"* pp. 13–14.

command friction. Care must be taken, therefore, to ensure that there are enough intelligence-gathering assets and communications equipment to satisfy anticipated operational needs. The technical components of the command system, furthermore, must be sufficiently reliable and functionally compatible to maintain uninterrupted service. The underlying command structure must also be unified and integrated to ensure coherent direction and coordination of the force. This unification requires strong vertical command links that allow the free and prompt flow of information and directives from top to bottom and vice versa, as well as lateral links among the elements of the force that must operate together. Decisionmaking authority should also be distributed in a way that permits high-level direction and control without compromising low-level responsiveness and initiative. Finally through training and exercise, command personnel can learn to cope with demanding and stressful conditions to reduce the likelihood of irrational and dysfunctional behavior.[100]

As such, these suggestions for enhancing command fluency amount to no more than generalized objectives for specific situations. They don't provide answers to such questions as, What is the best method for improving the survivability of a command system? How much intelligence and communications are enough? What is the right organizational balance between centralization and decentralization? Unfortunately there is no holy writ that says how to design a perfect, universally applicable command system. As one of the more insightful scholars of the historical evolution of command systems has concluded,

> No single communications or data processing technology, no single system of organization, no single procedure or method, is in itself sufficient to guarantee the successful or even adequate conduct of command in war. In the past, command systems radically different from each other have led to equally good results. Conversely, the success of a given command system at any one time and place constitutes no guarantee of its success in others, even where technological and other circumstances are not fundamentally different. It has been shown quite possible for a command system to be more successful at one level than at another (indeed, for success in command at one level to cancel out failure on another, deliberately or otherwise), or in one phase of operations than in the next. To paraphrase Frederick the Great's remark about commanders, the ideal command system, like Plato's Republic, exists only in heaven.[101]

100. See Chris Bellamy, *The Future of Land Warfare* (St. Martin's Press, 1987), p. 266.
101. van Creveld, *Command in War*, pp. 261–62.

While the perfect command system may not exist for all times and all occasions, it is possible, nevertheless, to consider how command requirements can vary according to different contexts and how these conditions should affect the design choices that are made about command survivability, technical sufficiency, and organization.

Since a command system in peacetime does not have to contend with enemy attack, the elements that would serve no useful function in wartime clearly do not have to be as survivable, if at all, as those that would be needed in war. Obviously the speed at which war could come should also dictate how fast the command system transforms itself from a peacetime to a wartime footing. For some critical components, the anticipated margin of warning time may be so short that peacetime operations have to be managed by the wartime command system. In other cases it may be sufficient only to maintain an alternative, more survivable, wartime command system to be activated at the appropriate time. Again the time necessary to effect the changeover should be determined by the amount of warning time that can be expected. Much also depends on whether the force is defensively or offensively postured and whether it is numerically inferior or superior to the potential adversary. The command system of a defensively oriented force will not only have to deal with greater uncertainty, thereby increasing reliance on timely intelligence collection and processing—especially for smaller-sized forces where the margin of error for low readiness and maldeployment may be narrower—but it may also have to withstand an initial, possibly massive, attack designed to degrade command and control. Command system survivability, therefore, whether through hardening or rapid reconstitution, should be a high priority. An offensively oriented force, however, has the benefit of knowing the time and place of the attack and can prepare its command system accordingly. Intelligence on enemy intentions is less important unless a preemptive response is considered possible. With operations known and planned in advance, the demand for information, and with it the stress on communications, is also likely to be lower.

Determining the right balance between centralized and decentralized control is not so clear and presents fundamental dilemmas. To prevent unauthorized, accidental, and otherwise unwanted uses of force in peacetime and especially in crises, a more centralized form of control seems preferable. For defensively oriented forces, however, particularly those that face the threat of surprise attack and that may also be deployed at a great distance from the center of decisionmaking, it makes sense to relax centralized control should hostilities appear imminent. Thus the forces' capacity to respond and adapt promptly to attack will be improved. However, this precaution may not only increase the risk of unauthorized and uncoordinated actions, but, for an inferior-sized force at least, it may also reduce the efficient deployment and application of defensive assets against the superior-sized force. Some means to reestablish centralized control therefore seems desirable. Similarly, offensive forces can afford to decentralize control once hostilities commence so that lower echelons have the discretionary authority either to exploit fleeting opportunities or to deal with unexpected setbacks. Again some means to exert overall direction and coordination when necessary is desirable to avoid the problems associated with allowing complete autonomy.

The key to knowing when to intervene from above comes from having an independent information collection system to monitor events without causing lower echelons to feel that they are under constant scrutiny. The "directed telescope," as some call this practice, has been used with notable success by commanders in the past.[102] During the Second World War, for example, both Montgomery and Gen. George S. Patton relied on roving intelligence officers to reconnoiter forward and report directly back to headquarters while others—notably some German officers—preferred to go take a look themselves. The Israelis have apparently adopted a similar approach to implement their system of optional control.

Other factors besides the balance of forces and doctrinal predisposition should be considered. A military force predisposed to conducting maneuver-type warfare needs a looser, more flexible command system than one that favors tactics of attrition.[103] Hardening and redundancy are more important survivability qualities for the latter, while mobility and deception are preferable to the former. The combat medium also makes a difference. Given the speed at which modern aircraft fly and the greater risk of accidents and misidentification, air operations require a high degree of centralized control and coordination. The information processing, decisionmaking, and communications components of the command system have to be more tightly integrated for the same reason. Too much high-level direction, however, can stifle the tactical initiative of the pilots during engagements. In contrast, the often geographically

102. van Creveld, *Command in War*, pp. 272–73.
103. Simpkin, *Race to the Swift*, p. 229.

dispersed nature of naval operations necessitates looser controls. This need is especially true for undersea operations where the difficulties of communication make continuous contact extremely hard if not totally impracticable. Similarly, where terrain or climate renders communications difficult, the command system has to be adapted accordingly. Finally the composition of force also affects command structure. Combined arms operations requiring the cooperation and synchronization of air, ground, and naval forces must obviously possess the necessary mechanisms to effect coordination at each phase from planning through implementation. This condition is even more important in coalition groupings where national as well as service interests have to be accommodated and coordinated.

In conclusion, command fluency does not mean just reducing command friction; it derives from matching the command system to mission requirements and likely contingencies in a way that also takes account of the nature of the force, its doctrine, and its structure.

CHAPTER FOUR

NATO: From Peace to War

THROUGHOUT the 1970s NATO became increasingly concerned with the buildup in the Warsaw Pact's offensive military capability and, more specifically, with the possibility that it could launch an attack against the alliance with little or no warning. Before 1978 the expectation had been that NATO would receive approximately one month's warning of an attack; after 1978 that estimate was revised and cut by half. The contraction in warning time exacerbated an already sensitive problem for NATO. For many years NATO defense planners had worried about the alliance's capacity to respond promptly and effectively to warlike preparations by the Warsaw Pact. They were concerned that the alliance would fail to reach the necessary consensus to authorize precautionary defensive measures that would either deter an attack or put NATO in a reasonable military position to defend itself should war occur. Certain members, it was feared, might question the evidence of hostile intent—some of which could be ambiguous—and therefore disagree with the assessment that an attack was imminent, while others might hesitate to approve raising the combat readiness of the active forces or mobilizing the reserves out of concern that such actions would appear provocative and make war more likely. NATO, as a consequence, might end up doing too little too late or, worse, start to unravel just when unity and resolve were most needed. The possibility of a short-warning attack sharpened these fears.

NATO, while recognizing that such problems were largely inevitable in an alliance of sixteen sovereign nations, responded to the revised warning estimate by improving its command arrangements to make the transition from peace to war more rapidly should this prove necessary. The facilities for collecting and sharing intelligence were upgraded along with the intra-alliance communications links to facilitate consultation and decisionmaking. New contingency plans and military response options were also crafted so that alliance leaders could more easily grapple with unpalatable decisions in a crisis. At the same time NATO's military forces began exercising their alerting and mobilization procedures more regularly and were also given greater authority to take precautionary measures in emergencies. As this chapter will reveal, however, important deficiencies remained in NATO's command arrangements for responding to the threat of war. Moreover, in its efforts to speed up the military responsiveness of the alliance, NATO unwittingly added to the danger of war breaking out inadvertently in a crisis.

The shortcomings of NATO's command arrangements for responding to the threat of war can best be explained by focusing on the three main processes that would underlie alliance action in such contingencies. The first is the intelligence-gathering and warning process. All crises begin with the observation and reporting of events that appear abnormal or threatening in some way. Information on the source of concern is collected and processed on a more or less continuous basis and then passed to the appropriate military and civil decisionmaking authorities. This step initiates the second process, high-level consultation and decisionmaking by alliance members. Various deliberative bodies meet to discuss the unfolding events and, with the approval of the member governments, decide what actions to take in response. Depending on the situation, the third process, placing the alliance's military forces and civil agencies on successively higher stages of alert and, if necessary, mobilizing the reserves, then begins.

The processes at work are not as discrete or the steps necessarily so sequential as implied here; in reality they would be heavily intertwined if not mutually interdependent once set in motion. As will also become evident, the diffusion of alerting authority throughout the alliance may also result in certain military measures being taken without direct political approval. For analytical purposes, however, the three main processes will be examined separately. The pitfalls and problems associated with each will be treated in turn. Before continuing, however, it is useful to have some basic understanding of the peacetime organization and operation of the alliance.

Peacetime Organization and Operations

After the signing of the North Atlantic Treaty in 1949, NATO took the unprecedented step of creating a peacetime multinational defense planning organization along with, though somewhat later, an integrated military command. While the size of this organization has expanded considerably since then, the basic structure, with some exceptions, remains the same. At its apex is the North Atlantic Council (NAC), which is chaired by the secretary general of NATO and includes representatives from each of the member nations. This group meets two or three times a year at the ministerial level to discuss general politico-military issues, although in exceptional circumstances the heads of state or government can also convene in this forum. The council meets every week, however, with the nations' permanent representatives (perm reps) to NATO in attendance. They also have frequent informal discussions among themselves, including weekly luncheons.

For consultations on specific military issues, the primary deliberative body of NATO is the Defense Planning Committee (DPC). Established in response to France's decision to withdraw from the integrated command structure in 1966, the DPC includes representatives from every country except France.[1] As is typical of the vagaries of NATO, Spain is a full participant in the DPC even though it is not part of the integrated military command. So too is Iceland even though it does not possess a defense force. Like the council, the DPC can meet at the ministerial or ambassadorial (perm rep) level, with such meetings usually taking place at irregular intervals. The DPC and the NAC have essentially equal authority except in matters that concern the military actions of the alliance; when it comes to approving increases in the military readiness of the alliance, the DPC is the primary deliberative body.

The NAC/DPC oversees a host of committees responsible for planning different aspects of the alliance's activities in peacetime.[2] One of these is the Military Committee. Though sometimes referred to as the "highest military authority of NATO," the Military Committee has no command authority and serves only to provide advice to the DPC through its

1. France, on request, can obtain the records of DPC meetings of interest to it.
2. For further details see *The North Atlantic Treaty Organisation: Facts and Figures* (Brussels: NATO Information Service, 1989), pp. 321–36; and *NATO Handbook* (Brussels: NATO Information Service, 1989), pp. 25–29.

chairman, who is also a permanent member of the DPC. Like the DPC, the committee meets two or three times a year at the more senior level with each nation's chief of defense staff present and on a weekly basis with their military representatives (mil reps) in attendance. Though criticized in the past for being largely redundant and moribund, the Military Committee has been reinvigorated in recent years to take a more active role in alliance planning and operations.[3] Another important but frequently overlooked committee is the Senior Civil Emergency Planning Committee. As its title suggests, this body is responsible for planning all aspects of NATO's civil emergency activities in crisis and war. Such is the enormity of this task, however, that the committee delegates much of this work to numerous planning boards and subcommittees.[4]

Supporting the NAC/DPC in formulating crisis response policy is the Council Operations and Exercises Committee. Besides controlling headquarters exercises, this committee also manages the NATO Situation Centre, which will be discussed later. The NAC/DPC and subordinate committees all meet at NATO headquarters at Evere in the northeastern suburbs of Brussels. This headquarters also houses the supporting international staff (civil), international military staff, and the sixteen delegations of the alliance members.

NATO's military command structure is organized according to three geographical areas of responsibility: Allied Command Europe (ACE), Allied Command Atlantic (ACLANT), and Allied Command Channel (ACCHAN).[5] Each is headed by a supreme allied commander—SACEUR, SACLANT, and CINCHAN, respectively, who are known collectively as the major NATO commanders. Beneath these officers are two other tiers in the NATO command structure: major subordinate commanders, who are typically responsible for specific areas of the main regions, and, below them, principal subordinate commanders, who are nominally in charge of large units of assigned forces such as army groups

3. See Gen. Gerd Schmückle, "Crisis Management in an Alliance of Sovereign States," Working Paper 56 (Washington: Wilson Center International Security Studies Program, 1984), pp. 15, 48–52; and David M. Abshire, *Preventing World War III: A Realistic Grand Strategy* (Harper and Row, 1988), p. 30.

4. For more information see Julius W. Becton, Jr., "Civil Emergency Planning: NATO's Hidden Strength," *NATO Review*, vol. 36 (August 1988), pp. 29–32.

5. The Canada-U.S. Regional Planning Group does not constitute a major NATO command.

or Allied Tactical Air Forces in each area. The NATO command structure and the peacetime location of each command's headquarters are illustrated in figure 4-1.

In peacetime the NATO military command structure is essentially a hollow one. With the exception of headquarters staff and some small multinational task forces, the military power of the alliance remains firmly under national control. Many of the senior NATO commanders are "dual hatted," however, in the sense that they are also in charge of national military contingents. All the principal U.S. military commanders in the European theater, for instance, hold key NATO positions, as figure 4-2 illustrates.

Similarly many of the senior British commanders in NATO are dual hatted: the commander in chief, Fleet, is also CINCHAN, and the commanders in chief of the British army of the Rhine and Royal Air Force (RAF) Germany also head the Northern Army Group (NORTHAG) and the 2d Tactical Allied Air Force (2ATAF) respectively. Though they are all NATO commanders, their responsibilities lie first and foremost with the national forces under their control.[6]

As indicated earlier, the major NATO commanders do control some small special-purpose military units in peacetime. These consist of two modest-sized naval task forces: Standing Naval Force Atlantic and Standing Naval Force Channel under SACLANT and CINCHAN, respectively, and the ACE Mobile Force under SACEUR's command. All three also have operational command of the NATO Airborne Warning and Control Force made up of AWACS aircraft. Similarly the system of ground-based radars that make up the NATO Air Defense Ground Environment is under multinational command in peacetime.

To facilitate consultation and coordination, the capitals of all the alliance members as well as the main military command centers are tied together by an extensive communications network that NATO developed and operates. The NATO Integrated Communications System, as it is known, consists of several communications satellites and associated ground stations, a chain of troposcatter and microwave relay towers known as Ace High that stretches the length of Europe from Norway to Turkey, as well as miscellaneous smaller networks that serve specific

6. David Fouquet, ed., *Jane's NATO Handbook, 1988–89*, first ed. (Coulsdon, Surrey, U.K.: Jane's Information Group Limited, 1988), pp. 69–103.

regions.[7] In addition NATO operates its own communications switching systems for routing message traffic throughout the alliance: the telegraph automatic relay equipment for data traffic, the initial voice switched network for telephone communications, and the NATO secure voice network for classified conversations.

Intelligence and Warning

The primary function of intelligence in NATO is to provide warning and assessments of incipient threats to the alliance. As a Rand Corporation primer on the alliance crisis management apparatus succinctly states:

> NATO depends upon its intelligence system to identify potential crises, to warn of crises in the early stages of development, and to define the nature and magnitude of crises that may evolve without being detected in their formative stages. The intelligence system signals NATO's consultative, decision, and action agencies to begin the transition from peace to crisis management. It provides the data on the basis of which NATO's political and military authorities can judge the scope and urgency of crises and decide what allied or national actions should be taken in response.[8]

Contrary to what many believe, however, NATO does not have an intelligence system in the sense of an independent freestanding organization that operates its own intelligence assets in support of alliance needs.[9] The task of monitoring Soviet and Warsaw Pact forces for the earliest signs of warlike preparations and possible hostile intent has always been a wholly national responsibility. The alliance, as a result, is entirely dependent on whatever intelligence its members are prepared to contrib-

7. The Ace High system is now being dismantled in a phased transition to the NATO Terrestrial Transmission System, consisting of an interlocking network of nationally owned military communications systems that NATO will lease for its own purposes. See chap. 5 for further information.

8. E. W. Boyd and others, NATO *Management: Peace-to-Crisis Transition*, R-2576/ 1-ISA/PA – &E/DOS, declassified NATO Secret Report prepared for the Office of the Assistant Secretary of Defense (International Security Affairs), the Office of the Assistant Secretary of Defense (Program Analysis and Evaluation), and the Department of State (Santa Monica, Calif.: Rand Corp., 1980), p. II-2.

9. The closest it has to one is the NATO-operated Airborne Warning and Control System (AWACS) aircraft and NATO Air Defense Ground Environment radars that would provide valuable intelligence on air activity in the area adjacent to NATO-controlled territory.

Figure 4-1. *NATO's Military Command Structure with Location of Peacetime Headquarters*

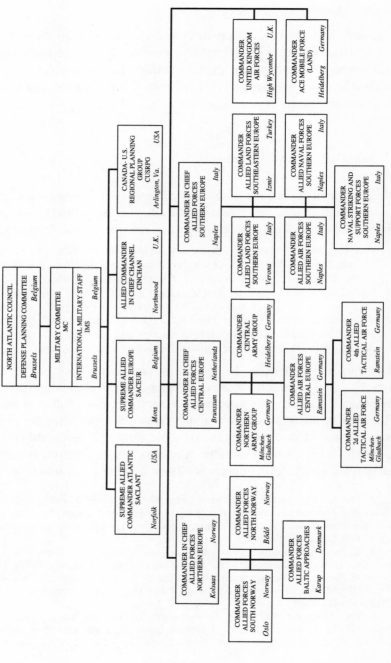

Source: *The North Atlantic Treaty Organisation: Facts and Figures* (Brussels: NATO Information Service, 1989), pp. 338, 345.

Figure 4-2. *U.S.-NATO Dual-Hatted Command Relationships*

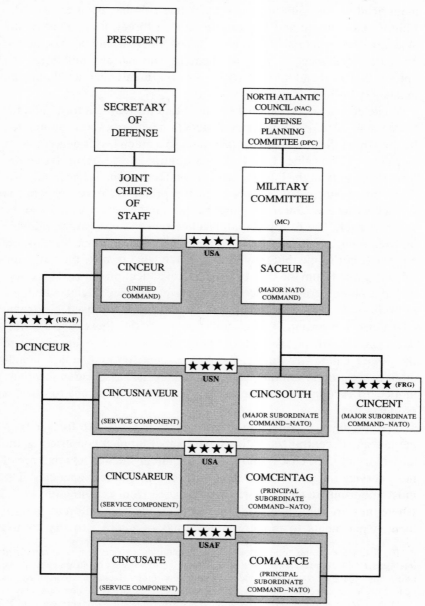

Source: Mitre Corp., "Board of Trustees' Visit to European Theater: Background Material," McLean, Va., March 1987, p. III-3.

ute. Although NATO does have its own intelligence staff assigned to the main headquarters, its principal peacetime role has been to brief the Military Committee and prepare the annual threat assessment of the Warsaw Pact. In a crisis, however, staff members would be expected to evaluate intelligence passed to them by the nations and brief the appropriate civil and military authorities on threatening developments in a timely fashion.

While each alliance member is committed to sharing information for the common defense, intelligence collection within NATO is dominated by the United States, Great Britain, and, to a much lesser degree, West Germany. [10] The value of the U.S. contribution, however, derives more from the quality of the intelligence supplied than from its sheer volume. The United States has always been the principal source of what is commonly termed "strategic" intelligence on the Soviet Union and the Warsaw Pact. The European intelligence services can gather valuable information from their embassy attachés and their contacts in Moscow and Eastern Europe, but they cannot match what is more regularly and reliably gained from the vast U.S. technical collection effort. This effort includes photoreconnaissance and signals intelligence (Sigint) satellites, as well as an elaborate set of airborne and ground-based electronic eavesdropping systems. [11] The span of coverage that these assets collectively provide—from the eastern borders of NATO to the far reaches of the Soviet Union—is without parallel. Except for some allied signals intelligence ground stations, non-U.S. intelligence assets are essentially limited to reconnoitering the areas immediately adjacent to NATO's borders.

The intelligence collection arrangements in NATO are further fragmented and decentralized within the principal supplier countries. In the all-important U.S. case, control over the intelligence assets that are of most service to NATO is divided among several different agencies. The most important strategic assets are managed from Washington, D.C., where they are subjected to competing demands from different government departments to monitor other areas of interest to the United

10. Estimates of the total amount vary. According to one retired senior U.S. intelligence officer interviewed, the United States provides 70 to 80 percent of the information reaching NATO. In confidential interviews other officials have disputed this figure but have not disagreed with the fact that the United States is the dominant player.

11. For more information on the U.S. intelligence collection systems see Paul B. Stares, *Space and National Security* (Brookings, 1987), pp. 18–22, 52–53; and Jeffrey T. Richelson, *The U.S. Intelligence Community*, 2d ed. (Ballinger, 1989), chaps. 7, 8.

States.[12] The U.S. intelligence collection effort in the European theater is also controlled by different authorities, some based in Washington, others in Europe. Each of the component service commands of U.S. European Command (EUCOM) operates its own collection management office (CMO), which is in turn responsible to the European collection management office (ECMO), run by a branch of EUCOM at its headquarters in Stuttgart. The ECMO acts not only as the central coordinating authority for U.S. military intelligence operations in Europe but also as the principal conduit for requesting the support of nationally controlled assets in Washington. Given its enormous area of responsibility, the ECMO has established a separate joint collection management office (JCMO) for the central region of Europe, which is colocated with the Allied Forces Central Europe (AFCENT) primary wartime headquarters at Boerfink in West Germany.[13]

Although NATO has no direct control over the intelligence-gathering activities of its members, it can exert some influence for the benefit of the alliance as a whole. Through the use of the NATO Collection Coordination Intelligence Requirements Management (CCIRM) System, NATO can channel intelligence requests from alliance members and NATO's senior commanders to those who can best provide assistance. The Intelligence Division at the Supreme Headquarters Allied Powers, Europe (SHAPE), is responsible for managing this system through designated officers at each of the main subordinate headquarters. Intelligence requests are passed from these officers to national intelligence representatives who in turn pass them on to their own national intelligence agencies. The main suppliers in fact operate what are generally referred to as national intelligence cells at SHAPE and at the AFCENT wartime headquarters. Thus the U.S. intelligence cell would pass requests to and from the U.S. ECMO at Stuttgart. Figure 4-3 shows the relationship between the U.S. and NATO intelligence collection management agencies.

12. See Richelson, *U.S. Intelligence Community,* for the most comprehensive description of the various U.S. intelligence agencies involved in this process.

13. NATO *Standardization, Interoperability, and Readiness,* Hearings before the Special Subcommittee on NATO Standardization, Interoperability, and Readiness of the House Committee on Armed Services, 95 Cong. 2 sess. (Government Printing Office, 1979), pp. 9–10. The U.S. collection management effort in Europe is currently undergoing major reorganization. In the future the ECMO will be replaced by a Joint Intelligence Center with subordinate centers for the northern, central, and southern regions of Europe. The above information has also been gleaned from confidential interviews.

Figure 4-3. *Organization of U.S. and NATO Intelligence Collection Management Agencies*

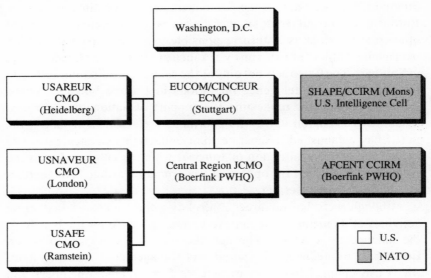

While NATO endeavors to exert some influence on the collection of intelligence, it has little effect on how it is subsequently disseminated. Collected intelligence flows within and among alliance members in several different ways and in several different forms, ranging from raw unprocessed data to finished assessments. It is important to distinguish three separate information flows within NATO. There are, first, the internal national flows where intelligence collected locally by tactical military units or nationally controlled assets is passed to higher authorities for processing and interpretation, and the reverse where intelligence collected and processed from strategic assets is passed down to lower command authorities. Depending on the distribution arrangements, tactical-type intelligence may also be passed laterally among national authorities at several levels.

The second type is nation-to-nation flows. Since the Second World War, much of the U.S. strategic intelligence effort has been carried out in concert with the United Kingdom and its Commonwealth partners: Canada, Australia, and New Zealand. In addition to setting a formal division of labor to monitor areas of mutual interest, the UK-USA agreement, as this arrangement is generally called, maintains special channels and procedures for exchanging intelligence. While the partnership between the United States and Great Britain continues to be the main axis of the agreement, a web of exchange arrangements evidently exists with other NATO countries, notably the Federal Republic of Germany, although the extent of its access to the gathered intelligence remains unclear.[14]

The third type is nation-to-NATO flows. Relatively low-grade intelligence, such as weekly summaries, is regularly released to NATO's intelligence staff either directly from the capitals or through the national intelligence liaison officers attached to the major headquarters. The real difficulty comes with furnishing more sensitive information, especially when it is still relatively raw or unprocessed. Since intelligence released to NATO under normal circumstances receives wide circulation, the principal suppliers are understandably reluctant to share sensitive intelligence without first "sanitizing" it to disguise the sources and methods used. In an effort to overcome this problem and provide a way for sensitive compartmented intelligence such as Sigint and communications intelligence (Comint) to be passed to the relevant authorities in a timely but more secure manner, NATO has established special handling detachments at each of the major military headquarters and also at Evere.[15] Consisting essentially of secure reading rooms, these detachments operate under strict rules governing the dissemination and use of the material made available.[16]

Many of NATO's senior officers and officials regularly obtain high-grade intelligence by virtue of the dual-hatted command arrangements mentioned earlier, as well as through official NATO channels. Thus all three of the major NATO commanders and many of the major subordinate

14. For more information see Jeffrey T. Richelson and Desmond Ball, *Ties That Bind: Intelligence Cooperation between the UKUSA Countries—the United Kingdom, the United States of America, Canada, Australia, and New Zealand* (Allen and Unwin, 1985), pp. 170–71. According to officials interviewed, French officials can evidently view U.S. satellite reconnaissance photos at the U.S. Embassy in Paris, but they cannot take the pictures away with them.

15. See Maj. Gen. Joachim M. Sochaczewski, "NATO Information Systems in Support of Consultation and Military Command and Control," in *Information and Consultation: Keys to Peace,* proceedings of the Eighth AFCEA Europe Symposium held in Brussels, 1987 (Brussels: AFCEA Europe, 1988), pp. 73–77, supplemented by information from interviews and command organization charts.

16. For example, information is released on the basis of a "no feedback" rule, that is, national representatives privy to the intelligence cannot transmit it back to their own domestic intelligence agencies.

commanders and principal subordinate commanders would be cleared to receive UK-USA "eyes only" intelligence. SACEUR, for example, would be kept abreast of developments by his U.S. EUCOM intelligence staff and also by a joint UK-USA secure facility operated by British and American officials at SHAPE. As in the case of the special handling detachments, cleared personnel would be able to examine intelligence in this room. Even though they could not disclose this information to their allied colleagues unless cleared to do so, key actors in the NATO decisionmaking process would nevertheless be kept informed by the principal suppliers of intelligence to the alliance. Similarly, the national permanent representatives and military representatives would receive national intelligence briefings, some of which might be deemed releasable to their NATO partners.

Given the need to draw together the many different sources of intelligence on the Warsaw Pact in a timely fashion, the United States took the lead in creating what have become known as Indications and Warning (I&W) centers. The purpose of these centers is to produce and display a composite picture of the day-to-day military readiness of the forces arrayed against NATO. This allows a general pattern of activity, such as changes in the readiness of disparate units, to be quickly identified and reported to higher authorities. The United States operates a network of I&W centers in Europe called the Warning Indications Systems, Europe (WISE), which is part of the much larger Worldwide Warning Indicator Monitoring System (WWIMS) run by the Department of Defense.[17] With its hub located at the EUCOM headquarters in Stuttgart, the WISE network is made up of independent centers run by each of the component commands at its peacetime headquarters. As one would expect, these centers specialize in monitoring activities that are of most interest to the parent service. Thus U.S. Army, Europe (USAREUR), at Heidelberg has traditionally concentrated on monitoring Warsaw Pact ground forces; the Fleet Command Center (FCC)–Fleet Ocean Surveillance Information Center (FOSIC) at the headquarters of U.S. Navy, Europe (USNAVEUR), in London, along with its component facilities in Rota, Spain, and Naples, Italy, pays attention to Soviet naval movements; and U.S. Air Force, Europe (USAFE), with its Tactical Fusion Center

17. Headquarters, U.S. European Command, "Intelligence: Missions and Responsibilities (U)," Directive 40-1, Stuttgart, January 4, 1987, p. 2; Headquarters, U.S. Army, Europe, and Seventh Army, "Organization and Functions, United States Army, Europe," USAREUR Regulation 10-5, Heidelberg, September 27, 1984, p. 16.

Figure 4-4. *U.S. Warning and Indications Systems, Europe*

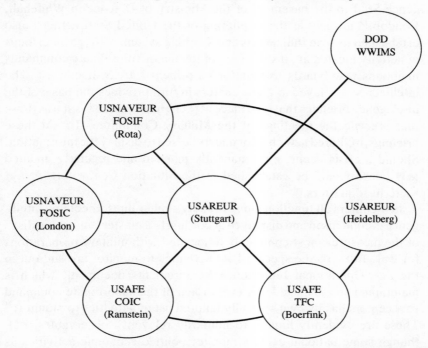

Sources: Based on Headquarters, U.S. European Command, "Intelligence: Missions and Responsibilities (U),"
Directive 40-1, Stuttgart, January 4, 1987; Headquarters, U.S. Army, Europe, and Seventh Army, "Organization
and Functions United States Army, Europe," USAREUR Regulation 10-5, Heidelberg, September 27, 1984; Jeffrey
T. Richelson, *The U.S. Intelligence Community*, 2d ed. (Ballinger, 1989); and interviews.

(TFC) at Boerfink and Combat Operations Intelligence Center (COIC) at
Ramstein Air Base in West Germany, focuses on the status of Warsaw
Pact air forces. The network is tied together by a special communications
circuit, which uses satellite and microwave links to exchange information
among themselves and also pass intelligence to and from Washington,
D.C.[18] Figure 4-4 shows the general configuration of the WISE network.

In a similar fashion but on a dramatically reduced scale, Britain and
Germany established their own I&W centers. Germany's is managed
by the Federal Armed Forces Intelligence Office at Bad Neuenahr-

18. Richelson, *U.S. Intelligence Community*, pp. 109–13; and miscellaneous inter-
views. In Washington, D.C., the National Operational Intelligence Watch Officers'
Network links together the U.S. government's intelligence centers. See Seymour M.
Hersh, *"The Target is Destroyed": What Really Happened to Flight 007 and What
America Knew about It* (Random House, 1986), pp. 66–67.

Ahrweiler close to Bonn, while Britain's is run by the Defence Intelligence Staff in the basement of the Ministry of Defence in Whitehall, London.[19] Largely at the prompting of the United States, NATO also established its own Indications and Warning system with the main focus of activity located at SHAPE. Each of the major subordinate commands maintains I&W boards to monitor its principal areas of interest. The intelligence displayed at these centers in turn provides the basis of the intelligence briefings that take place at NATO headquarters, such as those that precede the meetings of the Military Committee. To aid these briefings, a colored I&W chart or matrix is used to display the information. Should a crisis occur, a permanently manned and regularly updated I&W board would be established in the Situation Centre (SITCEN) at NATO headquarters.[20]

I&W centers all function along broadly similar lines. Incoming intelligence is condensed and displayed according to a master "indicators list" of the measures most commonly associated with military preparations for war. In NATO the specific Pact activities to monitor are laid out in the ACE Operational Intelligence Requirements document, which is maintained and managed at SHAPE. Each of the subordinate command I&W centers has its own specially tailored list of activities to monitor.[21] These are evidently limited to militarily relevant "observables," although some national centers monitor politico-economic activities as well (table 4-1).

With the aid of these lists, the daily readiness of opposing military units is displayed on either a manually operated or electronic indications board, depending on the sophistication of the center (most of the NATO boards are manually operated). The U.S. system, which NATO and other allied countries have adopted, uses a color coding scheme to classify military units, with green, yellow, and red denoting increasing states of

19. The German title of the Federal Armed Forces Intelligence Office is the Amt Für Nachrichtenwesen der Bundeswehr. See Jeffrey T. Richelson, *Foreign Intelligence Organizations* (Ballinger, 1988), pp. 28–29, 142–43; and Federal Minister of Defence, *White Paper 1985: The Situation and the Development of the Federal Armed Forces* (Bonn: Federal Minister of Defence, 1985), p. 231.

20. See Lt. Gen. James A. Williams, "Intelligence Support to NATO," *Signal,* vol. 38 (December 1983), pp. 87–90.

21. One report states that NATO's I&W system monitors 500 indicators of Warsaw Pact mobilization. See "The Military Balance," a staff study in Joseph Wolf, ed., *Strengthening Deterrence: NATO and the Credibility of Western Defense in the 1980s* (Ballinger, 1981), p. 118.

Table 4-1. *Typical Warning Indicators*

Politico-economic related

Withdrawal of diplomats and their dependents from certain countries.

Imposition of travel restrictions on Western diplomats and tourists.

Unusual industrial and trade activity aimed at increasing stocks of war-related equipment and materials.

Heightened civil defense preparations.

Military related

Force deployment indicators

Cancellation of leave and previously announced training exercises.

Heightened activity at military bases.

Call-up and mobilization of reserves.

Deployment from peacetime quarters and movement to assembly areas.

Dispersion of military aircraft and evacuation of naval vessels from port.

Concentration of forces in sensitive areas, movement of artillery and air defense units to forward positions.

Clearing/marking of attack routes.

Logistics indicators

Stand down of forces for maintenance and servicing.

Replenishment of ammunition; petrol, oil, and lubricants; and other war stocks.

Assembly of transportation vehicles, conversion of civil assets to military use.

Movement of bridging equipment and ammunition stocks to forward areas.

Intelligence indicators

Heightened intelligence collection efforts by reconnaissance satellites, aircraft, and patrols.

Increased counterintelligence efforts.

Evidence of deception.

Command and control indicators

Heightened communications activity.

Activation of wartime headquarters.

Evidence of new communications nets, call signals, and frequency changes.

Source: This list is compiled primarily from Richard K. Betts, *Surprise Attack: Lessons for Defense Planning* (Brookings, 1982), pp. 191–92; and Gen. Glenn K. Otis and Maj. Dewey A. Browder, "Tailoring Deterrent to Threat," *Army*, vol. 34 (October 1984), p. 141.

military readiness.[22] These rules, however, have had to be periodically reviewed and modified since some anomalous indicators can become a regular aspect of peacetime operations.

NATO has never been unduly concerned that it might fail to detect changes in the military readiness of Warsaw Pact forces. Quite the

22. According to interviews, the color assigned to a specific unit or organization changes on the basis of an elaborate set of rules for interpreting the incoming intelligence data. For example, a Soviet division would be classified with a particular color according to the readiness of its component regiments. If two were to leave their garrisons

contrary. With all the sophisticated sensors at its disposal and the increasing transparency in world affairs, such activity is extremely difficult to hide. Rather, the principal intelligence challenge to NATO has been to pull together disparate intelligence from many national sources, make sense of it, and disseminate it to the appropriate authorities in a comprehensible form and in a timely fashion. Unfortunately, despite some improvements, the mechanisms and procedures that NATO established to fulfill this requirement suffer from several deficiences, which raise serious doubts about the operational performance of NATO's early warning system in a crisis.

As already indicated, member nations are understandably reluctant to share source-sensitive intelligence with their NATO allies. Although NATO has made progress in facilitating this process with such innovations as the special handling detachments, the barriers to sharing intelligence— frequently referred to as the "green door" problem—still remain. The principal suppliers of high-grade intelligence to NATO have to go through a time-consuming review to determine what is releasable. One senior U.S. military intelligence officer admitted that he spent 75 percent of his time trying to get intelligence to the allies.[23] Although it is reasonable to expect that the barriers will come down in a serious crisis when, it is hoped, common interests will prevail, other bottlenecks and sources of friction are likely to affect the timeliness of the transfer and its eventual reception.

In particular NATO's resources for receiving, collating, and evaluating compartmented intelligence are apparently woefully inadequate. The NATO intelligence staff is reportedly "seriously undermanned and under-trained in peacetime."[24] Should the faucet controlling the flow of intelligence to NATO—principally from the United States—suddenly open, it is extremely doubtful whether the present system could handle

---

suddenly, then the division would be classified as green. This would change to yellow if another regiment left, and finally to red if the remainder moved from their peacetime quarters. The same kind of rules apply to the color coding of larger combat groupings and their associated command organizations.

23. *Alliance and Defense Capabilities in Europe*, Hearings before the Subcommittee on Conventional Forces and Alliance Defense of the Senate Committee on Armed Services, 100 Cong. 1 sess. (GPO, 1988), p. 58.

24. John P. Crecine, "C³I across the Seams of Military Organizations," in Gen. Jack N. Merritt, Gen. Robert Reed, and Roger Weissinger-Baylon, eds., *Crisis Decision Making in the Atlantic Alliance: Perspectives on Deterrence* (Menlo Park, Calif.: Strategic Decisions Press, 1987), p. 26–18. This observation has been corroborated in several interviews.

the likely torrent of information. According to several informed officials, the number of communications channels and appropriately cleared personnel that are required to handle sensitive intelligence is gravely insufficient for the task and would most likely become quickly overwhelmed by any sudden influx. Well before the peacetime staff and communications system could be augmented by mobilized personnel and additional circuits, the system could conceivably become so inundated with information that it could no longer keep up with events and might grind to a halt.

Even if the system held together, there are additional doubts about the capacity of NATO's intelligence personnel to make use of much of the information they receive. Peacetime training and exercises evidently do not prepare them for evaluating the latest types of satellite imagery or esoteric sources of signals intelligence. As one senior British officer has remarked, "Intelligence staffs would have to deal with intelligence abounding in quality and quantity with which they were completely unfamiliar. That factor in itself could well lead to further and very unwelcome delay in producing assessment consensus."[25] While these delays could prove immensely frustrating to the United States, since it will clearly be the principal supplier of this kind of intelligence to the alliance, it will need to handle this responsibility in a very delicate manner. A mixture of suspicion and resentment that the United States effectively controls so much of the information funneled into NATO could grow and prove yet another impediment to alliance consensus building.[26]

Depending on the nature of the events that sparked the crisis, the process of reaching a commonly accepted alliance assessment may prove acrimonious and slow. This problem is especially likely in a crisis that originates well beyond NATO's borders but which nevertheless threatens to spill over into Europe. In these cases asymmetries in the intelligence

25. Air Chief Marshal Michael Armitage, "Intelligence Assessment," in Merritt, Reed, and Weissinger-Baylon, *Crisis Decision Making in the Atlantic Alliance,* p. 6-3. See also Richard K. Betts, *Surprise Attack: Lessons for Defense Planning* (Brookings, 1982), p. 196. Persons interviewed have also remarked on the low status afforded to intelligence positions in the alliance.

26. According to several interviews, concern over this problem has apparently led the United States to use surrogates on some occasions for passing intelligence to NATO. The various bilateral intelligence arrangements that the United States maintains with its NATO allies can also cause problems. Intelligence made available to one country may at a later stage be fed into NATO channels, causing some confusion over whether it is new evidence that confirms the original or just recycled information.

assets of alliance members will really matter and national differences of opinion will probably be greater than ever.[27] Peacetime exercises apparently are not geared to simulating the formation of alliancewide intelligence assessments because the exercises are scripted and known by everyone in advance. Transforming what is essentially a small peacetime operation into one that can put together good assessments under pressure in a crisis takes time, which is precisely what NATO may not have.

The principal risk of a prolonged effort to reach a common assessment within NATO is that the whole process could become hopelessly overtaken by events. The chief suppliers could also conceivably become so frustrated with NATO's inability to process and make use of new intelligence that they cease to feed more information into official channels. Marked variations and differences could then develop between the situation assessments of those countries with direct access to intelligence and those heavily reliant on NATO. Direct capital-to-capital flows of intelligence and other back-channel transfers might mitigate this problem, but this solution is more likely to occur among the countries that already enjoy established arrangements for exchanging intelligence. The likelihood of considerable variations in the level of access to intelligence could seriously hinder the process of consensus building. Worse still, it could prompt unilateral actions that complicate and even contradict NATO's handling of the crisis.

Consultation and Decisionmaking

The principal forum for alliance consultation and consensus building in a crisis will be either the North Atlantic Council or the Defense Planning Committee. Any alliance member can use its permanent representative to request a meeting of the NAC/DPC if it believes there is

27. See Armitage, "Intelligence Assessment." See also Brig. Kenneth Hunt, "Crisis Management and Consultation," in John Garnett and others, *Peace to Crisis in Europe: Preparedness and Transition,* Whitehall Papers 2 (London: Royal United Services Institute for Defence Studies, 1986). As Hunt indicates, "Allies will not care to be steam-rollered by, say, an American interpretation and will have their own political assessments, particularly where some strong national interest is at work." p. 21.

an imminent threat to alliance security that warrants collective action. The ambassadors, or permanent representatives, are reportedly able to meet at two hours' notice at any time of the day or night and on any day.[28] If the situation is not so pressing, a formally inscribed item can be put on the agenda of the NAC/DPC, backed up with a supporting paper distributed beforehand. With certain exceptions, only the DPC has the authority to declare military and civil emergency measures on behalf of the alliance and then only with the unanimous approval—or at least passive acquiescence—of the member states. It is an inescapable fact of alliance life that national governments, not their representatives at the NAC/DPC, make the actual decisions.

Other NATO committees besides the NAC/DPC are likely to meet in a crisis, with some groups playing a more active role than others. The Political Committee might convene to discuss possible diplomatic and economic-related actions. According to officials interviewed, a list of potential options known as the Inventory of Preventive Measures has been drawn up for this purpose and includes such measures as diplomatic sanctions, economic embargoes, and the withdrawal of trade representatives from designated capitals. Friendly countries might be asked to apply diplomatic and economic pressure as well.[29] The Political Committee would take the initiative in choosing what actions from the list of measures appeared desirable and practicable, which would then be passed to the NAC/DPC for discussion and approval. These steps might precede or be implemented concurrently with whatever military actions are taken by the alliance. Meanwhile, the Military Committee would probably convene to discuss the security implications of the crisis. As noted earlier, the meeting would begin with an intelligence briefing on the current situation that included an I&W assessment of opposing military forces. On the basis of the discussion that followed, the Military Committee would recommend to the DPC measures drawn from its Catalogue of Potential Military Response Options. Although the Military

---

28. *North Atlantic Treaty Organization: Facts and Figures,* p. 324. The former U.S. ambassador to NATO also notes that "during holidays standby representatives, diplomatic and military, could meet in council session at any time, day or night, within an hour." Abshire, *Preventing World War III,* pp. 21–22.

29. NATO's plans have evidently at one stage included the destabilization of the Polish economy to hinder Soviet mobilization plans. See Patrick Tyler and R. Jeffrey Smith, "Study Finds NATO War Plans Outdated," *Washington Post,* November 29, 1989, pp. A1, A22.

Committee has no authority to authorize military readiness measures, it would most likely be used by the major NATO commanders to support such requests to the DPC and the nations' capitals.

Should a crisis reach a point at which the implementation of military readiness measures seems likely, the Senior Civil Emergency Planning Committee and its various subordinate planning boards would also be activated. Their primary role in a crisis would be to ensure that the alliance takes the necessary civil emergency measures to allow the alerting and mobilization process to run smoothly. This is a vital and much underappreciated component of NATO's preparations for war. As in the case of NATO's other crisis response measures, the DPC would be presented with packages of initiatives to be approved with the consent of the nations. These would cover a wide range of activities, including civil communications, shipping, surface transportation, aviation, petroleum, food and agriculture, industrial preparedness, and civil defense.

Another important body that would be convened in a crisis is the Committee on the Implementation of the NATO Alert System, more generally referred to as the Alerts Committee. This little-known committee made up of national representatives drawn from the permanent headquarters staff is activated to support the operations of the DPC. Its main responsibilities are to process requests to raise the military readiness of the alliance from the major national commanders or member countries, seek their approval from the national capitals through their delegations in Brussels, and afterward inform the DPC of the measures that had not been unanimously approved. Depending on the urgency of the situation and the nature of the disputed measures, the Alerts Committee would endeavor to reach a consensus among it own members. However, in an effort to speed up the process and bring additional pressure to bear on recalcitrant states, the disputed measures would be put on the secretary general's agenda for discussion in the DPC. Furthermore, through a recently computerized system, the Alerts Committee would try to keep track of where each of the alliance members stood with regard to its implementation of alert measures. The committee is not required to inform the DPC of every measure accepted since its members would keep their permanent members apprised of the situation, but it does have to notify the DPC when a higher stage of alert is requested. The Alerts Committee would also perform similar duties for NATO's civil emergency measures, contingency operations plans, and rules of engagement in a crisis.

Finally, a Crisis Operations Cell would be activated in the Situation Centre, ostensibly to monitor relevant events and receive information from alliance members. This cell would operate around the clock with a considerably expanded staff. As noted earlier, an I&W board would also be established.

The different NATO crisis consultation bodies and the process by which the alliance would approve the various civil and military alert measures are depicted in figure 4-5.

In recent years NATO has instituted a series of regular exercises to practice procedures for consultation and crisis management. In particular the large-scale biannual winter, civil emergency, and high-level exercises (WINTEX/CIMEX and HILEX) have evidently proved extremely useful for acquainting officials with NATO's contingency plans.[30] Though generally welcomed by alliance members, the exercises have nevertheless been criticized for the way they are formulated and managed.[31] As one report concluded, "Because the emphasis in these exercises is on testing the system rather than simulating an actual crisis, a degree of artificiality has been introduced into these exercises which is not helpful. As a result, participants too often base their actions on assumptions that may prove unwarranted in a real crisis."[32] Apparently, the scenarios chosen each year have been wedded, until fairly recently, to the standard contingency of reacting to the threat of aggression in central Europe. Other, arguably more plausible, scenarios that emanate from hypothetical events on the flanks of NATO or in Eastern Europe have never been used as the basis of these exercises. The reason for this stems in part from a certain wariness about indicating areas that NATO considers potentially dangerous. Some countries are also reluctant to confront sensitive issues even in a simulation for fear of having to disclose their true intentions in advance. Another important criticism is that NATO is fixated on exercising the procedures for

30. HILEXs are usually held in even-numbered years and practice political consultation procedures in a crisis; the WINTEX/CIMEXs are held in odd-numbered years and entail exercises for decisionmaking in crisis and wartime, including nuclear release procedures.

31. Unless otherwise indicated, the following information on NATO exercises has been derived from interviews.

32. Project on a Resources Strategy for the United States and Its Allies, *NATO: Meeting the Coming Challenge. An Alliance Action Plan for Conventional Improvements and Armaments Cooperation* (Washington: Center for Strategic and International Studies, 1987), p. 21.

Figure 4-5. *NATO Crisis Consultation and Alerting Mechanisms and Processes*

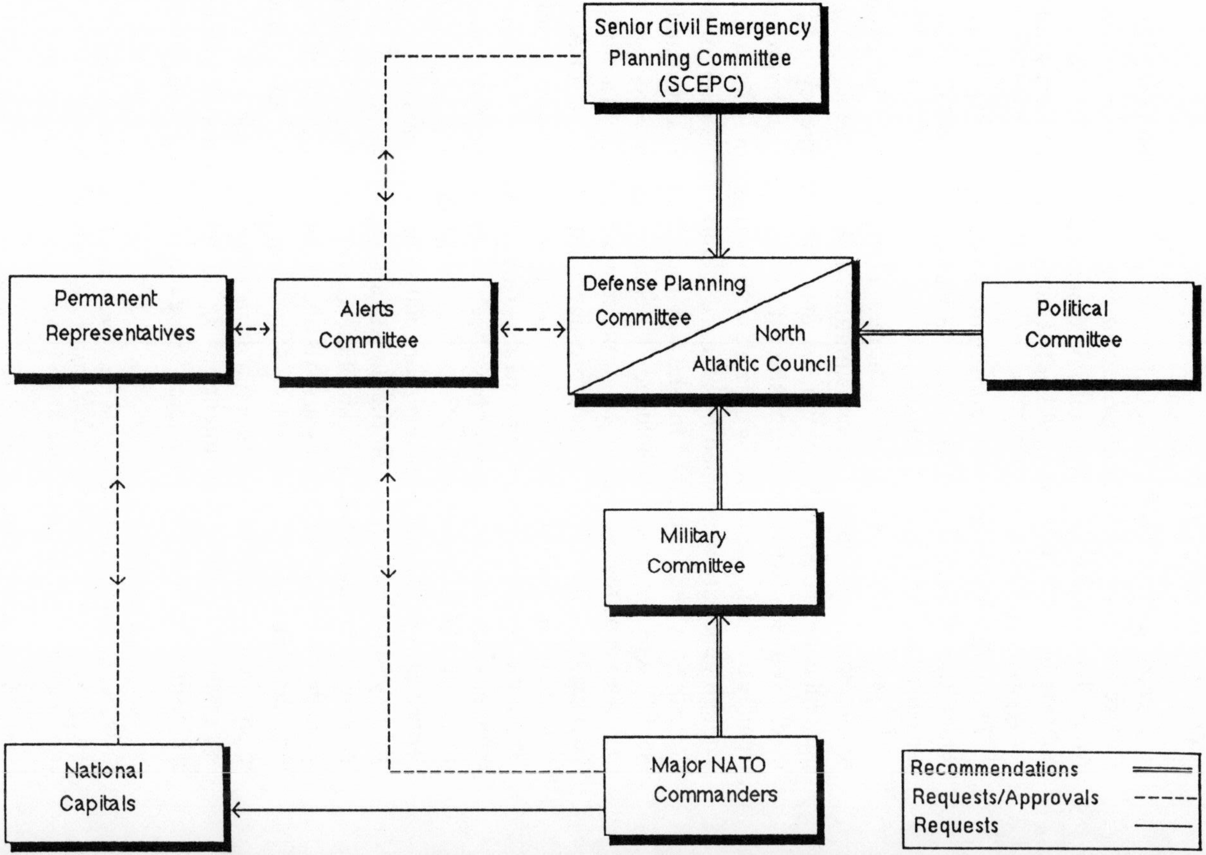

going, as one participant described it, "from tranquility to holocaust" in twelve days. Little or no attention is paid to practicing how NATO might help diffuse a crisis and put the brakes on the alerts process.[33]

The seriousness with which certain countries approach these exercises also varies widely among alliance members. For instance, some nations regularly send junior officials to play senior roles, while the heads of government of other countries have been known to participate on occasion.[34] As a result, familiarity with NATO's elaborate plans and procedures reportedly varies considerably among senior officials, including even the permanent representatives.[35]

Moreover, those participating are not subjected to the time pressures that typically characterize real crises. The exercises apparently work within the normal nine-to-five routine of the NATO bureaucracy and can often be held up when crucial decisions are referred to national capitals that happen to lie outside Brussels' time zone. While the urgency of a real crisis would presumably force the immediate attention of government bureaucracies, the effect that differences in time zones may have on alliance decisionmaking is not fully appreciated. As one retired senior official remarked, "People think and act differently at 2 a.m. than at 10 in the morning."

Despite the artificialities of NATO exercises, they have been sufficiently realistic in certain basic respects to indicate some of the most difficult challenges facing the alliance in a real crisis. The problems associated with reaching alliance consensus on what measures to take, as others have observed, stands out as the largest obstacle to collective action. Even when the threat of war has been absent, serious disputes have occurred over the need to implement military preparations in response to hypothetical Warsaw Pact movements. During HILEX 12 in 1986, for example, several European countries balked at SACEUR's

33. See also Ambassador Gordon S. Smith, "Some Notes on How NATO Would Go to War," in Gen. John T. Chain, Gen. Robert Dixon, and Roger Weissinger-Baylon, *Decision Making in the Atlantic Alliance: The Management of Political-Military Crises* (Menlo Park, Calif.: Strategic Decisions Press, 1986), p. 21.

34. For instance, former Prime Minister Margaret Thatcher participated in one HILEX exercise. The United States, on the other hand, is known for regularly sending junior personnel. One participant in these exercises observed that the officials taking the part of key decisionmakers tended to think and act like bureaucrats rather than like the politicians that would occupy these positions in a real crisis.

35. Schmückle, "Crisis Management in an Alliance of Sovereign States," pp. 13–14. This has been corroborated in several interviews.

request to implement the Rapid Reinforcement Plan to mobilize NATO's reserves, in the belief that it was premature and too provocative.[36] More recently the WINTEX 89 exercise proved especially controversial partly because of West Germany's delay in mobilizing its forces but more importantly because of disagreements about nuclear targeting.[37] Similar arguments have broken out among the allies over the associated civil emergency measures that in many instances have to be put into effect before many of the military readiness measures can be implemented. The disruption to airports, seaports, and major transportation routes that many such measures would create ensures considerable domestic debate if not outright opposition.

While NATO sees the difficulty of reaching a consensus as largely unavoidable in a sixteen-member alliance, NATO leaders have always hoped that the exigencies of the situation and the importance of maintaining unity and demonstrating resolve would prevail in a serious crisis. Officials have always believed that there is enough flexibility to NATO arrangements and procedures to overcome potential logjams of this kind. While the approval of every member state would always be sought, "The NAC/DPC has never operated in a manner implying recognition of the right of any member to veto actions acceptable to a 'coalition of the willing' among the Alliance, *nor are there any rules of procedure requiring an active expression of unanimity to arrive at a consensus.*"[38] As Gordon S. Smith, the Canadian ambassador to NATO, admitted, "Although one never likes to talk about such things, it is possible someone will be left behind. I do not therefore believe that, in a real crisis, NATO would be hobbled by the veto of a recalcitrant country refusing to join a consensus."[39]

Nevertheless, the responsiveness of the DPC in a crisis ultimately rests on the timeliness of national governmental deliberations, which could vary considerably. According to several participants in the NATO

36. Similar problems occurred in HILEX 11 in 1984. Interviews; and James A. Winnefeld, "Crisis De-Escalation: A Relevant Concern in the 'New Europe'?" N-3153-CC (Santa Monica, Calif.: Rand Corp., 1990), p. 2.

37. See "Schlag zuviel," *Der Spiegel,* March 13, 1989, pp. 15–16.

38. Boyd and others, *NATO Management,* pp. I-17–I-18 (emphasis in original). The provision of rules and voting requirements was deliberately excluded during the negotiation of the North Atlantic Treaty to ensure maximum flexibility so that "no government could be forced to take action against its will but that, conversely, no government could prevent other governments from taking such collective action as they agreed to take."

39. Smith, "Some Notes on How NATO Would Go to War," p. 22.

exercises, some countries are clearly better prepared and more profes-sional in establishing national crisis management machinery to support their delegations in Brussels.[40] Countries with coalition governments may also have to deal with the added burden of reconciling the potentially divergent views of various factions, some of whom may occupy key positions of responsibility with access to different sources of information. Furthermore, constitutional ambiguities over the power of certain domes-tic political bodies in a crisis can also affect how quickly a country might respond. Italy is reportedly one example of a country that has suffered in the past from this particular problem.[41]

Significant legislative hurdles will also have to be overcome in some countries before certain military readiness measures—notably mobilization and the transfer of command authority—can be approved. The situation for the alliance as a whole is extremely varied and complicated. In certain countries the head of state has some authority to call up reserves while in others the minister of defense retains similar powers. Most NATO countries, however, require parliamentary approval at some stage. For example, the president of the United States can call up 200,000 reservists for active service for up to ninety days without declaring a national emergency, after which congressional authorization is required. In Germany full mobilization requires the declaration of a state of defense by the Bundestag along with a proclamation signed by both the chancellor and the president of the Federal Republic. The minister of defense, however, can call up some reserves to "standby readiness." The Dutch minister of defense has similar authority in that he can recall short-leave units without parliamentary approval.[42] The U.K. minister of defense, in contrast, evidently does not require a parliamentary vote to implement the full range of mobilization options (table 4-2). Similar constraints affect the national governments' latitude to relinquish command authority over their forces to NATO. The Danish

40. Great Britain, for example, with its recent experience in the Falklands War is evidently better prepared than most. To make matters worse, confusing schisms have even been evident in the national delegations to NATO. On several occasions the statements of one country's military representative has been known to contradict directly the expressed views of its civilian permanent representative.

41. See Stefano Silvestri, "Crisis Management in the Mediterranean: Italy and Cooperation with Allied Nations," in Merritt, Reed, and Weissinger-Baylon, *Crisis Decision Making in the Atlantic Alliance*, pp. 11-6–11-7.

42. See Federal Minister of Defence, *White Paper 1985*, p. 75; and "Mobilization of the Dutch Army," *NATO's Sixteen Nations*, vol. 33 (October 1988), p. 59.

Table 4-2. *Mobilization Authority in Participating NATO Nations*

Member	Minister of defense	Cabinet	President	Parliament
Belgium	Partial	Full	Full[a]	. . .
Canada	. . .	Full	Full[a]	. . .
Denmark	Partial, full	. . .	. . .	. . .
Federal Republic of Germany	Partial	. . .	. . .	Full
Italy	. . .	Partial	. . .	. . .
Netherlands	Partial[b]	Full	. . .	. . .
Norway	Partial	Full	Full[a]	. . .
Turkey	. . .	Partial	. . .	Full
United Kingdom	Partial, full	. . .	. . .	. . .
United States	. . .	. . .	Partial	Full

Source: E. W. Boyd and others, *NATO Management: Peace-to-Crisis Transition*, R-2576/1-ISA/PA&E/DOS, declassified NATO Secret Report prepared for the Office of the Assistant Secretary of Defense (International Security Affairs), the Office of the Assistant Secretary of Defense (Program Analysis and Evaluation), and the Department of State (Santa Monica, Calif.: Rand Corp., 1980), p. IV-14.
a. King through council (Belgium); governor in council (Canada); and king in council (Norway).
b. Strictly speaking, the Dutch minister of defense cannot implement military measures involving mobilization; rapid call-up measures available to the minister include only trained conscripts on extended leave.

parliament, for example, has to approve the transfer of command authority by a two-thirds majority.[43]

Crisis decisionmaking could also likely be delayed, and perhaps seriously hindered, by the limited capacity of NATO communications links to and from the national capitals. They have evidently proved in exercises to be wholly inadequate for the sudden demands of a crisis. Available communications channels quickly become overloaded, causing long delays in the transmission and receipt of messages. This problem is not helped, moreover, by the reported inclination of many officials to send lengthy cables, sometimes to a long list of addressees. Although NATO operates a message priority system, it is often abused as frustrated officials inflate their messages' true level of precedence to ensure preferential handling.[44] These communications problems affect certain members of the alliance more than others. Some countries depend almost wholly on official NATO channels to their delegations in Brussels while others, like the United States, can use their extensive independently

43. Abshire, *Preventing World War III*, p. 61.
44. NATO evidently can employ rudimentary "minimizing" procedures to allow important messages to get through, but these have been only partially effective when used. Persons interviewed in general spoke of a widespread ignorance of NATO's crisis communications procedures that entail precise message formatting and also include specific guidelines for ensuring communications security.

operated communications systems. Although the use of public post, telegraph, and telephone (PTT) networks is an option, these too are likely to be overloaded in a crisis. Finally the possibility of deliberate interference of NATO communications prior to hostilities cannot be ruled out.

The inadequacy of external communications is matched by the archaic and inefficient state of the technical support systems within NATO headquarters. As one senior official lamented, "NATO is ten years behind the standards of most modern business organizations." The operations of many key offices are only now beginning to be computerized, while automatic data links among key committees have still not been fully implemented. As a result, most of the reports that are generated in a crisis would have to be typed and hand delivered or verbally delivered.[45] Furthermore the staff supporting the operations of the DPC is apparently quite small and would probably soon become overwhelmed and exhausted by a prolonged crisis.

Should NATO's consultation and decisionmaking process become particularly bogged down in a crisis, there is every likelihood that the formal alliance mechanisms will be bypassed in favor of bilateral arrangements. Many believe, for instance, that the top tier of NATO countries—the United States, the Federal Republic of Germany, Great Britain, and France—would not wait for complete consensus if delay might prejudice the timely implementation of measures they consider essential. Instead they will decide among themselves what action needs to be taken and then carry it out with the approval of as many NATO countries as they can get. Indeed an informal consultative arrangement among these four countries is known to exist, but for obvious reasons it is not openly acknowledged by them. Known as the "Quad," this arrangement evidently evolved from quadripartite consultations on Berlin to discussions on other issues.[46] Although the foreign ministers

45. One person interviewed attributed this lack of modernization to a reluctance to be perceived as "feathering one's own nest." NATO has also had problems with its efforts to modernize automatic data processing systems. The company with whom NATO contracted for new equipment reportedly went bankrupt.

46. See Norman Gelb, *The Berlin Wall: Kennedy, Krushchev, and a Showdown in the Heart of Europe* (Times Books, 1986), p. 127. The existence of the Quad, confirmed by interviews, is also somewhat obliquely referred to by former Secretary of State Alexander M. Haig, Jr., in Haig, *Caveat: Realism, Reagan, and Foreign Policy* (Macmillan, 1984), p. 249, and in Lincoln Gordon, "Convergence and Conflict: Lessons for the West," in Gordon, with Brown and others, *Eroding Empire: Western Relations with Eastern Europe* (Brookings, 1987), p. 320. One former NATO foreign minister

of these countries meet privately—usually on the eve of NATO ministerial summits—it is unclear whether this arrangement extends to contingency planning for crisis and war.[47] In some NATO planning documents, however, there are reportedly hints of "emergency escape clauses" that would permit action without universal approval.[48] Similarly, the numerous bilateral Wartime Host-Nation Support agreements, which many NATO countries have signed to facilitate the movement and operation of military forces in their territory, represent in many respects a desire to operate independently of formal NATO mechanisms.

Alliance members have also no doubt developed their own plans in the event that NATO unravels in a crisis. The United States, for example, has prepared contingency plans to direct military operations in Europe independent of NATO. According to a report issued by the General Accounting Office, "U.S. plans . . . contain provisions for the United States to assume centralized direction of U.S. *and allied forces* should NATO fail to function in wartime." Moreover, "the United States might have to temporarily exercise such direction until the NATO members approve military action."[49]

While these independent initiatives may address the question of alliance vacillation in a crisis, they do not remove the problem altogether. There is no guarantee that the major nations will be united in their views and recommendations, as past crises have illustrated. Even if their unity remains intact, many of the military readiness measures they may want to implement could still be dependent on the acquiescence of states that do not share their views. The reinforcement of forces along the central

---

interviewed also referred to this group as the "directorate," evidently after de Gaulle's abortive proposal to Britain and the United States in 1958 to create such an organization. For details see Alfred Grosser, *The Western Alliance: European-American Relations since 1945*, trans. Michael Shaw (Continuum, 1980), pp. 186–88. For economic discussions the Quad became the basis for the G-7 group of nations.

47. Quadripartite consultations evidently took place during the Polish crisis of 1981 and before the Ottawa summit in February 1990 to discuss the unification of Germany. Although Italy is not a regular member of the Quad, according to interviews it was apparently included in the discussions held by this group on the modernization of intermediate-range nuclear forces in the late 1970s. See Lincoln Gordon, "Interests and Policies in Eastern Europe: The View from Washington," in Gordon, with Brown and others, *Eroding Empire*, p. 119.

48. Hunt, "Crisis Management and Consultation," p. 23.

49. General Accounting Office, *Relationships between U.S. and NATO Military Command Structures—Need for Closer Integration*, LCD-77-447 (October 1977), p. 29 (emphasis in original).

front, for instance, requires the active cooperation of several nations to open up the vital lines of communication. Vacillating countries, therefore, can still make life difficult.

Alerting and Mobilization

The military forces that make up the combined military strength of NATO can be alerted and made ready for war in several different ways. There are, first, the nationally established procedures and mechanisms for alerting forces. These are authorized and implemented under the direction of the national command authorities of each country and can be taken independently of alliance actions. National military commanders, furthermore, often have considerable discretionary power in certain circumstances to alert forces under their control. The second category of alert procedures are the commonly approved NATO measures, which encompass several discrete but largely interdependent areas of activity related to elevating the readiness of active military forces, implementing civil emergency measures, and ensuring the rapid reinforcement of NATO. Although most of these measures can be authorized only by the DPC with the approval of national governments, senior NATO commanders also have the predelegated authority to take certain steps to alert and employ forces under their control.

National Alert Measures

Each country in NATO has established its own alert procedures to raise the readiness of its military forces and if necessary put its entire political and economic infrastructure on a wartime footing. Given the sensitivity that surrounds this issue, public details of these national plans are extremely scarce. It is unclear, moreover, how much information the allies have shared among themselves about their emergency planning.

The U.S. alert system is probably the most well known of any NATO country, principally because of the public scrutiny that has attended the several instances in which U.S. nuclear forces were put on higher states of alert. This attention, however, has been focused almost solely on the system operated by the Joint Chiefs of Staff (JCS) and then only on one part of these procedures. Besides the five defense readiness conditions, there are two emergency conditions: Defense Emergency and Air Defense Emergency, which have in turn three attack warning conditions:

red, yellow, and white. Furthermore, the United States has established a separate alert system for civil emergency preparedness known as civil emergency readiness levels.[50] The purpose and application of the JCS alert system has been described as follows:

> The Alert System of the Joint Chiefs of Staff is designed for use in crisis management. It is adaptable to a full spectrum of crises—from general war and execution of the Single Integrated Operational Plan (SIOP) to operations and regional tensions in a limited area, with or without the use of nuclear weapons. It is intended to be used as a directive as well as an authorization for the commanders of the unified and specified commands to implement preplanned actions to increase force readiness which may include the execution of portions of some plans or entire plans during a particular alert condition (LERTCON).[51]

In accordance with JCS guidelines both U.S. commander in chief, Europe (USCINCEUR), and commander in chief, U.S. Atlantic Command (USCINCLANT), have established alert procedures for their own commands. These measures have been tailored specifically to the forces and geographic area under their control.[52] The European Command alert procedures are very similar to the NATO alert measures to the extent that they even use the same nomenclature.[53] Forces under the control of these commanders could be raised unilaterally to successive states of readiness, either in response to orders from Washington, as several previous crises have illustrated, or at the behest of the unified commander.[54] While the normal practice would be to seek authorization from the JCS to implement measures beyond the most basic actions to raise military readiness, *the unified commanders nevertheless have discretionary power to take whatever measures they consider necessary to preserve the security of the forces under their command,* including

50. This information comes from the sanitized version of Joint Chiefs of Staff, *Alert System of the Joint Chiefs of Staff, Part 1: Concept (U)*, SM-410-74 (Washington, January 1981), pp. 1-1, 2-1. There are three civil emergency levels: Communications Watch, Initial Alert, and Advanced Alert. See the sanitized version of JCS, *Major NATO Commanders Alert System Procedures for the Joint Chiefs of Staff (U)*, SM-1-79 (Washington, January 1979), pp. 9-1–9-3.

51. JCS, *Alert System*, p. 2-1.

52. See the sanitized version of JCS, *Major NATO Commanders*.

53. Interviews. For historical interest see Headquarters, U.S. European Command, "USCINCEUR's Defense Readiness Conditions," declassified Secret Report, Stuttgart, November 7, 1959, reproduced as "Emergency Readiness Plans," CCS 3180, April 20, 1959, Record Group 218, National Archives, Washington.

54. During the 1970 Lebanon crisis and again in the Yom Kippur War, U.S. conventional forces in Europe went to a higher state of alert.

moving them from their peacetime locations to anywhere in their area of responsibility.[55] The commander in chief of USEUCOM could also request that U.S. dual-based forces be returned to the European theater as is practiced in the annual REFORGER (Return of Forces to Germany) exercises. While the United States evidently does not need the approval of the allies to do this, as a practical matter the allies' assistance is required to receive the forces when they arrive.

Less is known about the alert systems of America's principal military allies in NATO.[56] The British procedures are laid out in the *War Book* produced by the cabinet office. Each government department also has plans that are cross-referenced with the nationwide and NATO levels of alert. The British government evidently practices these procedures in parallel with the HILEX/WINTEX exercises. As for Britain's military forces based in Germany, again there are no constraints on them being placed on alert unilaterally, including having the forces leave their barracks.[57] The Federal Republic of Germany's national alert system, like most others, has separate military and civil emergency components. Even though its forces have been formally committed to the defense of NATO, under the Bundeswehr Alarm Plan they can be put on alert independent of alliance decisions. According to interviews, the measures laid out in this plan, however, are very similar to NATO's. While members of the alliance are requested to keep one another informed of any such unilateral alerting, such courtesy is not obligatory.

In addition to these unilateral alert measures, numerous bilateral agreements exist among members of NATO. Most of these concern Wartime Host-Nation Support (WHNS) arrangements to ensure that reinforcements can pass smoothly and quickly through ports, airports, and rail and road lines. Although WHNS agreements have been reached in the context of alliance planning to facilitate the rapid reinforcement of Europe in the event of war, they are not formal NATO documents. Neither is their implementation tied to the NATO alert system, partly

---

55. This discretionary authority is discussed in Bruce G. Blair, "Alerting in Crisis and Conventional War," in Ashton B. Carter, John D. Steinbruner, and Charles A. Zraket, eds., *Managing Nuclear Operations* (Brookings, 1987), pp. 116–17. The U.S. Army in Europe, for instance, regularly practices the rapid dispersal of forces that have been "uploaded" with ammunition from their barracks.

56. The following information on European alert systems was gathered during several interviews.

57. The "ground dumping" of ammunition outside of their storage areas, however, apparently requires the German government's approval.

because some of the agreements apparently have contingency plans in the event that certain NATO countries refuse to make their facilities available to others.[58] As a consequence, only the signatories are aware of their contents. The existence of other classified bilateral contingency-based alerting agreements that fall outside of the formal NATO framework should not be discounted either.

NATO's Alert Measures

NATO's alert measures can be arbitrarily divided into two basic categories: those that can be implemented without the consent of higher political authorities and those that require their approval. It is a somewhat fuzzy distinction since the two sometimes overlap.

As described earlier, the major NATO commanders have operational control of some military forces in peacetime, albeit all of modest size. In a crisis the ACE Mobile Force and the standing naval task forces could be dispatched and used at their discretion. Similarly, the fleet of AWACS aircraft could be directed to carry out additional surveillance missions where appropriate. The headquarters staff at each of the major NATO commands could also be placed on a higher state of readiness. Leave could be canceled, while the operations and intelligence centers could be manned on a twenty-four-hour basis, which is apparently what occurred during the 1980-81 Polish crisis, according to officials interviewed. Preliminary discussions among officers with NATO responsibilities would most likely also take place along with an initial review of contingency plans. At the army group-ATAF level, the commander could call subordinates together for an exchange of views about the situation, although they would not be bound by the commander's orders at this stage.

If the military situation became more threatening, senior NATO commanders could authorize on their own initiative further enhancements to the alliance's military readiness. Under a plan known as Closed Fence, the commander, Allied Air Forces, Central Europe (COMAAFCE), has the predelegated authority to implement a variety of defensive measures against surprise air attack, including dispersal of aircraft, arming of missiles, and more permissive rules of engagement. While the

58. See Robert R. Ulin, "Belgium: The Strategic Hub," in Jeffrey Simon, ed., *NATO-Warsaw Pact Force Mobilization* (Washington: National Defense University Press, 1988), p. 411.

commander in chief, Allied Forces, Central Europe (CINCENT), evidently has no equivalent authority with regard to ground forces, SACEUR can declare what are referred to as "No-Notice Readiness Exercises" that would in effect activate NATO's military command system—headquarters, communications, and so on—to wartime readiness levels, but such exercises would not involve the movement of combat forces. However, NATO corps commanders can call corps readiness exercises for their specific areas of authority, which evidently could entail the "practice" movement of forces to their general defense positions.

In the event that any of the major NATO commanders consider war imminent they also have the power to invoke special emergency procedures that would otherwise require the approval of the DPC. Known as the Counter Surprise Military System (CSMS), it is designed to allow NATO's military forces to take purely protective measures to reduce their vulnerability in the event of a surprise attack. Two discrete conditions of readiness (State Orange and State Scarlet) can be declared, depending on how imminent the attack is considered. The former is measured in hours, the latter in minutes.[59] Depending on the available time, the types of steps to be taken under the CSMS include dispersing aircraft and concentrations of vehicles, vacating barracks, and taking cover. Since these measures are highly disruptive to operations and could not be sustained for an extended period without compromising readiness, the forces would be fully or partially stood down in accordance with NATO's other alert procedures. While the CSMS alert states can be declared by the major NATO commanders, they have already delegated this authority (with the acquiescence of the DPC) to certain senior officers in their commands. This almost certainly includes the major subordinate commanders like COMAAFCE and his subordinate ATAF commanders.

While the CSMS can be invoked independently, it is technically part of the main NATO system for alerting forces known formally as the major NATO commanders' Alert System.[60] This system is made up of 193

59. Under the 1959 USCINCEUR alert measures, "State ORANGE will be declared when information received indicates a possible enemy attack within one or more hours with maximum time approximately 36 hours," while "State SCARLET will be declared when information received indicates an enemy attack within a few minutes." Headquarters, U.S. European Command, "USCINCEUR's Defense Readiness Conditions," p. 11. These same timelines are evidently still in force.

60. Actually its correct title is SI-E/72, March 9, 1972, *Alert System of SACEUR, SACLANT, and CINCHAN*. See JCS, *Major NATO Commanders*, p. E-1. As a result of several revisions, the document's classification number has changed; according to one

measures spanning four discrete gradations of alert from Military Vigilance through Simple Alert and Reinforced Alert to, finally, General Alert, which is equivalent to a state of war. In addition to specifying increasing levels of military readiness, the associated spectrum of civil emergency measures that would need to be implemented at each stage have apparently been added to make it a more integrated system.[61] Only those measures associated with Military Vigilance, however, can be declared by the major NATO commanders; the rest must be approved by the DPC with prior national concurrence. Under what is called the Status of Negotiations document, each nation has declared in advance its intention either to execute, withhold, or consult on individual measures within each stage of the alert system. In practice any nation can also choose to stand aside and allow NATO as a whole to declare certain states of alert without necessarily implementing the associated measures. Thus substantial variation is possible in the alert postures assumed by each country.

By all accounts, the major NATO commanders' Alert System is a very flexible instrument capable of being applied selectively in a wide range of contingencies. For instance, certain alert measures can be declared for specific commands and not others, while naval units could conceivably be at a different level of readiness from the ground and air forces in the same region. Furthermore, the DPC can choose to implement each measure step-by-step or all at once. It can also choose to adopt certain measures from higher stages of alert without formally declaring them. Flexibility, however, has been acquired at the cost of simplicity. According to one account, "The system is neither simple nor easy to understand and use."[62]

Although precise details of the measures associated with each level of alert remain classified, it is possible to construct some idea of the types of activity that would take place. Their implementation would also obviously depend on the nature of the situation.[63]

---

senior NATO official interviewed, it is now SI-E/80. The document is also often referred to as the "Blue Book," after the color of the loose leaf-binder that contains it.

61. NATO's alert system is evidently not organized according to numbered alert conditions, as some public descriptions have implied. Unless specified, information for this section was collected during several interviews.

62. Boyd and others, *NATO Management*, p. I-24.

63. This section draws on material acquired in interviews in addition to several open sources: Blair, "Alerting in Crisis and Conventional War," pp. 75–120; Alexander L.

MILITARY VIGILANCE. As just noted, Military Vigilance can be declared unilaterally by any of the major national commanders for their specific command area. If the DPC wished to, however, it could extend the alert to other regions. The measures that fall into this category are virtually indistinguishable from those that can be implemented at the discretion of NATO and national commanders. Thus leave would be canceled and personnel recalled to their barracks. Some preliminary stocktaking of equipment inventories to ascertain shortfalls would probably also take place as part of a general accounting of unit readiness. Additional maintenance would begin and logistical requests would be prepared where required. The tempo of operations would be stepped up within NATO's military headquarters: I&W and other intelligence centers would be manned around the clock and special crisis management cells or committees would probably also be activated to review contingency plans and discuss different options. NATO's ground forces would still be confined to their barracks but on standby to move out. Thus equipment would be packed and transport readied. Troop and ammunition movement plans would also be prepared for delivery to the local civil authorities. The guiding principle for all military actions at this stage is to avoid measures that would be externally observable. This guideline is likely to be difficult to meet when it comes to intelligence gathering, however. Unless the DPC believed it unduly provocative, surveillance of the relevant areas will most probably be stepped up.

At NATO headquarters in Brussels the NAC/DPC and the Military Committee would meet to hear the latest intelligence and discuss the evolving situation. The Alerts Committee would also be activated along with the Situation Centre to support their deliberations. Similarly the consultants to the Senior Civil Emergency Planning Committee, which would represent the advance party or "crisis elements" of NATO's Civil Wartime Agencies, would also be summoned to Brussels for discussions.

SIMPLE ALERT. At Simple Alert military preparations become more noticeable. Ground forces would begin to move out from their barracks

---

George and others, *Inadvertent War in Europe: Crisis Simulation,* a special report of the Center for International Security and Arms Control (Stanford University, June 1985), pp. 60–61; and Friedrich Wiener, *The Armies of the NATO Nations: Organization— Concept of War, Weapons and Equipment* (Vienna, Austria: Herold Publishers, 1987), p. 369.

to their nearby assembly areas where they would be matched up with their component units. Some elements of the covering force may also be deployed to forward positions. At air bases a higher proportion of aircraft, particularly for air defense duties, would be put on alert to take off on short notice. Maintenance and servicing of equipment in general becomes a high priority; logistics requests would now be submitted to bring these forces up to certain sustainable levels.

Simple Alert also marks the stage at which the transfer of command authority from national to NATO commanders would commence. As a rule only forces that are classified as combat ready by their national commands are "chopped" to NATO. The timing of the transfer has been meticulously planned and specified on a master schedule, but, as noted earlier, considerable uncertainty surrounds the relinquishing of national command authority. As part of the chop-over process, the senior NATO commanders would move to their wartime command posts where they would begin to assemble their battle staffs. Communications to and from these headquarters would be expanded, and liaison teams would be formed to facilitate coordination among the national units. Heightened security arrangements would also take effect to protect key facilities and communications. Additional communications security procedures, for example, would be implemented.

At Simple Alert a host of civil emergency measures would also commence. The crisis elements of NATO's Civil Wartime Agencies would begin to assemble at their wartime locations and start preliminary preparations. The communications system linking these bodies would also be activated. While independent of the major NATO commanders' Alert System, preparations to implement the various Host Nation Support agreements would most likely also take place at this stage in the alerts process. Similarly, SACEUR would most probably request that the DPC approve implementation of the Rapid Reinforcement Plan.

REINFORCED ALERT. With the declaration of Reinforced Alert, the troops already in their assembly areas would begin moving to their assigned general defense positions and commence preparations to defend their immediate area against attack. Troops would dig in, begin clearing fields of fire, lay mines, and complete the preparation of bridges and roads for detonation. As part of the Central Region Barrier Plan some detonations of the civil infrastructure, such as bridges and power lines in forward areas, may take place at this stage, although that would presumably be delayed for as long as possible for obvious reasons.[64] Patrolling activity and intelligence gathering in general would be intensified, and lateral communications would be established with adjoining units. Wartime communications procedures would also take effect. Rules of engagement would be relaxed to allow forces to fire in self-defense.

By this stage of alert the chop-over of command authority will also have been completed. The evacuation of dependents and a variety of civil defense measures will also be at an advanced stage. Finally, NATO's Civil Wartime Agencies would by now have been fully constituted at their wartime locations.

GENERAL ALERT. NATO is effectively at a state of war with the declaration of a General Alert. At this stage, the DPC is also expected to give Border Crossing Authority and make a Hostile Nations Declaration so that the rules of engagement can be amended accordingly.

No mention has been made so far of the measures related to nuclear weapons at each of the stages of alert. From what can be gathered from public sources, the readiness of these weapons would be largely unaffected until Simple Alert had been declared, excluding of course the possibility of nationally authorized activities.[65] At this stage preparations to disperse the land mobile forces would most likely begin, while the special communications systems to control these weapons and authorize their release would start to be activated. At Reinforced Alert they would then leave their peacetime bases and move to their covert wartime locations to await further orders.

NATO's alert system represents the product of many years of thought and planning on how the alliance can respond to military threats in a careful, measured, and timely manner. Nevertheless, serious questions remain over how well NATO could implement these measures even if it managed to overcome the obstacles in the way of reaching alliance consensus for their approval. NATO's limited experience in alerting its forces is in many respects compounded by reluctance to test some of

64. See Office of the Assistant Secretary of Defense for Program Analysis and Evaluation, NATO Center Region Military Balance Study, 1978–1984, declassified NATO Secret Report (Department of Defense, 1979), p. I-51.

65. This discussion draws heavily on Blair, "Alerting in Crisis and Conventional War." See also Catherine McArdle Kelleher, "NATO Nuclear Operations," in Carter, Steinbruner, and Zraket, Managing Nuclear Operations, pp. 445–69.

these measures, in part because of the considerable cost and disruption that it would entail but also because of a general loathing to open a Pandora's box. Much the same can be said about implementing the multitude of bilateral Host-Nation Support agreements. Since the details of many of these accords are politically sensitive, they have never been centrally coordinated or fully tested. As a result NATO's logistics planners have no clear idea of the potential gaps and shortcomings if the process is ever activated.[66]

Besides these big unknowns, there are other disquieting problems that concern the coordination and compatibility of the many different alert plans that could take effect if war was threatened. In particular the unilateral implementation of national alert measures—whether taken by local military commanders or by political leaders—could differ considerably from the formal NATO posture and might conceivably contradict it. For example, certain U.S. measures in the system for defense readiness conditions are likely to precede the declaration of equivalent measures under the major NATO commanders' Alert System. Similarly, while Germany's military alert procedures parallel NATO's very closely, Germany nevertheless reserves its right to implement its own national measures, which again might diverge from NATO official declarations at the time. As the European response to the Chernobyl nuclear reactor accident illustrated, countries react to events in very different ways.[67]

Even when countries alert their forces in conformity with NATO procedures, wide variations in the overall posture of the alliance could still occur. Besides the possibility that certain members might bow out of implementing particular measures, other countries might decide unilaterally to move to much higher states of alert than the DPC had formally declared, which apparently happened in a NATO exercise in 1988. At one point, according to several observers of the exercise, NATO was still formally at Military Vigilance while Norway was at Simple Alert and Turkey had gone even higher to Reinforced Alert. Needless

66. For an excellent account of this problem see James Kitfield, "The Host-Nation Support Gamble," *Military Logistics Forum,* vol. 4 (October 1987), pp. 30–36. After one exercise Gen. Bernard Rogers, while still the supreme allied commander, Europe, evidently complained bitterly about the proliferation of WHNS agreements, saying that he had little control over them and in some cases was unaware of them.

67. This problem is compounded by the transnational reach of news media, which can cause considerable public confusion, as Chernobyl also showed.

to say, such an outcome in a real crisis could appear confusing and contradictory to an outside observer.

Overview: The Danger of Inadvertent War

By the end of the 1980s NATO had built up an elaborate system to respond to the threat of attack, including, if necessary, going to war. By focusing on the threat of calculated aggression by the Warsaw Pact, however, NATO largely overlooked the possibility of war occurring inadvertently. As Ambassador Gordon S. Smith warned in 1986, "In 'normal circumstances,' NATO could make the transition quite well from peace to war. I am less optimistic that we are as ready as we should be for something unplanned. Although every effort has been made to build in flexibility and assure political control, we need decision makers and others to be more sensitized to such dangers as inadvertent war."[68]

During the early 1980s that likelihood increased markedly for several reasons. As already discussed, NATO became progressively concerned during the 1970s that the buildup in the Warsaw Pact's offensive military power had given it the capability to launch an attack against the West with little preparation and consequently little warning. NATO responded by bolstering its conventional defenses, notably the capacity to strike deep at targets in Eastern Europe and the Soviet Union. The latter reflected a doctrinal shift during the same period that emphasized targeting the rear echelons of attacking Warsaw Pact forces at the outset of a conflict to retard their forward momentum and prevent them from gaining overwhelming superiority against NATO's forces on the battlefield. NATO, at the same time, embarked on a significant nuclear weapons modernization program, largely in response to similar deployments by the Soviet Union. Though intended to buttress deterrence, these weapons nevertheless threatened nuclear attack with little or no warning. Naturally, NATO's military responses caused considerable concern in the Warsaw Pact.[69]

---

68. Gordon S. Smith, "Some Notes on How NATO Would Go to War," in Chain, Dixon, and Weissinger-Baylon, *Decision Making in the Atlantic Alliance*, p. 23.

69. Soviet anxieties over U.S. and NATO intentions apparently reached their peak in 1983. According to reports from the Soviet defector Oleg Gordievski, the KBG increased its efforts to detect signs of war preparations by the West. See Gordon Brook-Shepherd, *The Storm Birds: Soviet Postwar Defectors* (Weidenfeld and Nicolson, 1989),

For both sides the growing threat represented by the increasingly offensive character and heightened readiness of each other's principal adversary placed an added premium on rapid military response at the earliest signs of hostile intent. At the same time, it also increased the danger that ostensibly defensive preparations taken in a crisis might be misperceived or misunderstood as offensive in nature, triggering, as a consequence, a rapid sequence of unintended military interactions between the two sides that propel them to dangerously high levels of combat readiness. In such volatile circumstances, the likelihood of further misunderstandings, as well as accidents between two such heavily armed and well-primed adversaries, would be very high.[70] Even more alarming is that preemption would likely become a more attractive option—certainly if war were considered inevitable—to avoid falling victim to the first and potentially devastating blow at the outset. As will be discussed in chapter 5, the widespread vulnerabilities of NATO's command arrangements to attack did little to dissuade preemptive action and arguably represented yet another source of crisis instability.

Something akin to this kind of crisis dynamic apparently took place during the 1983 NATO Able Archer command post exercise held to test new alliance nuclear release procedures. Warsaw Pact intelligence officers reportedly mistook the exercise as a NATO deception plan to hide preparations for the real thing, causing them, to the horror of Western intelligence officers monitoring events, to sound the alarm in Moscow.[71] Although it is unclear whether Moscow ordered any concrete measures in response, or even whether NATO hurriedly assured the Soviet Union that it was just an exercise, this incident nevertheless shows how actions can be dangerously misinterpreted in a certain climate of relations.

Although NATO had always been sensitive to the problem of striking the right balance between deterrence and reassurance in a crisis, it remained largely ignorant of how deficiencies in its command system

---

pp. 330–34. See also Michael MccGwire, *Perestroika and Soviet National Security* (Brookings, 1991), pp. 387–92.

70. See Scott Sagan, *Moving Targets: Nuclear Strategy and National Security* (Princeton University Press, 1989), pp. 143–48, for historical examples.

71. See Brook-Shepherd, *Storm Birds*, pp. 329–330; and MccGwire, *Perestroika*, pp. 390–91.

might seriously compromise the efforts of the alliance to send a clear signal of its intentions. The difficulties associated with collating and disseminating nationally derived intelligence, the inadequacies of NATO's communications and data handling facilities, and the unpreparedness and unfamiliarity of certain members with NATO's crisis procedures and contingency plans continued to be some of the most serious problems. Together they threatened to complicate and delay the vital process of alliance consensus building in a crisis, which in turn increased the likelihood that individual member nations might take unilateral actions that would project a potentially confusing, contradictory, and even highly ambiguous image of NATO's intentions.

Furthermore, many of the initiatives introduced to speed up NATO's military responsiveness to the threat of short-warning attack—some of which, paradoxically, were implemented to prevent the alliance from becoming paralyzed by indecision over whether to authorize potentially provocative defensive measures—unwittingly added to the danger of an acute crisis escalating inadvertently. The creation of Indications and Warning Centers undoubtedly increased the sensitivity of the alliance to slight changes in the military readiness of Warsaw Pact units. But the fragmented organization of the centers and their direct links to senior national and NATO commanders invested with the discretionary authority to raise the military readiness of the forces under their jurisdiction increased the opportunity for potentially uncoordinated and ambiguous unilateral actions to be taken in a crisis. Such actions might stimulate offsetting responses by an equally sensitive Warsaw Pact, producing a spiral of progressively escalatory behavior.

NATO's computerized I&W boards developed to fuse together incoming intelligence on the military readiness of the Warsaw Pact added to the danger of inadvertent escalation. From their inception they were really only intended to display changes in the military readiness of the Warsaw Pact rather than help explain them. Some intelligence analysts became concerned, however, that NATO was growing too dependent on them and, moreover, using them as substitutes for an understanding of the events they depicted. In an apparent reference to this concern, Michael Herman, a retired senior British intelligence official, remarked, "The essence of all intelligence is understanding, and warning is a matter of achieving it by bringing proper insight to bear on current evidence, in conditions of speed and stress. Excessive emphasis on methodology could distract attention from this search for understanding."[72] In a similar vein, others warned that NATO's I&W centers were too focused on monitoring military indicators, with consequently insufficient attention paid to political and economic events.

NATO's search for understanding in a crisis also risked being compromised by the nature of its alerting system. To account for the impact of NATO activities on the behavior of the Warsaw Pact, allied intelligence analysts needed to be kept fully apprised of what had been authorized and implemented either independently or collectively by alliance members. Given NATO's system for reporting and monitoring alerting activity, however, the analysts were likely to remain uninformed and even misinformed in a crisis. Alliance members are under no obligation to inform one another of their *national* alert measures. Even the information they do share could be misleading or out of date. As past crises have shown, national command authorities have not always been fully aware of the steps that their *own* military forces have taken with predelegated authority. The Alerts Committee is supposed to keep track of and monitor the measures approved by the alliance and implemented by each country, but this vital task has not been automated. Measures are reported and registered manually, a process that is obviously time consuming, prone to error, and subject to being rapidly overtaken by events.[73] Overall, it is conceivable that NATO's intelligence analysts and decisionmakers have remained dangerously ignorant of NATO's effect on Warsaw Pact behavior. As Herman has also observed, "In practice the Allied community probably underrates the extent to which Soviet activities are influenced by their perceptions of Western activities. Intelligence peers into the fish tank—often a murky tank with strange and evasive fish in it—without realising how much the inhabitants are themselves reacting to what is going on outside."[74]

In high states of combat readiness, both sides also face the problem of maintaining control over their forces. For NATO, with its more

---

72. Michael Herman, "Warning: Some Practical Perspectives," in Merritt, Reed, and Weissinger-Baylon, *Crisis Decision Making in the Atlantic Alliance*, p. 7-3. One person interviewed, who is familiar with the way I&W boards operate, described them as "a social science response to a non-social science problem" and expressed concern that they have become "technological crutches."

73. The numerous measures are laboriously entered on a long spreadsheet. The United States has repeatedly recommended that NATO automate the alerts reporting and monitoring process, but this proposal remains under study.

74. Herman, "Warning," pp. 7-2–7-3.

decentralized command arrangements, the task of orchestrating and controlling the actions of its forces is a much greater problem. In peacetime exercises NATO regularly experienced problems with keeping in contact with its forces once they left their barracks. Not only do tactical communications nets take time to establish, especially if undertaken at short notice, but the standard practice of enforcing strict radio silence in units at forward positions to avoid compromising their position to an enemy is an added limitation. In a real crisis this constraint would not only reduce the degree of high-level control, but it would also constrict the amount of information being passed back. Under these conditions the relevance of orders to the realities of the situation could become progressively disconnected.[75] Moreover, the risk of independent, and possibly unwarranted, actions being authorized at the discretion of the local commander on the spot also grows.

The problem of maintaining connectivity with forces in the field is not likely to be helped by NATO's complex plans to transform its high-level command relationships in a crisis. The U.S. command structure, in particular, would undergo a very complex transformation. At some stage in the alerts process, the headquarters staff of the U.S. European Command in Stuttgart would be split up, with some joining SACEUR's staff at SHAPE and the rest moving to High Wycombe in England. Similarly, some of the headquarters staff of U.S. Army, Europe, would travel to the Central Army Group's wartime command post while the others relocated to a bunker at Massweiler, West Germany, where the wartime headquarters of USAREUR would be constituted.[76] Although such movements have been practiced, they are not comparable to what would take place in a real crisis. Indeed, there is little evidence to suggest that the numerous national and NATO contingency plans have ever been coordinated and that the necessary level of orchestration and synchronization required to implement them effectively was ever fully appreciated.

75. This same argument is made by Blair, "Alerting in Crisis and Conventional War," p. 117.

76. Daniel Charles, *Nuclear Planning in NATO: Pitfalls of First Use* (Ballinger, 1987), pp. 127–28.

CHAPTER FIVE

NATO at War

FROM THE LATE 1960s until fairly recently, NATO had publicly declared its intent to defend its territory as far forward as possible to its border with the Warsaw Pact. Driven to a large extent by political and geographical considerations, the doctrine of forward defense presented NATO's military commanders with significant operational challenges. To avoid being decisively outnumbered and overwhelmed at the outset of a war, NATO not only had to mobilize and ready its forces in a timely manner but also anticipate when and where the main blows would fall so that it could concentrate those forces accordingly. Failure to do so would almost certainly doom NATO's chances of defending itself by conventional means alone.[1] Although NATO could predict the most likely avenues of attack from telltale preparations, considerable uncertainty attended the task of divining enemy intentions in time to make the necessary defensive adjustments. NATO, furthermore, faced the monumental task of orchestrating a defensive campaign involving the air, ground, and naval forces of many different countries, each speaking a different language and operating, in many cases, very different equipment according to different operational practices. All had to be coordinated and synchronized for the alliance to realize full combat potential or at least prevent dangerous rifts from occurring among the allies.

NATO's chances of overcoming these operational challenges and successfully repulsing a Warsaw Pact attack rested, therefore, not just on the quantity and quality of its manpower and weaponry, but on how effectively they were employed in battle. This capacity in turn hinged

---

1. The operational consequences of NATO maldeploying its forces are discussed more fully in Joshua M. Epstein, *Conventional Force Reduction: A Dynamic Assessment* (Brookings, 1990), pp. 12–24.

on the performance of NATO's command system. This system, after all, would be responsible for promptly detecting and identifying enemy concentrations, for passing this intelligence in an equally timely manner to NATO's senior commanders, for relaying their movement and targeting decisions to subordinate forces, and ultimately for coordinating and directing their activities in battle. To perform effectively, however, NATO's command system had to be able to overcome or reduce to manageable proportions the most likely sources of command friction. More specifically, the Warsaw Pact could be expected to make every effort to mask its operational intentions and directly impede the collection of accurate intelligence by the alliance. The importance of NATO's command system, furthermore, marked its key physical components (command posts, intelligence centers, and communications facilities) as obvious targets for a massive and concerted assault by the Warsaw Pact at the outset of a war. To these external sources of friction could also be added the self-generated variety, particularly those associated with coalition warfare. Again, the Warsaw Pact could be expected to do everything to encourage and exploit divisiveness in the allied war effort.

The following assessment of NATO's wartime command system, which was carried out prior to the recent demise of the Warsaw Pact, reveals many deficiences and raises many doubts about its capacity to support the alliance's wartime goals as traditionally defined. Key components of the command system do not meet minimal standards of survivability, while other problems, notably in the dissemination of intelligence, also exist. Collectively, they represent a serious and persistent neglect by the alliance. The shortcomings of NATO's command system can best be analyzed by focusing on the theater, operational, and tactical levels of command, with war on the former central front as the base case.

The theater level refers, in essence, to the role and responsibilities of the supreme allied commander, Europe (SACEUR), in providing overall direction of a campaign in Europe. However, the day-to-day management of operations in the central region is the direct responsibility of the commander in chief, Allied Forces, Central Europe (CINCENT), in coordination with the commander in chief, Allied Air Forces, Central Europe (COMAAFCE). These two officers along with their subordinate army group and Allied Tactical Air Force commanders constitute the operational level of command. Below them, the tactical control of the ground battle is left to the national corps commanders and their subordinate officers, while the planning and supervision of air operations is the responsibility of senior air force officers operating from specific command centers. The air and land battle at the tactical level will be discussed separately.

Each level is analyzed according to a common framework. Following an introduction that sets out the associated command responsibilities and requirements, the primary components of the supporting command system—its wartime command structure, intelligence-gathering assets, information processing systems, and communications facilities—are described in turn. Drawing on the types of command friction that each level could reasonably be expected to encounter, each section concludes with an assessment of the overall adequacy of the command arrangements for that level.

The Theater Level

In wartime SACEUR's primary role is to oversee and provide military direction to NATO's prosecution of the war. While operational command of NATO's central region forces engaged in the fighting will be delegated to CINCENT, SACEUR is responsible nevertheless for allotting resources, setting priorities, and providing specific guidance for the campaign. Moreover, he will command the nuclear phase of operations, for which planning is sure to start at an early stage. In preparation for the use of nuclear weapons, he would seek nuclear release authority from higher political authorities so that he could respond to similar requests from below should the military situation deteriorate.[2] SACEUR's staff would also oversee and coordinate the reinforcement and resupply effort between the relevant national and alliance agencies. The logistical effort involved represents an incredibly daunting and much underappreciated challenge to NATO. The sheer size of the movement alone is staggering. Estimates of the number of forces that would be transported to Europe from the United States vary between 1 million and 1.5 million men plus 1 million tons of stores, and from Great Britain some 130,000 men and

2. See Catherine McArdle Kelleher, "NATO Nuclear Operations," in Ashton B. Carter, John D. Steinbruner, and Charles A. Zraket, eds., *Managing Nuclear Operations* (Brookings, 1987), pp. 457–64.

100,000 tons of stores.[3] On top of this can be added the movement of men and matériel from the other NATO countries to the central front. All this activity would have to be carefully synchronized and managed to prevent what would soon degenerate into an utterly chaotic and hopelessly entangled situation. The need for optimum performance from the relevant movement control and coordination bodies cannot be overstated. As one former NATO logistics officer bluntly observed, "In a future conflict, all aspects of logistical support must be capable of functioning at peak efficiency immediately reinforcement begins. Unless this can be achieved the RRP [Rapid Reinforcement Plan] will soon be halted, Europe will be littered with an accumulation of undelivered freight and the fighting troops will rapidly run out of ammunition, fuel and spares. In a word NATO would have lost."[4]

For the initial stage of a war, SACEUR can be expected to direct operations from the Supreme Headquarters Allied Powers, Europe (SHAPE), Command Center (SCC) immediately adjacent to peacetime headquarters at Casteau on the northeast outskirts of Mons in Belgium. Known also as SHAPE's primary wartime headquarters (PWHQ), the SCC was completed in the early 1980s and consists of a hardened bunker that is apparently capable of withstanding all but a direct nuclear strike.[5] A mobile alternate command post for SACEUR, code-named Fast Break, is currently under development as part of a general effort to improve NATO's theater command and control system, especially its facilities for wartime headquarters. While original plans called for deployment of approximately 150 large trucks and trailers sometime in the early 1990s, SACEUR's mobile headquarters is currently being scaled back in size to reflect the changed circumstances. In wartime, as is standard practice in NATO, one part of the headquarters would function as the main or "active" command post (CP) while another would be on standby in reserve at a different site to assume control when the main CP moves to another location. A small advance party, known in NATO circles as a leapfrog unit, would be responsible for setting up communications at the

3. These figures and the following discussion draw heavily on the impressively thorough but unpublished study by Brig. F. A. L. Alstead, "Ten in Ten?: A Study of the Central Region Transport Capability in Crisis and War," which was completed while the author was a NATO fellow in 1986–87, p. 16, app. L.

4. Alstead, "Ten in Ten?" p. 355.

5. Unless otherwise indicated, the following account is drawn from various interviews.

new site before the command vehicles arrive. Specific operating locations for Fast Break have already been presurveyed in southern Belgium. One of the deputy SACEURs would most probably travel with the alternate command post.[6]

Plans have also been drawn up for SACEUR to direct operations if need be from the bunker of the commander in chief, U.K. Air Forces (CINC UKAIR's) (code-named Broad Shield) at High Wycombe to the northeast of London. This location is very close to the EUCOM primary wartime headquarters in a separate facility at High Wycombe. This three-story underground bunker was originally built in the 1960s and underwent major refurbishment in the early 1980s to strengthen it and proof it against chemical and biological attack. It is most likely hardened to the same standards of survivability as SACEUR's PWHQ at Casteau.[7] As noted previously, this headquarters, which would also be at SACEUR's disposal by virtue of his dual-hatted command responsibilities, becomes fully activated once operations have been wound down at the peacetime facility in Stuttgart. In his role as commander in chief, Europe (CINCEUR), he has also at his disposal a fleet of four EC-135 airborne command posts code-named Silk Purse that in peacetime are based at RAF Mildenhall in Suffolk, England, but would be dispersed in a crisis to other locations. These aircraft, however, would be used primarily for relaying nuclear employment orders in wartime.[8]

The provision of intelligence—like logistics—remains firmly in national hands even after a nation's combat forces have been chopped to NATO. As in peacetime, most of the intelligence reaching SACEUR will come either directly from the United States or indirectly from EUCOM's European Collection Management Office (ECMO)-Joint Intelligence Center (JIC), which presumably will have moved from Stuttgart to High

6. See also "Mobile HQ to Aid NATO Survivability," *Jane's Defence Weekly*, August 26, 1989, p. 328.

7. Duncan Campbell, *The Unsinkable Aircraft Carrier: American Military Power in Britain* (London: Michael Joseph, 1984), pp. 186–87.

8. One aircraft is always ready to be sent airborne at short notice. Lajes Air Base in the Azores is evidently one of the dispersal sites. See NATO Standardization, Interoperability, and Readiness, Hearings before a Special Subcommittee on NATO Standardization, Interoperability, and Readiness of the House Committee on Armed Services, 95 Cong. 2 sess. (Government Printing Office, 1979), p. 1075; Bruce G. Blair, "Alerting in Crisis and Conventional War," in Carter, Steinbruner, and Zraket, *Managing Nuclear Operations*, p. 86; Campbell, *The Unsinkable Aircraft Carrier*, pp. 184–86, 241; and interviews.

Wycombe.[9] Other national intelligence cells at SHAPE, notably the British and German ones, will also be feeding him information from their national organizations. While SACEUR has no control over the exploitation of allied intelligence assets, he can utilize NATO's Collection Coordination Intelligence Requirements Management (CCIRM) system to request information from allied sources.

Supporting the processing of incoming intelligence and its subsequent dissemination is an automated command and control information system (ACCIS) at SHAPE. This system employs equipment purchased from the United States that was originally designed for SHAPE's Worldwide Military Command and Control System (WWMCCS). It is directly tied by way of a dedicated communications link to the Allied Forces Central Europe (AFCENT) CCIS computer at Boerfink.[10] Since 1986 the War Headquarters Information Dissemination and Display System (WHIDDS) has also been operational at SHAPE. This system is designed to superimpose intelligence about current enemy force dispositions onto computer-generated maps that can then be distributed within the headquarters. Similar decision aids are being introduced at some of NATO's other wartime command posts.[11]

For receiving political guidance and military intelligence as well as for directing the alliance's military operations, SACEUR will depend on a variety of NATO-owned and -leased communications systems. The backbone of NATO communications is the Ace High system, noted in chapter 4, that runs from northern Norway to southern Turkey, as illustrated in figure 5-1.

The PWHQ at Casteau is linked by land lines (including a new underground fiber optic cable) to three nearby microwave radio relay towers that are in turn connected to the Ace High system. SACEUR can also use NATO's communications satellites. SHAPE is linked to the NATO

9. One report indicates that the vacated cruise missile site at Molesworth, England, will also be the site for a new U.S. intelligence center currently located in Stuttgart. See Michael Evans, "UK Base to Be U.S. Intelligence Centre," *London Times*, January 12, 1990, p. 1.

10. For a comprehensive account of the various NATO CCIS systems and improvement projects see Maj. Gen. Joachim M. Sochaczewski, "NATO Information Systems in Support of Consultation and Military Command and Control," in *Information and Consultation: Keys to Peace*, proceedings of the Eighth AFCEA Europe Symposium held in Brussels, 1987 (Brussels: AFCEA Europe, 1988), pp. 73–77.

11. "NATO Set to Upgrade SHAPE System," *Jane's Defence Weekly*, April 22, 1989, p. 685.

Figure 5-1. *The NATO Ace High Communications Network*

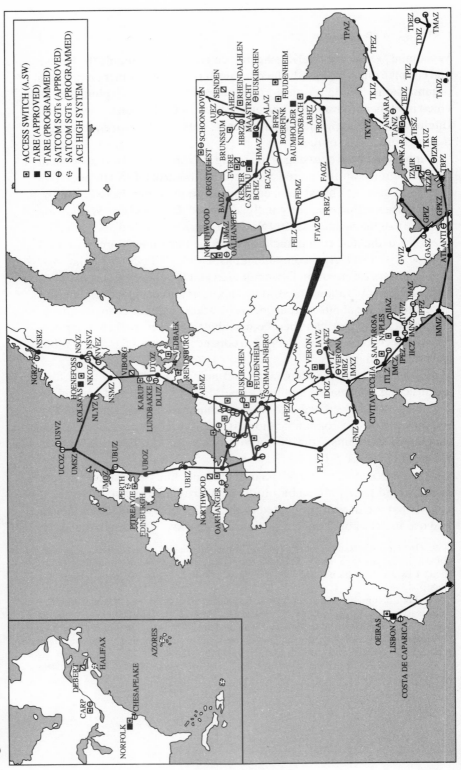

satellite ground station at Kester outside of Brussels, which also serves the main headquarters at Evere.[12] Through special cooperative arrangements, NATO can also use the U.S. Defense Satellite Communications System (DSCS) III and the new British Skynet IV satellites. These communications systems allow SACEUR to talk and exchange data directly with the national capitals and with the wartime headquarters of NATO's subordinate commanders.

The PWHQ at Casteau is also tied into Belgium's postal, telegraph, and telephone (PTT) system, which provides access to Europe's entire public communications network. NATO makes extensive use of Europe's PTT systems in peacetime through numerous leasing arrangements reached between an extremely important but not commonly known organization called the Allied Long Lines Agency and its national affiliates. Of the approximately 10,000 communications circuits used by NATO, about a third are leased from the PTTs, according to officials interviewed.[13] As will become more and more evident throughout this chapter, the PTT networks are expected to play a vital support role in wartime. These communications links act as carriers for several automatic data exchange systems, including the CCIS networks and the Status Control Alerting and Reporting System used to disseminate nuclear release orders.[14]

In the event that the primary terrestrial and satellite systems fail, SACEUR will rely on an emergency overlay network of high-frequency (HF) radio links to maintain "connectivity" with his forces. Two networks are available for this contingency: Bright Dawn, which serves as a general broadcast system and the other called, somewhat apocalyptically, Last Talk, for authorizing the use of nuclear weapons.[15] A new Allied Command Europe (ACE) emergency overlay system employing high-frequency (HF) radio and very-high-frequency meteor burst communications is currently under development.[16]

---

12. SHAPE also has a heavy transportable satellite ground station located in its vicinity.

13. Approximately 3,000 are leased from national military communications systems.

14. See John Morgenstern, "C³ for Tactical Nuclear Forces in Europe," *Signal*, vol. 35 (December 1980), pp. 57–58.

15. See declassified portions of Department of Defense, *Report on the Nuclear Posture of* NATO, Secret (May 1984), p. IV-9; and Campbell, *The Unsinkable Aircraft Carrier*, p. 184.

16. See Daniel J. Marcus, "SHAPE Readies Bids on Meteor Burst System for Battle Communications," *Defense News*, July 18, 1988, pp. 3, 37; and Dan Boyle, "Long

When dispersed in the field, SACEUR's mobile alternate command posts will be able to tie into NATO's communications networks through transportable microwave radio towers and small satellite ground terminals. The presurveyed sites will evidently also have special connections to allow the communications vehicles to plug into the PTT networks. And like the PWHQ, HF radio will provide the final back-up means of communications.

Besides the NATO-owned or -leased communications systems, SACEUR can also take advantage of the extensive collection of U.S. communications facilities in the European theater. The SHAPE PWHQ is linked to the Digital European Backbone (DEB) network at Flobecq, which is part of the U.S Defense Communications System (DCS). From here messages can flow westward across Belgium to Britain or eastward to Germany. The AFCENT wartime bunker at Boerfink is also tied into this system. A separate DCS microwave "tail" runs from SHAPE to the NATO facility at Chievres to connect into the Ace High system.[17] In addition to the elaborate DCS microwave network, SACEUR can also take advantage of the available U.S. satellite communications facilities, notably the DSCS satellite for wideband traffic and the Air Force Satellite Communications System (AFSATCOM) transponders hosted by the Fleet Satellite Communications (FLTSATCOM) System. The latter are used, furthermore, for a dedicated nuclear-related communications network known as Flaming Arrow.[18] Like NATO, the United States also operates its own HF system called Regency Net for disseminating nuclear release orders to its forces.[19] Finally, the United States has leased what is in many respects a more elaborate network of PTT circuits known as the European Telephone System (ETS), which links together all the U.S. military facilities in Europe. SHAPE is tied into this network through the facility at Chievres.[20]

Distance Communications—Back to Ionization," *International Defense Review,* vol. 12 (May 1988), p. 491.

17. According to the U.S. AUTOVON telephone directory, Chievres is also the location for the European Command Nuclear Interface Element (EUNIEF). U.S. Defense Communications Agency, *Defense Communications System Global AUTOVON Telephone Directory* (GPO, January 1986), p. 34.

18. See Paul B. Stares, *Space and National Security* (Brookings, 1987), pp. 30–31, 70.

19. This has replaced an earlier system called, believe it or not, Cemetery Net. See "Regency Net Contract," *Signal,* vol. 38 (April 1984), p. 72.

20. Robert T. Hanson and Klaus Strassman, "The U.S. Armed Forces European Telephone System," *Signal,* vol. 41 (October 1986), pp. 61–63. See also diagram of

Table 5-1. *Primary U.S.-NATO Theater Communications Systems*

Type of communications	NATO	United States
Terrestrial microwave	Ace High	Digital European Backbone (Defense Communications System)
Satellite	NATO III/IV (DSCS III/Skynet IV)	DSCS III, FLTSATCOM (Flaming Arrow/AFSATCOM)
High-frequency radio	Bright Dawn Last Talk	Regency Net
Postal, telephone, telegraph	PTTs (leased)	European Telephone System

Source: See text.

Should SACEUR need or decide to direct the war effort from either of the High Wycombe bunkers, he can take advantage of virtually the same set of U.S.- and NATO-owned communications systems. The principal communications systems available to SACEUR/CINCEUR are listed in table 5-1, and the specific links at the SHAPE PWHQ and the EUCOM/UKAIR PWHQ are illustrated in figures 5-2 and 5-3.

As the senior NATO commander in Europe, SACEUR would serve as the principal point of contact between the alliance's higher political authorities and its military chain of command. Where and how the alliance will collectively formulate its wartime policy is something of a mystery, however, even to some of its senior military commanders. As James Eberle, a former allied commander in chief, channel (CINCHAN) has remarked, "As a NATO military commander, I frequently discussed with the other commanders where the political authority would lie and how it would be exercised after a general alert. There is a great lack of understanding as to where political decisions will be taken. . . . In my view, this whole area of command and control in NATO operations has been almost totally ignored because it is so difficult to resolve. Yet it is of great importance that these issues be discussed, and their complexity is one more reason to address them."[21] Although the WINTEX/HILEX-CIMEX exercises practice NATO consultation procedures from the begin-

ETS in Maj. Gen. Clarence E. McKnight, "The Army's National Role in NATO's Communications," *Signal,* vol. 35 (December 1980), p. 46.

21. Admiral James Eberle, "Crisis Management Issues in the Employment of Theatre Nuclear Forces," in Gen. Jack N. Merritt, Gen. Robert Reed, and Roger Weissinger-Baylon, *Crisis Decision Making in the Atlantic Alliance: Perspective on Deterrence* (Menlo Park, Calif.: Strategic Decisions Press, 1987), p. 24-3.

Figure 5-2. *SHAPE PWHQ Connectivity*

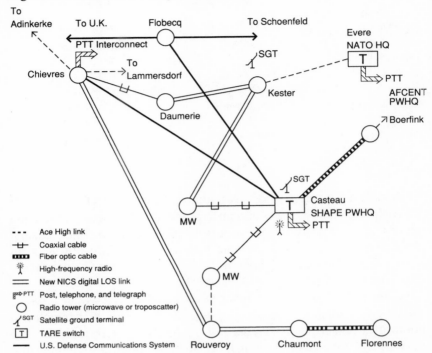

Sources: Maj. Gen. Giovanni Battista Pesci, "NATO Communications Systems in Support of Consultation and Military Command/Control," in *Information and Consultation: Keys to Peace*, proceedings of the Eighth AFCEA Europe Symposium held in Brussels, 1987 (Brussels: AFCEA Europe, 1988), p. 83; and U.S. Defense Communications Agency, *Defense Communications System/European Communication Systems: Interoperability Baseline* (Washington, February 1981), pp. 7-20–7-21. Map is not drawn to scale.

ning of a crisis to the early stages of a war, the North Atlantic Council-Defense Planning Committee (NAC/DPC) and their headquarters support staff do not relocate to a special wartime facility, unlike the national government authorities that repair to dedicated underground bunkers. The reason is simple: no such NATO facility exists to house them in wartime. Numerous proposals to build a wartime counterpart to Evere have been made, but all failed to secure the necessary support and funding even though it is commonly known that the present peacetime headquarters building could not withstand military attack or even, for that matter, some forms of sabotage. The communications links in and out of this headquarters are also extremely vulnerable to attack.

SACEUR's ability to direct and coordinate the reinforcement and resupply effort is also open to serious question. Despite the vital

Figure 5-3. *EUCOM PWHQ Connectivity*

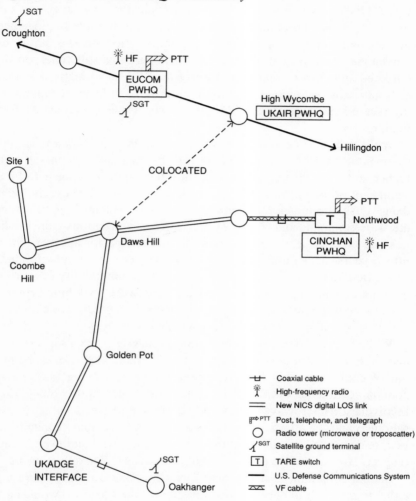

Source: Pesci, "NATO Communications Systems," p. 83.

importance of this task to NATO's wartime operations, there is currently no central coordinating authority under SACEUR's jurisdiction to oversee the movement of forces and equipment. Since logistics is a national responsibility, each country has set up its own set of plans and timetables. NATO has endeavored to coordinate national planning by establishing several agencies for this purpose that are responsible for specific regions, but their responsibilities evidently overlap in a confusing and inefficient way.[22] One major consequence of these organizational arrangements is that SACEUR has no unified data source that can provide his logistics officers with up-to-date and accurate information on the status of movements to the central front. NATO apparently still relies on an outdated and slow manual reporting system. To make matters worse, each nation has developed its own computerized data bases and monitoring systems, none of which is directly interoperable to exchange information.

With such a wide range of command posts and communications systems at SACEUR's disposal, the task of maintaining contact with higher and subordinate command authorities does not appear to be a significant problem. This assessment, however, would be overly if not dangerously optimistic. Despite recent improvements, NATO's theaterwide command and control system suffers from serious vulnerabilities and other deficiencies that will not be rectified for another ten to fifteen years, depending on whether current projects are fully funded. This evaluation is reached after examining the vulnerability of NATO's wartime command posts, communications network switching centers, and associated transmission systems to deliberate attack (see appendix A for a discussion of the type of threats that NATO faces).

While SACEUR's PWHQ is probably able to survive conventional strikes and even nuclear near misses, it can, for all practical purposes, be put out of commission—at least temporarily—by destroying the nearby communications access nodes. As figure 5-2 indicates, approximately six relatively soft microwave towers serve the bunkers that are vulnerable to sabotage and air attack. Although NATO does have some capacity to restore destroyed communications links, it is not well endowed in this respect. How quickly service could be reinstated is also questionable.

Should communications outages force the PWHQ to cease operation either temporarily or permanently, direction of the war effort would pass to either High Wycombe or the mobile alternate headquarters dispersed in the field. Although the intention is to hide the mobile headquarters as well as possible and, moreover, take advantage of their mobility to

22. For example, there is the Agency for Coordination of Transport in Central Europe, which is a NATO Civil Wartime Agency located near Maastricht, the Cross Channel Coordinating Committee, and the Joint Movement Control Centre at AFCENT with subsidiary centers at NORTHAG and CENTAG headquarters. See Alstead, "Ten in Ten?" pp. 23–29.

frustrate enemy targeting, this task will not be easy. Besides the large numbers of vehicles (over fifty per command post) and the telltale antennas, the miscellaneous communications and electronic equipment would radiate a distinctive electromagnetic signature that could betray their location. NATO hopes to minimize this risk by locating the communications facilities ten to fifteen kilometers from the main CP but connected by fiber optic cable. If the mobile headquarters are discovered in time to be attacked, their chances of survival are not high, given the vulnerability of unprotected vehicles.

The transfer of command between different headquarters could also upset the continuity of operations, particularly if it also entails a change of personnel. While the two deputy SACEURs are technically next in the chain of command, they are not American officers (one is British and the other German) and therefore would take over only temporarily until the U.S. president nominated a replacement, should SACEUR for whatever reason be incapacitated. In the meantime SACEUR's nuclear responsibilities apparently would shift to his deputy, a four-star U.S. Air Force general, while overall direction of air operations would be transferred to CINC UKAIR in High Wycombe.

After NATO's command posts, the next most lucrative targets are the communications switching centers that determine the routing of voice and message traffic throughout the alliance. These along with the locations of other key NATO command and control facilities are listed in table B-1 of appendix B. Many of the NATO switches are located within hardened wartime headquarters and would therefore be protected from most forms of attack. Those outside, however, would clearly not fare so well.[23] In comparison the U.S. AUTOVON or AUTODIN switches are evidently more vulnerable to air attack and sabotage. The control centers that manage the day-to-day operation of the communications networks represent another set of highly attractive targets. These are listed in table B-1. Many of these sites—particularly those supporting the DCS network—can be considered soft targets.

The fixed communications transmission sites of the respective net-

23. The key NATO switches at Baumholder and Senden, Germany, and Maastricht, in the Netherlands, may fall into this latter category. See table of TARE switches in U.S. Defense Communications Agency, *Defense Communications System/European Communication Systems: Interoperability Baseline* (Washington, February 1981), pp. 3–37. Some people interviewed believed that the location of many of the switches inside the hardened headquarters is a liability since it makes them doubly attractive targets.

works are even less survivable. As one NATO communications expert has observed, "Communications facilities are easy targets. They are distinctive, usually physically remote and difficult to defend, and can be thought of as "soft" in every sense. Many of the more important facilities radiate and can be easily identified and found. Indeed most of the facilities are registered with international agencies and many require frequency coordination with potential enemy nations."[24] A notable case is the chain of Ace High microwave and tropospheric scatter radio stations. When this system was conceived in the 1960s, wartime surviv- ability was not one of the primary design criteria. The NATO Integrated Command System (NICS) Stage II improvement program was supposed to rectify this vulnerability, but it was never funded. It is more appropriate, therefore, to use the metaphor of a single thin strand of thread than a communications backbone when describing the Ace High system. The unanimous assessment of those experts interviewed was that it would not survive more than a few days in a high-intensity war in central Europe.[25] NATO's capability to reroute traffic around damaged or de- stroyed communications facilities or restore them is apparently "rudi- mentary."[26] For instance, there are only a limited number of spare antennas to replace those destroyed.

The alliance is clearly pinning its long-range hopes on the creation of the NATO Terrestrial Transmission System (NTTS). Rather than replace Ace High with a completely new and expensive system, NATO intends to link each of Europe's national military communications systems together to form a super network for the alliance's use. NATO will pay user fees to individual countries, as well as build and maintain the cross- border links (CBLs) that will connect the system.[27] The divestiture phase,

24. Hans van Gelder, "Improving the Survivability of NATO Communications," *Signal*, vol. 37 (May 1983), p.148. See also comments of Gen. Joachim M. Sochaczewski in "NATO Planning Enhanced C³ over Decade," *Aviation Week and Space Technology*, November 7, 1983, p. 81.

25. One of the people interviewed even suggested that *spetsnaz* units could disable the system in twelve hours.

26. Joachim M. Sochaczewski, "The Role of Communications in NATO," *Military Technology*, vol. 8 (June 1984), p. 154; and interviews. NATO evidently uses a system known as Automatic Alternative Routing. See Giovanni Battista Pesci, "NATO Communications Systems in Support of Consultation and Military Command/Control," in *Information and Consultation: Keys to Peace*, p. 81.

27. For more information on the NTTS see Gope D. Hingorani and Rupert Brand, "Architectural Framework for the Evolution of NATO Integrated Communications System," *Signal*, vol. 40 (October 1985), pp. 55–65; Ian Mason-Smith, "The NATO Terrestrial Transmission System (NTTS)—An Overview," in *Command, Control, Commu-*

to which some liken this process, has already begun. Norway turned off its Ace High circuits in 1988 and switched on the new Norwegian Defense Digital Network (NDDN). Other countries will follow suit in a planned transition that is expected to finish up in southern Europe sometime in the late 1990s.[28]

Given the alliance's perennial funding shortfalls, the NTTS plan is a practical solution to NATO's future communications needs. For a relatively small investment NATO gets a modern digital communications network that is far more survivable than the current system. Nevertheless, NTTS will have its weaknesses. For the foreseeable future NATO will continue to use the existing TARE-IVSN switches to route data and voice traffic. Of greater concern, however, is the potential vulnerability of the microwave and cable cross-border links. If the published configurations of the NTTS connectivity plan are any indication, there may be no more than twenty links for the whole alliance and even fewer for the central region, all of which would be obvious targets in wartime.[29] Unless NATO makes the appropriate provisions to replace or repair these vital connections in wartime, then the network's ability to meet theater command and control needs will be put in jeopardy.

Until the NTTS becomes fully operational, the U.S. Defense Communications System in Europe would serve as the principal terrestrial-based alternative to Ace High. Despite a recent modernization program to convert the links from analog to digital communications, the DCS appears only marginally more survivable. For a start there are just eight access points connecting the two systems.[30] The DCS transmission system, moreover, is designed in star-shaped patterns in many areas. Destruction of the central communications hub, which usually corresponds with the

nications and Management Information Systems, Conference publication 275 (London: Institution of Electrical Engineers, 1987), pp. 203–28; Gope Hingorani, Ronald Knight, and Alberto Loffreda, "NATO Communications Rationalization and Interoperability— An Architectural Framework," in Information and Consultation: Keys to Peace, pp. 51–56.

28. For a list of the candidate national subnetworks see Mason-Smith, "NATO Terrestrial Transmission System," p. 206.

29. See diagram in Pesci, "NATO Communications Systems," p. 84.

30. Those points are Casteau, Belgium; Bonn, Germany; Cold Blow Lane and Mormond Hill, Great Britian; Aviano and Naples, Italy; and Izmir and Incirlik, Turkey. These interconnects are all furnished (except for Izmir) by buried cable leased by local PTTS. Four other locations have also been approved: Elmadag and Yamanlar, Turkey; Mt. Pateras, Greece; and Bagnoli, Italy. See U.S. Defense Communications Agency, Defense Communications System/European Comunication Systems, pp. 7–11.

location of the DCS technical control facilities listed in table B-2, would effectively put the local network out of commission. The communications links between these central nodes also depend on radio relay stations, many of which are unattended, unprotected, and located in remote areas. According to a U.S. Air Force report on the Belgian portion of the DCS, which can be considered representative of the rest of the network, the "existing facilities do not have blast protection and could not survive near misses by conventional bombs. There is inadequate lighting to detect or deter potential intrusion, and existing fences have deteriorated to a point where routine maintenance is no longer cost effective."[31] While a systematic program to improve the security of each of the main DCS sites is under way, confidence in the DCS being able to survive for very long in a conventional war is not high among those U.S. officials interviewed. Most concurred with the conclusion of a 1983 report to Congress that stated, *"The Defense Communication System is highly vulnerable to sabotage and air attack and is not survivable in wartime."*[32]

With both the main terrestrial military communications networks in Europe vulnerable to attack, it is not surprising, though somewhat ironic, that many expect the extensive European postal, telegraph, and telephone system to bear the burden of NATO's communications needs in wartime. With their comparatively well-endowed network of switching centers and dense grid of microwave and cable transmission links that offer multiple routing possibilities across Europe, the PTTs are less likely to fail catastrophically than their military counterparts should this system also come under attack. While undoubtedly the PTT system offers a valuable wartime communications asset to NATO and may ultimately prove its salvation, it would be wise not to depend too greatly on its service in wartime.[33]

31. *Military Construction Appropriations for 1985,* Hearings before the Subcommittee on Military Construction Appropriations of the House Committee on Appropriations, 98 Cong. 2 sess. (GPO, 1984), pt. 3, p. 875.

32. *Department of Defense Appropriations for 1985,* Hearings before the Subcommittee on the Department of Defense of the House Committee on Appropriations, 98 Cong. 2 sess. (GPO, 1984), p. 905 (emphasis in original). The report, which was conducted by the House Surveys and Investigations Staff, goes on to state, "The lack of survivability [sic] of DCS C³ facilities is so acute and the expectation that C³ will be an early target is of such concern that, as one Air Force official put it, 'I fully expect that one of the first signals that the Soviets are invading Europe will be when we pick up the phones and the lines are dead.' " p. 932.

33. The following discussion draws heavily on interviews.

Some national PTT networks, such as the Deutsche Bundespost in Germany, are indeed well endowed with multiple routing options, but others apparently are not. The bulk of communications traffic in Belgium, for instance, evidently passes through the major hub at Brussels. Furthermore, although the NATO Integrated Communications System Central Operating Authority (NICSCOA) has already reached agreement with the various PTT authorities to release commercial circuits to NATO in wartime, some experts privately wonder how responsive they will be to the needs of the military when the time comes. The most commonly voiced problem, however, concerns the cross-border gateways that tie the various networks together. As one senior NATO communications official has remarked, "The cross-border conectivity is very often poor, relying heavily on a few *very soft* choke points."[34] The location of these "vulnerable bottlenecks," as some describe them, is well known since they are registered with the International Telecommunications Union in Geneva and listed in their publicly available reports. Table B-3 lists the relevant intra-European cross-border links. Overall, while the PTTs may prove immensely useful for wartime communications within NATO countries, their availability for theater command and control should not be taken for granted.

Satellite communications systems provide the primary alternative to vulnerable terrestrial transmission networks. NATO, however, is only now taking steps to ensure that it can take advantage of its communications satellites in wartime, having previously considered them primarily for peacetime use only. Like many of NATO's other commonly funded communications projects, survivability was not a high-priority requirement when the satellite communications program was originally conceived. Thus the existing NATO III satellites are susceptible to electronic countermeasures, particularly jamming, while the fixed ground stations that serve them are all exposed to attack. In comparison the new generation of U.S. DSCS III satellites are more resistant to electronic interference, but their associated DCS ground stations are vulnerable.[35] The locations of U.S. and NATO fixed satellite communications ground stations in the European theater are listed in table B-4. Until NATO deploys its new class of satellites (NATO IV) and, moreover, procures the planned set of highly transportable terminals in the 1990s, the alliance

34. Sochaczewski, "Role of Communications in NATO," p. 154 (emphasis added).
35. For further details on the vulnerability of the U.S. and NATO satellites see app. A of Stares, *Space and National Security*, pp. 187–99.

simply cannot depend on the support of satellite communications in wartime.[36] U.S. forces in Europe, however, are currently in a better position, having already deployed mobile and therefore more survivable satellite ground terminals. The United States can also use a variety of ultra-high-frequency satellite links via other space systems.

If all else fails, SACEUR can use the various HF systems at his disposal to communicate with his forces. High-frequency radio is not without drawbacks, however. Signals transmitted at this frequency travel over long distances and are therefore susceptible to interception and location by enemy direction-finding equipment. With its limited bandwidth, HF radio is also only suitable for minimum essential communications; it is certainly not adequate for managing the type of high-intensity military operations envisaged by many defense planners.

The automated command and control information systems that need high-capacity data links to exchange the vast amounts of intelligence generated from allied sources will clearly suffer the most should NATO's main communications channels become inoperable in wartime. As it is, these CCIS systems suffer from problems of their own. A series of unplanned and uncoordinated decisions taken at different times has left each of the regional commands in ACE with its own individual CCIS equipment and software, none of which is fully interoperable. Even the SHAPE data processing system, which is directly linked to the AFCENT CCIS that uses the same WWMCCS hardware, cannot exchange information automatically. In this case the reason is that the two systems operate at different security classifications.[37] Although NATO is in the process of establishing common standards for the next generation of CCIS systems under the System Design and Integration Contract (SD & IC) study, these will not be implemented until the mid-1990s at the earliest. Meanwhile, several commands, notably AFNORTH and UKAIR, have already fielded new information systems that will not be compatible—at least initially—with the new standards.[38] Furthermore, since the central region mobile alternate wartime headquarters are to be fitted with a new CCIS system,

36. See Pesci, "NATO Communications Systems," p. 83.

37. Sochaczewski, "NATO Information Systems," p. 76; and interviews.

38. Sochaczewski, "NATO Information Systems." See also Lt. Gen. R. J. Donahue, "C³ Architecture Challenges NATO CIS Agency," Signal, vol. 43 (June 1989), p. 36; "NATO Develops CCIS Acquisition Plan," in Defense Electronics and Computing Supplement to International Defense Review, vol. 22 (March 1989), pp. 7–8; and James B. Schultz, "Northern Europe to Receive New Battle Management System," Defense Electronics, vol. 17 (May 1985), pp. 64–68.

they too cannot become fully operational until the SD & IC study is completed and accepted.[39]

Overall, NATO's present theater command and control arrangements suffer from some major shortcomings that threaten to compromise SACEUR's ability to execute his primary command responsibilities. The commitment to build more survivable headquarters and robust wartime communications is beginning to reach fruition and will help matters, but there is still considerable room for improvement.

The Operational Level

Though it is not widely appreciated—especially in the United States—operational command of NATO forces in the central region during wartime is the responsibility of the commander in chief, Allied Forces, Central Europe (CINCENT). Since France left NATO's integrated military command structure, this post has been filled by a four-star West German general. His mission and command responsibilities are enormous. Besides having to defend a front that covers all the most likely invasion routes into Western Europe, the ground and air forces of seven nations (including presumably France) will come under the command of this officer (see figure 5-4). Directly assisting CINCENT in carrying out his wartime tasks will be the commander in chief, Allied Air Forces, Central Europe (COMAAFCE), who is a four-star U.S Air Force general. While COMAAFCE is technically subordinate to CINCENT in the chain of command, they would essentially direct and coordinate operations together.

Immediately below these two officers are the commanders of the two army groups and associated Allied Tactical Air Forces: NORTHAG-2ATAF and CENTAG-4ATAF. They directly command the actions of the army corps and the Allied Tactical Operations Centers and Sector Operations Centers, which manage, respectively, offensive and defensive air operations in their regions.

As stated earlier, the alliance's defensive goal in the event of an attack is to repel the lead echelons of an invading force as close as possible to NATO's eastern border. NATO currently plans to use a relatively light, forwardly deployed covering force to delay and disrupt a Pact attack to

39. Daniel J. Marcus, "NATO Delays Command Post Development," *Defense News,* September 28, 1987, pp. 1, 48.

Figure 5-4. *The Central Front with Location of Major NATO Wartime Headquarters and Corps Groupings, 1990*

Netherlands I

NORTHAG
2ATAF   West Germany I

British I

Belgian I

CASTLE
GATE   West
Linnich   Germany III

Bonn

NORTHAG/2ATAF
PWHQ   United
Maastricht   States V

AFCENT
PWHQ
Boerfink   United States VII

CENTAG/4ATAF
PWHQ
Ruppertsweiler   West Germany II

CENTAG
4ATAF

Source: Adapted from William P. Mako, *U.S. Ground Forces and the Defense of Central Europe* (Brookings, 1983), p. 33.

buy time for further defensive preparations in the rear. Their engagement will also help differentiate the primary axes of the offensive from those that are merely feints. The main defensive battle, however, is expected to be fought to the rear of the covering force where the bulk of each of the corps ground forces will have been assembled and readied for action. Depending on how these forces fare in repulsing the attack, the army group and ATAF commanders will deploy their reserves and allocate air power according to the needs of the individual corps commanders.[40] In doing so they will be monitoring the situation not only at the front but also deep in the enemy rear so as to divine the Pact's operational intentions in time for the necessary responses to be set in motion. Their assessment will then become the basis for their requests for reinforcements and air power from CINCENT.

While the army groups have their own reserves that are taken from forces already allocated to each commander, the region's main operational reserves are under CINCENT's control, to be used at his discretion.[41] These reserves are currently composed of the U.S. III Corps that, with the exception of one forwardly deployed brigade in northern Germany, would have to be deployed from the United States in wartime. Though categorized as the AFCENT Reserve Force, the U.S. III Corps has been slated for operations in the NORTHAG area. In addition to these assigned forces it is widely expected that French forces would provide the bulk of CINCENT's operational reserves, although there is no formal commitment to do so. The First French Army would almost certainly deploy to support COMCENTAG in southern Germany while the French III Corps and Force d'Action Rapide would likely help COMNORTHAG in the north.[42] The Canadian Fourth Mechanized Brigade

40. See Gen. Nigel Bagnall, "Concepts of Land/Air Operations in the Central Region: I," *RUSI Journal for Defence Studies,* vol. 129 (September 1984), pp. 59–62; and Gen. Martin Farndale, "The Operational Level of Command," *RUSI Journal for Defence Studies,* vol. 133 (Autumn 1988), pp. 23–29.

41. Under the newly instituted "concept of operations," several of the corps in NORTHAG will commit certain units under their command in wartime to form an army group operational reserve that can be used at COMNORTHAG's discretion. The units that make up this force are believed to be the West German Third and Seventh Panzer Divisions, the U.K. Third Armored Division, and a Belgian Mechanized Brigade. There is evidently no such arrangement in CENTAG, although it is believed that the reinforcing U.S. First and Fifth Armored Divisions might operate collectively once they arrive in the theater; and interviews.

42. See David C. Isby and Charles Kamps, Jr., *Armies of NATO's Central Front* (London: Jane's Publishing Company, 1985), pp.29–30. See also Jacques Isnard,

Group is another designated reserve force to be used at COMCENTAG's discretion.

The commitment of operational reserves clearly requires sound judgment and careful planning based on the fullest appreciation of enemy intentions. A force the size of an army corps cannot be deployed from its assembly area in the rear without considerable preparation, which inevitably takes time. Logistical arrangements, communications plans, and movement schedules have to be worked out in detail to ensure that the full military potential of the force is realized at the time and place it is most needed. This preparation is likely to take several days to which must also be added transit time to the point of contact.[43] What in peacetime exercises may be a relatively straightforward maneuver can become in wartime an extremely challenging task. Besides the general congestion of communications routes from forward-moving supplies and rearward-moving refugees, key bridges and railway viaducts over major physical barriers may have been destroyed and would have to be replaced or circumvented.[44] The need to disguise the movement of the reserves from enemy intelligence may impose additional restrictions on travel. And finally, if discovered, the force may be subjected to direct attack that may further impede movement.

All these considerations put a premium on the earliest possible identification of the enemy's main axes of attack to enable the reserve force to arrive at the intended place at the intended time. The associated dilemmas are clear: to commit the reserves to the wrong sector will not only mean that they will fail to lend support to the most endangered portions of the front, but they could also be left ripe for encirclement from breakthroughs elsewhere. Once movement plans have been set in motion, there is not a great amount of flexibility for change. Yet to wait until the main threats have been unambiguously identified may leave the reserve forces with insufficient time to prepare a concentrated and

"Reorganisation Ahead for French Army," *Jane's Defence Weekly*, July 1, 1989, p. 1347.

43. See Col. Ted A. Cimral, "Moving the Heavy Corps," *Military Review*, vol. 68 (July 1988), pp. 28–34.

44. According to one expert, "Along a given axis of advance in West Germany a body of troops will encounter a minor water obstacle on an average of every 5 to 10 km, a medium water obstacle up to 100m wide every 30 to 60 km and something bigger like the Weser, the Inn, the Rhine or the Danube (100 to 300m wide) every 100 to 150 km." Hugh Farringdon quoted in Diego A. Ruiz Palmer, "Countering Soviet Encirclement Operations-Emerging NATO Concepts," *International Defense Review*, vol. 21 (November 1988), p. 1416.

coordinated counterattack that stands a reasonable chance of success.[45] The importance of intelligence assets that can look deep into enemy-held territory and discriminate, as quickly as possible, primary ground threats from feints cannot be overstated. It is a prerequisite to NATO's prosecuting a successful defensive campaign.

The challenge facing the alliance's intelligence system at the operational level, therefore, is to detect and identify the main axes of a Warsaw Pact offensive sufficiently far in advance for NATO's senior commanders to prepare and move their reserves to cover the most threatened sectors of the front. How far in advance is a function of the anticipated time to prepare and move a reserve force into position as well as the estimated time of arrival of the Pact follow-on forces that threaten to create and exploit a breakthrough.[46] Depending on their state of readiness and the location of their assembly area, a corps-sized NATO reserve force may take anywhere from two to five days to organize itself and move into place to counterattack.[47] NATO can hope that air interdiction slows down the advance of Pact forces to the front and that its ground forces hold them for as long as possible once they get there, but NATO's senior commanders must still anticipate by several days, on the the basis of the best available intelligence, where the main points of effort will be so they can set their reserves in motion. The situation at the front may indicate the Pact's operational intentions, but it doesn't necessarily follow that the location of the initial attacks will also be where the main effort is to be applied. Feints and other maneuvers aimed at deceiving NATO intelligence and pinning its reserves to a particular sector of the front should be expected. The main focus of attention to NATO intelligence at

45. There are more tactically related dilemmas that have to do with deciding the timing and main axis of the counterattack. See the remarks of Martin Farndale, a former COMNORTHAG, quoted in Palmer, "Countering Soviet Encirclement," p. 1416.

46. The following discussion assumes the commonly accepted configuration for a Pact offensive against NATO in which advancing forces are "echeloned" so that secondary and tertiary waves can exploit whatever success is achieved by the lead elements. See chap. 4 of Office of Technology Assessment, *New Technology for NATO: Implementing Follow-on Forces Attack,* OTA-ISC-309 (Washington, June 1987), pp. 55–80. According to Western defense analysts, breakthrough operations are also to be carried out by independent combined armed forces called Operational Maneuver Groups, which would be specially constituted in wartime. See *Department of Defense Authorization of Appropriations for Fiscal Year 1984, and Oversight of Previously Authorized Programs,* Hearings before the House Committee on Armed Services, 98 Cong. 1 sess. (GPO, 1983), pt. 3, pp. 1781–87. This concept of operations has been superseded, evidently as a result of the proclaimed switch to emphasizing a predominantly defensive posture.

47. Interviews. See also Cimral, "Moving the Heavy Corps."

the operational level will be the movement and concentration of the Pact's second and third echelons well to the rear of the front. Unless the Pact's campaign plans fall into the hands of the alliance, it is the commitment of these forces to particular avenues of approach that offers NATO intelligence the best indication of Pact intentions.

To render this kind of advance warning, NATO intelligence must be able to gain an accurate picture of the situation approximately 150 kilometers behind the front. Warsaw Pact forces at this distance from the front would take an estimated two days to arrive, although their approach march, as indicated earlier, can be slowed by military attacks from NATO's air forces.[48] Depending on the effort made by NATO to disrupt and delay their movement, the second- and third-echelon forces may take much longer, however. Delaying tactics, therefore, allow NATO to buy time to compensate for ambiguous intelligence.

Besides the ground reserves, CINCENT's other principal operational asset is air power. For obvious reasons air power is a more flexible and responsive military instrument to influence the outcome of battle. At the same time it is a more complex instrument to employ. More than 2,000 aircraft of different mission types, some of which overlap, would need to be told what to do and where to go on a daily if not hourly basis. As one retired COMAAFCE explained, "The operational challenge for employing air is at the level of apportionment and allotment. Here we determine how many and what kind of aircraft should be used for what air missions to best meet the theater commanders' overall objectives. Since there are just not enough aircraft to go around, . . . we strive to concentrate firepower at the right times and places to meet overall campaign objectives."[49] More specifically, apportionment and allotment

48. This figure is arrived at by assuming that a motorized rifle division moves at an average pace of approximately 15 kilometers per hour with a thirty-minute rest every three hours. If as expected the approach march would be carried out in the hours of darkness (say between 1900 and 0600 hours), then two nights would be needed. See app. B of Philip Feld, James A. Semrad, and Gail D. Williams, *Joint Surveillance Target Attack Radar System Intervisability: Final Report (U),* prepared for Electronic Systems Division, Air Force Systems Command, Hascom AFB (McLean, Va.: BDM Corp., 1984), pp. B-1–B-4; U.S. Army Intelligence and Threat Analysis Center, *Soviet Army Operations* (Washington: Department of the Army, 1978), pp. 3-20–3-21. The area beyond 150 kilometers is generally considered—in the United States at least—the primary interest of echelons above corps. See Col. William V. Kennedy and others, *Intelligence Warfare: Today's Advanced Technology Conflict* (London: Salamander Books, 1983), p. 150.

49. Gen. Charles L. Donnelly, "A Theater-Level View of Air Power," *Air Power Journal,* vol. 1 (Summer 1987), p. 4.

entail, first, determining the proportion of total air assets given to each
ATAF commander and, second, judging the relative emphasis given to
each of the main mission categories: defensive or offensive counterair,
battlefield interdicton, close air support, and reconnaissance. Decisions
are arrived at through joint consultation between CINCENT and COM-
AAFCE, who base their judgment on their own requirements and sources
of information as well as on the requests put to them from the army
group and ATAF commanders who together have established their needs
and priorities.[50]

Like the ground battle, decisions on the commitment of air power are
full of trade-offs and dilemmas. While some aircraft are best suited to a
specific mission like close air support or reconnaissance, other types
can be used in several ways. The achievement of air superiority, for
example, which is widely considered one of NATO's primary objectives
in wartime, can be attained in two ways: through the use of fighters that
intercept enemy aircraft over NATO territory (defensive counterair), or
the use of long-range ground attack aircraft that destroy enemy air forces
at their home bases (offensive counterair). The latter option may have a
higher payoff in the number of enemy aircraft destroyed, but it may
entail more attrition to friendly forces than the former since the Warsaw
Pact's own air defenses have to be penetrated. The expected payoff from
attacking airbases must also be balanced against the utility of hitting
other targets in the Pact's rear, such as communications choke points
and key command and control facilities. Such attacks may help slow
down and degrade the combat potential of the follow-on forces coming
into the theater, but this longer-range consideration must in turn be
balanced against the more immediate needs of NATO's ground commanders at the front. Finally, these trade-offs have to be calculated in relation
to the specific requirements of each region and sector.[51]

In the opening stages of a conflict in central Europe, NATO's air forces
will be preoccupied initially with repulsing the opening Pact air attack.
Certain prepackaged offensive responses will most probably then be put

50. Donnelly, "Theater-Level View," pp. 4–5; and Air Marshal Patrick Hine,
"Concepts of Land/Air Operations in the Central Region: II," *RUSI Journal for Defence
Studies,* vol. 129 (September 1984), pp. 65–66.
51. Hine, "Concepts of Land/Air Operations: II." See also Malcolm W. Hoag,
Strengthening NATO Capabilities: A "Hi-Lo" Ground Force Mix for Area Defense, R-
2039-AF (Santa Monica, Calif.: Rand Corp., 1977), p. 8; and "Beyond the Corps Battle
in NATO's Central Region," *International Defense Review,* vol. 22 (February 1989),
p. 169.

into effect. After that NATO simply does not have enough aircraft to pursue a particular employment plan for very long if the cost is not translated into meaningful results. With probably two to three sorties possible each day, NATO's senior air commanders must have a complete, reliable, and up-to-date picture of the evolving situation before they can commit further resources to a particular course of effort. This capacity means having rapid postattack assessments of the damage inflicted on enemy targets and, moreover, information on the attrition suffered in the process. There is little latitude for suboptimal choices. According to one senior allied air commander, "Today, at typical NATO sortie rates, a 5 percent attrition will halve the available force in five days and 10 percent will halve it in a little over three days. At 20 percent attrition, the graph of remaining force size is descending on an impressive incline."[52]

Information is critical to the prosecution of the war at the operational level. Figure 5-5 provides an overview of the expected information flow among the principal NATO commanders in the central region, which in turn helps in assessing the possible impact of vulnerabilities and deficiencies in NATO's operational-level command system.

By the time of the outbreak of hostilities CINCENT and COMAAFCE plan to have transferred operations from their respective peacetime headquarters at Brunssum and Ramstein to the AFCENT PWHQ at Boerfink in Germany. Known also by the code name Erwin, this multistory hardened bunker is located approximately 60 kilometers to the northwest of Ramstein Air Base. Although originally built for the West German air force, it was made available to NATO in 1977.[53] In 1985 NATO also made the decision to replace the old mobile AFCENT alternate war headquarters (AAWHQ)—which was still using equipment from the era when CINCENT was a French commander—with a modern, fully capable command post. Although the trucks and some of the communications equipment had been delivered by 1988, the AAWHQ (or "85 buy" as it is unofficially known) is not expected to become fully operational until the central region CCIS modernization issue has been resolved, which means

52. Air Vice Marshal John R. Walker, "The Air Battle:The First Hours," NATO's Sixteen Nations, vol. 33 (September 1988), p. 30.

53. See Dan Boyle, "C³—The Essential Ingredient to Air Defense," International Defense Review, vol. 11 (June 1978), p. 862; and Nato Standardization, Interoperability, and Readiness, p.385. See also "Headquarters, Allied Forces Central Europe," NATO unclassified organizational chart, Brunssum, June 1988.

Figure 5-5. *Wartime Information Flow among NATO Operational-Level Commanders*

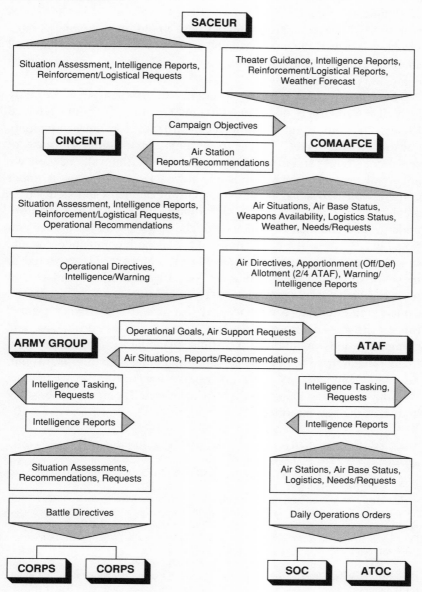

sometime in the mid-1990s. In the interim, CINCENT will have to make do with the equipment that has already been fielded, which resides in peacetime at Tapijn Kasserne in Maastricht, Holland.[54] Like SACEUR's mobile headquarters, this command post would move among presurveyed sites in wartime, most probably in the eastern part of Belgium and southern Holland. The same procedure of deploying a main and reserve command post will also be employed.

The primary wartime headquarters of NORTHAG/2ATAF is presently located at Cannerberg on the outskirts of Maastricht.[55] Though referred to formally as the Joint Operations Center (JOC), it is more commonly known as "the cave," owing to its physical location. Because of space constraints and unsatisfactory conditions (the walls of the cave apparently are beginning to fall in), however, a new PWHQ is under construction across the border in Germany at Linnich-Glimbach. Codenamed Castle Gate, the new facility reportedly consists of a six-story underground complex of bunkers, which is expected to become operational by 1991.[56] In the early stages of a war, both commanders would operate from this complex. COMNORTHAG, however, is expected to move forward to his mobile command post to stay in closer contact with his subordinate corps commanders. This too has two separate elements: a main and alternate command post that would move every night.[57] Since COM2ATAF is more dependent on the large data processing and communications facilities at the static headquarters, he would most likely remain there to oversee and coordinate the air battle. He would, however, send a deputy forward with COMNORTHAG to stay in contact with the static headquarters by way of a dedicated communications link known as the "air interface."[58]

54. Given its incomplete state, the AAWHQ has been used with mixed results in the annual NATO CPX and field exercises.

55. William M. Arkin and Richard W. Fieldhouse, *Nuclear Battlefields: Global Links in the Arms Race* (Ballinger, 1985), p. 227.

56. According to one report the new facility will be able to operate independently for months, sealed from the outside world with its own water supply and air-renewal ventilation system. See Clemens Range, "Die NATO grabt sich an der Rur ein" ("NATO Digs Itself In on the Ruhr"), *Die Welt,* April 27, 1988, p. 4. Whether the Maastricht cave will remain in caretaker status as a backup is unclear.

57. Bagnall, "Concepts of Land/Air Operations: I," p. 60. Gen. Bagnall's successor, Gen. Martin Farndale, also instituted the practice of using helicopters to stay within thirty-minutes' flying time of each of the main corps headquarters. See Farndale, "Operational Level of Command," p. 26.

58. Hine, "Concepts of Land/Air Operations: II," p. 66.

COMCENTAG and COM4ATAF would control operations from their PWHQ at Ruppertsweiler, located just to the west of the major U.S. communications hub at Pirmasens. This is a relatively new underground facility, which has replaced the old PWHQ at Kindsbach in the vicinity of Ramstein Air Base to the north. Kindsbach, however, still serves as the CENTAG-4ATAF alternate wartime headquarters.[59] Finally, COMCENTAG can also use his U.S Army mobile command post, which would operate much like NORTHAG's.[60]

While the precise capabilities of NATO's intelligence assets are, for obvious reasons, difficult to gauge, table 5-2 lists the publicly known NATO reconnaissance systems that seem capable of gathering information approximately 150 kilometers behind the front, which is of the most interest to NATO's operational-level commanders.

As table 5-2 indicates, the intelligence assets for monitoring the movement of Warsaw Pact forces in the rear are controlled by the United States and to a lesser extent by Great Britain and West Germany. Not surprisingly these three countries have been responsible for creating the present NATO organizational structure for collecting, processing, and exchanging intelligence in the central region.

Beginning with the main center of operations, the United States, the Federal Republic of Germany, and Great Britain have each established national intelligence cells within the AFCENT PWHQ at Boerfink.[61] These cells act as two-way conduits to supply nationally gathered intelligence to CINCENT-COMAAFCE and also to receive their specific collection requests by way of the central region CCIRM channels described earlier. The assistant chief of staff for intelligence would oversee and coordinate this effort. A special handling detachment (SHD) is also available for passing the most sensitive intelligence. The British National Intelligence Cell (BRITNIC) is directly linked to the British Intelligence Support System (BRISS) attached to COMNORTHAG's headquarters. This connection is the central fusion center for the British intelligence collection effort in northern Germany and for receiving intelligence from London, including UK-USA eyes-only information. Given its dependence on large

59. "Headquarters, Central Army Group," NATO unclassified organizational chart, Heidelberg, July 1988.

60. Lt. Col. Edward R. Baldwin, Jr., NATO Ground Forces Communications Interoperability from the American Perspective, Study Project (Carlisle Barracks, Pa.: U.S. Army War College, 1980), p. 19. This post is apparently being upgraded.

61. Unless indicated, the following information is drawn from miscellaneous interviews.

Table 5-2. *NATO Central Region Long-Range Intelligence Assets*[a]
Greater than 150 kilometers

Platform	Function[b]	Designation or name[b]	Country and agency[b]	Estimated number
Space based	Photint, Imint	KH-11, advanced KH-11[c]	U.S.: NRO	2–5
		Lacrosse	U.S.: NRO	4[d]
		Spot	FR	2
	Sigint	Magnum	U.S.: NRO	4
		Jumpseat	U.S.: NRO	2
Air based	Photint, Imint	U-2[e]	U.S.: USAF	14–17
		TR-1[e]	U.S.: USAF	12+
		Tornado F.3	U.K.: RAF	
		Canberra PR9	U.K.: RAF	2
	Sigint	RC-135 (Rivet Joint)	U.S.: USAF	25+
		EC-130 (Coronet Solo Comfy Levi)	U.S.: USAF	8–10
		Senior Scout Senior Ruby Senior Spear	U.S.: USAF	n.a.
		Nimrod R1/R2P	U.K.: GCHQ, RAF	3
		Tornado ECR	FRG: GAF	35
		Gabriel C-160G	FR: FAF	2–4
Ground based	Sigint	AN-FLR.9	U.S.: NSA	3
		Comfy Shield	U.S.: USAF	n.a.
		n.a.	U.K.: GCHQ, UKA	n.a.
		n.a.	FRG: BND, GA	n.a.
		n.a.	FR	n.a.

Sources: Paul B. Stares, *Space and National Security* (Brookings, 1987), pp. 15–22, 38, 53–66; Col. William V. Kennedy and others, *Intelligence Warfare: Today's Advanced Technology Conflict* (London: Salamander Books, 1983), pp. 76–165; *Jane's All the World's Aircraft, 1988–89*, and *Jane's Weapons Systems, 1988–89* (London: Jane's Information Group, 1988); International Institute for Strategic Studies, *The Military Balance, 1988–89* (London, 1988); Paul Stares and John Pike, "The Contribution of U.S. C³I to the Defence of NATO," in Jane M.O. Sharp, ed., *Europe after an American Withdrawal: Economic and Military Issues* (Oxford University Press in association with the Stockholm International Peace Research Institute, 1990), pp. 402–05, 407–11, 413–15; and Jeffrey T. Richelson, "The Future of Space Reconnaissance," in *Scientific American*, vol. 264 (January 1991), pp. 38–44.

n.a. = Not available.

a. Excludes French, NATO naval, and human intelligence assets.

b. BND, German federal intelligence service; FAF, French Air Force; FR, France; FRG, Federal Republic of Germany; GA, German army; GAF, German Air Force; GCHQ, Government Communications Headquarters; Imint, imagery intelligence; NRO, National Reconnaissance Office; NSA, National Security Agency; Photint, photographic intelligence; RAF, Royal Air Force; Sigint, signals intelligence, covers both communications intelligence and electronic intelligence; UKA, army of the United Kingdom; and USAF, U.S. Air Force.

c. KH-11 is being phased out; advanced KH-11 became operational in 1989.

d. Estimated number for full constellation.

e. Also carries Sigint sensors.

information processing equipment and high-capacity communications facilities, BRISS would operate from the PWHQ in wartime, although a scaled-down version would also move around with COMNORTHAG's mobile command post.[62] The German National Intelligence Cell (GENIC) is likewise linked to its principal source of information, namely, the Federal Armed Forces Intelligence Office (FAFIO) at Bad Neuen-hahr-Ahrweiler.[63] In addition to feeding information to the GENIC at Boerfink, FAFIO supplies the German intelligence cells at the NORTHAG/2ATAF and CENTAG/4ATAF wartime headquarters as well as their army corps by way of a dedicated communications link called the automated data exchange (ADX).

The U.S. intelligence architecture in central Europe is a more complex arrangement, which is currently undergoing some major restructuring. The U.S. Central Region Joint Collection Management Office (CRJCMO) at Boerfink, which coordinates U.S. intelligence activities with the NATO CCIRM system, is to be superseded by the Central Region Joint Intelligence Center (CRJOIC). The principal hub for U.S. intelligence reaching AFCENT headquarters, however, is the Tactical Fusion Center (TFC). One of its primary missions—since it is mainly a U.S. Air Force, Europe (USAFE) facility—is to provide an up-to-date picture of the air battle. Intelligence garnered from multiple sensors is fused with the assistance of the Kaleidoscope data processing system, which in turn displays the position of friendly and enemy air forces.[64] Located within the TFC is another data fusion system known as OASIS (Operational Applications of Special Intelligence Systems), which combines data on the air and ground battle from sensitive U.S. sources for an overall assessment.[65]

62. BRISS's communications capability has recently undergone modernization under Project Gemini. Interview and "C³I System Planned for UK Commanders in West Germany," *Jane's Defence Weekly*, July 22, 1989, p. 112.

63. According to a former director of the DIA a "joint U.S./West German correlation center" will also be established here. See Lt. Gen. Leonard H. Perroots, "New Approaches to C³ Interoperability in the Intelligence Community," *Signal*, vol. 43 (September 1988), p. 33. FAFIO is also very close to the West German government's wartime bunker at Marienthal in the Ahr valley to the south of Bonn.

64. See *Department of Defense Appropriations for 1980*, Hearings before the Subcommittee on the Department of Defense of the House Committee on Appropriations, 96 Cong. 1 sess. (GPO, 1979), pt. 3, p. 816. Positional data are usually displayed in alphanumeric form, although a geographic representation is also possible.

65. "Martin Marrietta to Lead Tactical Intelligence Effort," *Defense Electronics*, vol. 17 (January 1985), p. 28; and William P. Schlitz, "C³ for the European War," *Air Force Magazine*, vol. 66 (June 1983), p. 68.

The TFC's principal source of intelligence is the USAFE Combat Operations Intelligence Center (COIC) located at Ramstein. This is not only the central processing center for photointelligence gathered by USAFE aircraft in the central region, but it is also directly linked to one of the most important U.S. Sigint ground facilities in Europe.[66] Known formally as the Tactical Reconnaissance Exploitation Demonstration System (TREDS), it is more commonly referred to by its code name, Metro Tango. In its present form, Metro Tango consists of a collection of vehicles with special signal-processing and high-capacity communications equipment situated close to Hahn Air Base, Germany.[67]

The intelligence collected by the TR-1, RC-135/Rivet Joint, EC-130 (Coronet Solo/Comfy Levi) and the ground-based Comfy Shield systems is all transmitted to this facility. A special data processing system known as Compass Jade for correlating the collected Sigint with reports from AWACS aircraft and other sources also functions here. The material gathered is then transmitted directly to the TFC at Boerfink. Though owned and operated by the United States, Metro Tango has been officially committed for NATO's use in wartime.

Another important and relatively new part of the U.S. intelligence infrastructure in Europe is the army's Echelon-Above-Corps Intelligence Center (EACIC). This facility is an outgrowth of a longstanding effort to establish a wartime army intelligence center that would act as the functional equivalent of USAFE's TFC or COIC. Although details of its operational characteristics are scarce, it is most probably located at the U.S. Army, Europe (USAREUR) wartime facility at Massweiler, which is close both to the CENTAG-4ATAF PWHQ at Ruppertsweiler and the U.S. communications center at Pirmasens. The EACIC will be USAREUR's central hub for receiving intelligence from U.S. national assets such as reconnaissance satellites.[68]

66. *Military Construction Authorization Fiscal Year 1982,* Hearings before the Subcommittee on Military Construction of the Senate Armed Services Committee, 97 Cong. 1 sess. (GPO, 1982), p. 374.

67. See U.S. Army Intelligence and Security Command, *Annual Historical Review, Fiscal Year 1985* (Arlington, Va.: U.S. Army 1986), p. 25. TREDS will eventually become known as the Tactical Reconnaissance Ground Station and move to a permanent location, most probably the vacated ground-launched cruise missile base at nearby Wuersheim. Evidently there are plans to establish a second site to serve the NORTHAG and BALTAP (Baltic approaches) regions. Interviews and Todd Shumway, "A Tradition of Tactical Reconnaissance," *Defense Electronics,* vol. 21 (September 1989), p. 66.

68. See discussion of EACIC's role in Department of the Army, *Corps Intelligence and Electronic Warfare Operations,* FM 34-25 (Washington, September 1987), p. 2-10.

Besides the intelligence that these U.S. fusion centers receive from collection assets in the European theater, information derived from U.S. national sources, notably satellites, will also be fed to them. Under a program known as TENCAP, for Tactical Exploitation of National Capabilities, the United States is developing the ground terminals, processing equipment, and comunications systems to speed up this process. Imagery and Sigint from space platforms will now be down-linked directly to ground stations in Europe or indirectly from Washington.[69]

NATO's intelligence organizational arrangements for the central region are depicted in figure 5-6.

Supporting the processing and passage of intelligence in the central region are a variety of NATO and nationally operated data exchange systems. The main NATO system is the central region CCIS network discussed earlier, which uses hardware originally designed for the U.S. WWMCCS system. The network centers around two large Honeywell 6060 mainframe computers located in the wartime headquarters at Boerfink and Maastricht. A third is to become operational at the Ruppertsweiler facility. Tied to these computers are a number of remote network processors or terminals at various locations, including corps headquarters.[70] While this network will remain the NATO central region's primary system for processing and exchanging data until it is replaced in the mid-1990s, several separate computer-based networks have sprung up in recent years, mainly as a result of U.S. initiatives to exchange intelligence among the allies.

The most established and widely used is the Joint Tactical Fusion-Limited Operational Capability Europe (LOCE) system. At the heart of this network is the central automated data processing facility located inside the COIC at Ramstein. This facility correlates intelligence received from sensor interface modules at key U.S. collection centers in Europe

---

The EACIC is also the likely recipient of the Single Source Processor-SIGINT (SSP-S), which is designed to analyze enormous quantities of Sigint data. See "Sophisticated Intelligence Processing," *Jane's Defence Weekly*, March 25, 1989, p. 521.

69. The large U.S. ground station at Augsburg, Germany, is a likely candidate facility to receive satellite imagery. For more information on TENCAP and associated systems see Paul Stares and John Pike, "The Contribution of U.S. C³I to the Defence of NATO," in Jane M. O. Sharp, ed., *Europe after an American Withdrawal* (Oxford University Press in association with the Stockholm International Peace Research Institute, 1990), pp. 402–20.

70. Sochaczewski, "NATO Information Systems in Support of Consultation and Military Command and Control," p. 76.

Figure 5-6. *NATO Central Region Intelligence Organization*

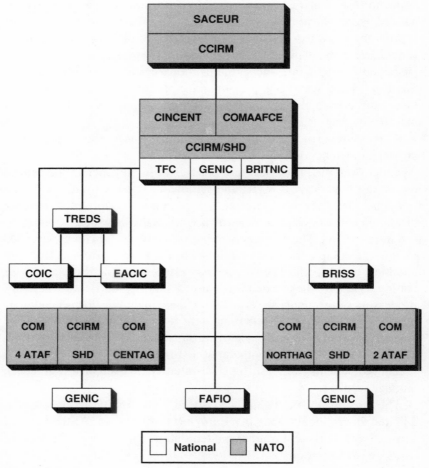

Source: See text.

and then transfers the processed (and presumably sanitized) information to remote display terminals at the main NATO headquarters in the central region.[71] Although originally designed to be a short-term demonstration system, LOCE has become a semipermanent feature of the intelligence architecture in central Europe. It will most likely form the U.S. gateway

71. Eldon Mangold, "Joint Tactical Fusion–Limited Operational Capability Europe," IEEE EASCON 83, pp. 327–29. As of 1981, sensor interface modules are located at Twenty-

into a planned NATO-sponsored project for exchanging intelligence known as the Battlefield Information Collection and Exploitation System (BICES). The intention is to establish a large NATO network of standardized ADP terminals capable of passing information from the main collection and processing systems directly to the relevant users.[72] The NATO Air Command and Control System (ACCS) program will provide the same service for air operations.

Another experimental network involved in the planning for BICES is the Battlefield Information and Targeting System (BITS), which was originally sponsored by the U.S. Defense Nuclear Agency. This is an IBM-PC based network with terminals at all the main allied intelligence centers. These terminals exchange information with a central computer at Boerfink. Although this system has evidently proved useful in exercises, it is unclear how long it will remain in operation.[73] Finally, under the NATO-sponsored Central Region Intelligence Communications Architecture (CRINCA) program, the same intelligence centers have established common data formatting procedures to exchange order-of-battle information among themselves. This system was again designed to test operational concepts for the BICES program.[74]

For controlling operations in the central region, NATO's operational-level commanders have a similar mix of communications systems at their disposal as SACEUR. The most important system in the AFCENT

---

sixth Tactical Reconnaissance Wing, 6911 Electronic Security Squadron, 330 Company (AS), V Corps, VII Corps, and the Tactical Fusion Center. Remote display terminals include AFCENT PWHQ, NORTHAG/2ATAF PWHQ, CENTAG/4ATAF PWHQ, EUCOM HQ, USAREUR HQ, V andVII Corps HQS. See also Stares and Pike, "Contribution of U.S. C³I," p. 417.

72. For more information on BICES see Lt. Col. K. A.W. Mackenzie, "BICES Advances Battlefield Information in NATO's Central Region," Defense Electronics and Computing Supplement to *International Defense Review*, vol. 22 (March 1989), pp. 24–26; Daniel J. Marcus, "NATO Intelligence System Faces First Major Review," *Defense News*, February 15, 1988, pp. 1, 28; and Gabriel Ferenczy, "A System of Systems—The Battlefield Information Collection and Exploitation System (BICES)," *NATO's Sixteen Nations*, vol. 32 (August 1987), pp. 43–45.

73. A related system that also uses IBM equipment is the Tactical Analysis and Planning (TAP) Management System, which serves U.S. forces in Europe. Though designed originally to support nuclear operations, it has evidently expanded its role to cover other missions. For information on BITS and TAP see James S. Cullen, "Evolutionary Development of Command and Control Information Systems (CCIS) in the United States," in *Information and Consultation: Keys to Peace*, pp. 102–05; and Mackenzie, "BICES Advances Battlefield Information," pp. 24–26.

74. Mackenzie, "BICES Advances Battlefield Information," p. 26.

region is the gridded network of microwave towers known as the Central Region Improvement Program (CIP-67). Though intended to be operational by 1967, like many projects in NATO, CIP-67 was not completed until much later, in this case 1983. As figure 5-7 indicates, CIP-67 extends from northern to southern Germany, with the rear portions of the network covering parts of Holland and Belgium. All the peacetime and wartime headquarters of the AFCENT region are linked together by this system. Although the front line of microwave towers was designed to be transportable, the antennas have been off-loaded, making the entire system fixed to its current location, according to several officials interviewed.[75]

Aside from the CIP-67 network, the only other NATO-operated systems used in the central region are the satellite communications terminals and the emergency high-frequency nets. The CIP-67 network, however, is augmented by miscellaneous national military communications systems that crisscross the region. These include the U.S. Defense Communications System (DCS), discussed earlier, which would be responsible, among other things, for passing U.S. intelligence to and from the main processing and fusion centers in the European theater. A dedicated net known as the Intra-Theater Intelligence Communications Network that would link facilities such as COIC, TFC, EACIC, and Metro Tango is being set up to run off the modernized AUTODIN system (known as the Defense Data Network, DDN).[76] In northern Germany, the British forces also have their own chain of microwave radio towers, known as STARRNET, that links their bases and provides them with rearward communications to the United Kingdom. Several interconnects exist to tie it in to both CIP-67 and the DCS.[77] The extensive German Air Force Automated Communications System, made up of microwave links and land lines, is also in West Germany.[78] This system is greatly relied on for coordinating NATO air operations.

75. Larry K. Wentz and Gope D. Hingorani, "NATO Communications in Transition," *IEEE Transactions on Communications,* vol. 28 (September 1980), p. 1533.

76. Maj. Gen. Schuyler Bissell and Lt. Col. Daniel G. Kniola, "Intelligence for War Fighting," *Signal,* vol. 41 (September 1986), pp. 48, 51.

77. CIP-67 interconnects are at Hehn and Roetgen, while the DCS is accessed at Adenau and Garlstedt. For more information on STARRNET see U.S. Defense Communications Agency, *Defense Communications System/European Communication Systems,* pp. 10-9–10-10.

78. See Lt. Col. Gerhard Huebner, "The German Air Force Automated Communications System (GAFACS)—Its Relationship to and Interfaces with NATO-Related Programs," in *NATO and Western Europe C³ National and International Aspects,* Fourth

Growing use is also made of the region's civil post, telegraph, and telephone networks. In particular most of the intelligence exchange networks just described—CCIS, LOCE, BITS, and CRINCA—use specially encrypted circuits leased from the Deutsche Bundespost. The West German automated data exchange is also borne by this system. In wartime an even greater reliance on the public telephone networks can be expected. Much of the operational traffic between the ATAF commmanders and their air bases, for instance, will go over these circuits.[79] The army group commanders are also likely to make great use of the PTTs for communicating with their mobile corps headquarters. Special pick-up points have been installed at selected locations throughout the central region for NATO's ground forces to plug into. Within the Federal Republic the Bundeswehr has created its own strategic communications network called the Grundnetz out of the Deutsche Bundespost system.[80] Hundreds of pick-up points throughout western Germany have been laid down, each of which is connected by specially protected landlines and controlled from hardened command centers. The Grundnetz is probably the most survivable communications system in central Europe.[81] The U.S. Army has likewise established its own network of PTT pick ups called the U.S. Command Grid Network (CG Net) that serves the area currently occupied by the two U.S. corps in southern Germany.[82] According to a senior NATO commander interviewed, the British have also established a specially leased circuit known as the Brahms link to communicate with the U.K. liaison officers at each of the corps in the NORTHAG region.

AFCEA NATO Symposium and Exposition, Brussels, 1983 (Washington: AFCEA International Press, 1983), pp. 72–79.

79. The West German and Dutch air forces, in particular, rely heavily on the PTT networks for interbase communications. See Michael J. Witt, "Europe Utilizes Public Networks for Defense Telecommunications," *Defense News,* October 31, 1988, pp. 10–11.

80. William F. de Dufour, *Army Communications Interoperability with NATO Nations,* MTR-8016 (McLean, Va.: Mitre Corp., 1979), p. 71.

81. For more information on the Deutsche Bundespost see U.S. Defense Communications Agency, *Defense Communications System/European Communication Systems,* pp. 11-5–11-7.

82. The CG Net does extend to other U.S. Army forces in Europe. See Maj. Erik W. Helgesen and others, "The USAREUR Tactical C^2 System at Echelons Above Corps," *Signal,* vol. 42 (June 1988), pp. 233–38. The U.S. forces' European Telephone System also relies on leased PTT lines. Each of the PTT terminals has access to ten to forty circuits, which are "dialed up" by the users. According to one expert interviewed, mobile CPs can access the pick up by way of land line (including fiber optic links) from as far as two kilometers away.

Figure 5-7. *The CIP-67 Network*

Source: Joachim M. Sochaczewski, "The Role of Communications in NATO," *Military Technology*, vol. 8 (June 1984), p. 152.

A composite overview of the communications links to and from the static wartime headquarters of the major NATO operational commanders is provided in figures 5-8 and 5-9. The same communications systems would be used by the mobile command posts. The two sections of AFCENT's AWHQ each have transportable microwave towers to link up with the CIP-67 system.[83] They will also be able to plug into PTT pick-up points at the presurveyed sites that the command posts would move between. And AFCENT's transportable satellite ground terminal would allow it to use the various NATO and U.S. communications satellites as well.

The communications arrangements for COMNORTHAG's mobile command headquarters are somewhat different, reflecting the dominant British influence.[84] The main and alternate command posts are connected to two separate but interlinked mobile communications centers (COMCENs), which essentially act as message switches. The second COMCEN was added for extra redundancy, but the communications needs of the mobile CP have evidently grown so much that now both are needed. Each of these nodes in turn has a single relay link into the CIP-67 network.[85] They can also tap into the PTT system, either through a single pick-up point at Senden that has multiple circuits available for use or through more austere PTT connections that have fewer lines. With its greater flexibility and reliability, increasing use is also being made of the British Ptarmigan tactical communications network to support army group needs.[86] With the exception of some high-frequency radio equipment used as backup, this description covers all the electronic means of communication for NORTHAG. Satellite communications facilities—certainly by way of NATO channels—are evidently not available.

83. Actually the main command post will have two microwave relay towers. As standing operating procedures dictate, these would be sited some distance away from the main command vehicles.

84. Responsibility for NORTHAG headquarters communications is actually shared between the 28 (U.K.) Signal Regiment and the 840 (GE) Signal Battalion. The former unit handles communications from the headquarters to the communications centers where the latter takes over. "Headquarters, Northern Army Group," NATO unclassified organizational chart, Moenchengladbach, Germany, January 1988.

85. The CIP-67 can apparently be accessed by a third roundabout route, but this is apparently not easy to do and is rarely practiced. Information on NORTHAG mobile HQ communications was obtained in interviews. See also Baldwin, *NATO Ground Forces Communications Interoperability,* pp. 20–21.

86. "British Army Experience with Ptarmigan and Wavell," *International Defense Review,* vol. 21, no. 5 (1988), p. 500.

Figure 5-8. *AFCENT/NORTHAG Wartime Headquarters Connectivity*

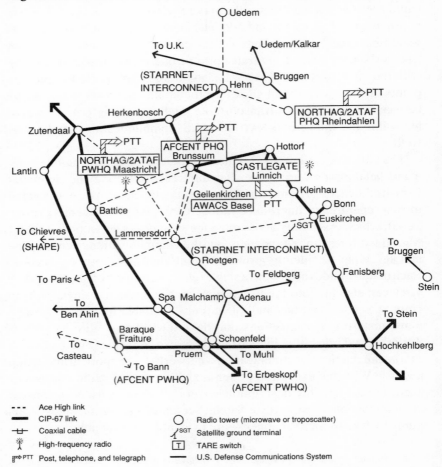

Sources: Sochaczewski, "Role of Communications in NATO," p. 152; U.S. Defense Communications Agency, *Defense Communications System/European Communication Systems*, pp. 7-21–7-22, 28; P. W. Hughes, B. R. Kuhnert, and S. M. Sussman, *Central Region Command and Control Communications Capabilities*, MTR-8167, sanitized version prepared for Electronic Systems Division, U.S. Air Force Systems Command (Bedford, Mass.: Mitre Corp., 1981); Larry K. Wentz and Gope D. Hingorani, "NATO Communications in Transition," *IEEE Transactions on Communications*, vol. 28 (September 1980), p. 1527; and interviews. Map is not drawn to scale.

In contrast the communications arrangements for COMCENTAG's mobile command post are somewhat different, reflecting the dominant U.S. influence.[87] While this post also relies on two mobile and interconnected switching centers known as Army Group Area Signal Centers to manage the flow of communications in and out of the headquarters, the two German corps are served by the CIP-67 microwave network. The two U.S. corps can also be reached through a separate system called the Tactical Automated Switching System (TASS). This system is a tropospheric-scatter link that employs U.S. joint tactical (TRI-TAC) communications equipment. The switches at these signal centers also provide access into the U.S. DCS network.[88] And like NORTHAG's command post, PTT links and high-frequency radio are also available.

In summary NATO's present operational level command and control system suffers from major shortcomings that raise serious doubts about the ability of NATO's senior commanders to provide coherent and effective direction of a campaign in central Europe. These deficiencies affect, moreover, every part of NATO's command system at this level of operations.

The first identifiable problem concerns the wartime command post arrangements. While the facilities at Boerfink, Maastricht, Linnich-Glimbach (Castle Gate), Ruppertsweiler, and Kindsbach are apparently hardened to withstand conventional attack and probably nuclear strikes near misses as well, most of their communications links to the outside world are extremely exposed and therefore vulnerable to attack in wartime.[89] The communications supporting the AFCENT PWHQ at Boer-

87. The responsibility for communications in the CENTAG region is also split between the U.S. 97th Signal Battalion and the 890th German Signal Battalion. Information on the CENTAG command post was obtained through various interviews.

88. These are the TTC-39 and the TYC-39 switches used for voice and data traffic respectively. The U.S. Corps can also be reached by way of a U.S. Army Area Signal Center (AASC) that uses essentially the same equipment. This can use the U.S. tactical satellite links to the corps if necessary. For more information on the TRI-TAC program see "Joint Tactical Communications Program," in *The C³I Handbook: Command, Control, Communications, Intelligence,* prepared by the editors of *Defense Electronics* (Palo Alto, Calif.: EW Communications, 1986), pp. 128–30; and Myron Fox, "'Quantum Leap': Force Modernization through Tactical Communications," *Signal,* vol. 38 (November 1983), pp. 17–20.

89. Not every one of those interviewed agreed that these facilities were immune to conventional attack. One senior NATO commander observed that certain types of nonnuclear weaponry delivered in a certain way could disable the Boerfink facility. Another noted how easy it is to locate and target this facility since a large car park was built nearby, and the method used to shield the bunker from nuclear EMP apparently

Figure 5-9. *AFCENT/CENTAG Wartime Headquarters Connectivity*

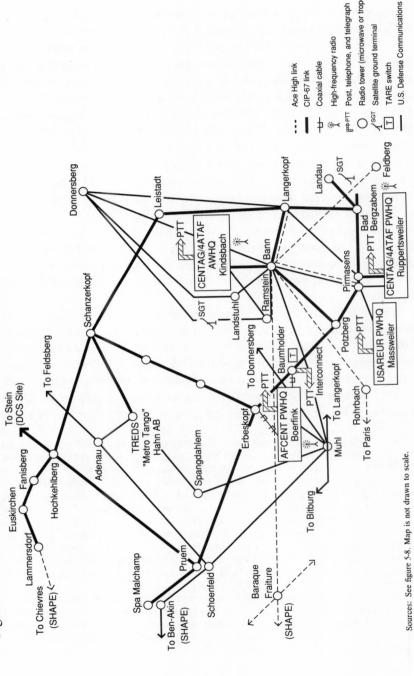

Sources: See figure 5-8. Map is not drawn to scale.

fink, for instance, were universally declared "extremely vulnerable" by all those interviewed. The reason stems to a large extent from the bunker's heavy reliance on the communications towers on top of the nearby Erbeskopf mountain. One retired senior NATO commander even went so far as to state that a single air-delivered 500-pound bomb would destroy the communications facilities at this site.[90] NATO's current capacity to replace damaged or destroyed antennas is severely limited. Not all of Boerfink's communications go by way of Erbeskopf, however. There are also several buried cables, including a fiber optic link to nearby communications facilities. Although many believe that these links would be able to survive conventional air attack, some experts consider them vulnerable to being cut by saboteurs.[91]

While the communications links at NATO's other static wartime headquarters are not considered as vulnerable as those at the AFCENT PWHQ, they may still become decapitated from their supporting systems by selective attacks at key network nodes. From figure 5-9 it would appear that destruction of just half a dozen major communications centers, notably at Erbeskopf, Muhl, Baumholder, Pirmasens, Bann, and Donnersberg, would severely hamper if not paralyze operations at the fixed AFCENT, CENTAG-4ATAF, and USAREUR command posts in the area. This situation appears even worse for the main NORTHAG-2ATAF headquarters.[92]

Should these fixed headquarters facilities be put out of commission for an extended period, then, as just noted, the management of operations would shift to the mobile command posts. However, these posts are not designed to substitute fully for the primary headquarters since space and other constraints limit the nature of the deployable equipment. How much of a difference these limitations would make to operational performance is hard to gauge. It seems clear, however, that those officers responsible for processing intelligence and for directing air operations

---

killed the adjacent vegetation that had helped screen it. As this person reflected, "It's as if it has a giant bullseye on it."

90. The towers are also clearly marked to help aircraft navigation.

91. According to one NATO signals officer interviewed, the cables are not buried very deeply and could be discovered easily by metal detectors.

92. COMNORTHAG apparently has a fleet of cars at his disposal, as well as his private helicopter, to act as couriers if communications go down. Given their proximity to one another, dispatch riders could also be used between the AFCENT and CENTAG/4ATAF headquarters, although this capability clearly would not compensate for the lost communications.

would suffer the most. As their information processing and communications demands have grown, so large, fixed command centers have become virtually indispensable to them. It is also difficult to assess how vulnerable these command posts are to detection and attack. While they would move around to avoid being targeted, this movement would have to occur more frequently than is reportedly practiced in exercises. The difficulty and the time taken to set up communications at each site have made command post operators resistant to frequent moves between different locations.[93]

Some additional protection for the mobile command posts might be gained from their chosen operating location. The AFCENT AWHQ will probably operate from a large industrial facility to help hide its distinctive electromagnetic signature, while the NORTHAG mobile command post has been known to operate in exercises from hardened aircraft hangars. This precaution will not help redress the real weakness of the mobile command posts, however. Both the NORTHAG and CENTAG command posts are dependent on only two mobile communications centers for channeling messages to and from the headquarters. In the NORTHAG case at least, should either one of these nodes be destroyed, the alternate headquarters would no longer be able to function at full capacity. The operational impact of this impairment is hard to gauge; the consequences of losing both, however, are clear.

Even if the various wartime headquarters survive, problems can be expected in coordinating the air-land battle at the operational level. Although NATO commanders talk of a jointly run campaign by a combined team of air and ground planning staff, the command arrangements at the army group-ATAF level are for all practical purposes bifurcated; the senior land commanders will operate from their mobile headquarters while the senior air commanders will generally stay put at their bunkers.[94] While coordination will take place through special communications links, this harmonization may not always be possible for the reasons just discussed. Maintaining a pool of well-trained battle staff to man the headquarters in wartime also presents problems for NATO. The regular

93. Several officers commented, for example, that "transportable" is a better description than "mobile" for the AFCENT AWHQ.

94. The situation is different at the AFCENT-AAFCE headquarters, where operational planning is apparently more directly coordinated. Incidentally, the permanent air battle staff is no longer tied to CINCENT's slower land-oriented twelve-hour decision cycle, which is the equivalent of two to three operational cycles of the air campaign. With his concurrence they can make decisions within this cycle.

rotation of senior officers in NATO means that the expertise built up over several years of working together on exercises has to be reestablished every few years.[95] On the positive side, however, rotation does encourage a regular influx of new ideas.

Assessing the adequacy of intelligence support to NATO's operational-level commanders without access to classified information poses obvious difficulties. Nevertheless, several conclusions can be reached on the basis of publicly available information. The first concerns the tasking of the allies' intelligence assets in support of NATO's collective needs in wartime. CINCENT and his intelligence officers, as noted earlier, have no control over national collection systems. While the CCIRM process exists for the purpose of requesting intelligence from the allies, it is apparently very bureaucratic and sluggish in operation, according to several NATO officials interviewed. It is unlikely to be sufficiently responsive to the fast-breaking conditions of a conflict on the central front. The situation has been summed up by Major General Edward B. Atkeson, a former assistant chief of staff for U.S. Army intelligence in Europe:

> The various ACE headquarters (army group, region, and so forth),...having no special intelligence collection capabilities of their own, would remain heavily dependent upon higher and lower echelons. In time of war the commmanders at these levels would be responsible for the conduct of the defense at the operational level, yet they would have no influence over how the supporting intelligence effort might be directed. They could not order subordinate national corps to steer their associated intelligence collection systems toward any particular targets. They might "request": they might cajole; but since they would have no institutional insight into how national intelligence systems operate, their influence, at best, would be blunt, diffuse, and slow.[96]

NATO's deep-looking intelligence assets can also be expected to suffer attrition once hostilities begin. Those operating from fixed and forwardly deployed locations—notably the peacetime eavesdropping stations in West Germany—are the most vulnerable. Their land mobile and airborne counterparts, however, are clearly less susceptible to attack. The Sigint aircraft, for instance, can stand off from enemy-controlled air space and

95. Training centers like the U.S. Warrior Preparation Center help in this regard. See "U.S. Simulated War Game Center Begins Operations," *Aviation Week and Space Technology,* September 3, 1984, pp. 201–13.

96. Maj. Gen. E. B. Atkeson, *The Final Argument of Kings: Reflections on the Art of War* (Hero Books, 1988), p. 207. See also John H. Cushman, *Command and Control of Theater Forces: Adequacy* (Washington: AFCEA International Press, 1985), pp. 27–28.

also operate from bases in the rear. The same flexibility applies to the TR-1 aircraft, which may also be given fighter escorts when flying close to the front. Some aircraft, principally the British and German Tornados, will have to penetrate Pact air space to fulfill their mission and are sure to suffer some losses from the heavy air defenses. The vulnerability of the vital space-based intelligence assets will depend on the course of future antisatellite developments. The latest generation of U.S. high-altitude, and to a lesser extent low-altitude, reconnaissance satellites are believed to be survivable against the current Soviet antisatellite (ASAT) threat. Should the U.S. begin fielding its own ASAT weaponry, it is reasonable to expect the Soviets to respond and develop further countermeasures. The security of U.S. and allied satellites is then likely to become progressively more difficult to maintain over the long term.[97]

Arguably the most lucrative targets for the Warsaw Pact will be the associated NATO intelligence ground stations, processing sites, and fusion centers. Some of these, as just described, are located within the hardened wartime headquarters; others, however, are not. The vital Metro Tango facility, for example, is completely exposed, although a permanent, hardened site is expected to be found for this facility. The COIC, while located inside an earth-covered bunker at Ramstein, is not considered very survivable by some knowledgeable officers interviewed.[98] In contrast, to give some idea of the misplaced priorities of NATO planning, the newly constructed F-16 avionics maintenance hangar nearby is heavily protected and capable of operating in a nuclear environment.

Even if it is assumed that these key facilities will escape destruction and stay operational, NATO faces additional problems when it comes to feeding the collected intelligence into alliance command channels. For a start, the NATO communications channels, which under normal circumstances do not have to bear much intelligence traffic, have evidently become quickly choked in exercises that approximate wartime conditions, leading to long delays before messages can be sent or received. It seems that the introduction of new intelligence assets into the theater that generate vast streams of data, as well as the growing capability to transmit imagery electronically, has not been met by a

97. See Stares, *Space and National Security,* pp. 174–200.
98. One officer even described it as a "mortar magnet," apparently because it is located close to the perimeter fence at Ramstein and vulnerable to attack from *spetsnaz*-type forces.

commensurate increase in communications capacity. Most of the officers interviewed indicated that it was not a dearth of intelligence that was the main problem, but that there was too much information to assimilate.

In particular, NATO's ability to process and disseminate the high-grade intelligence that it receives in a timely fashion is open to question. While the three principal intelligence suppliers to the alliance have a direct interest in providing their best product to NATO's senior command-ers—most of whom happen to come from the same countries—the time-consuming arrangements and procedures that have evolved in peacetime to protect sources and permit the release of sensitive national intelligence into NATO channels are simply not conducive to the expected pace of wartime operations. Events will be moving too quickly for there to be enough time for the usual sanitization of national intelligence. In short, unless NATO adapts quickly to wartime conditions, the incoming intelli-gence will build up faster than it can be processed.

The technical support systems will have to undergo an equivalent transformation if they are to be able to handle high-grade intelligence. The various automated data processing systems for exchanging intelli-gence—CCIS, LOCE, BITS, and CRINCA—can only handle and distribute intelligence classified to a level no higher than Secret. The same will apply to the much-heralded BICES system for exchanging battlefield intelligence. Although a general downgrading of classification can be expected in wartime, it is still doubtful whether especially sensitive intelligence, notably Sigint, can be accommodated on this system. How NATO intends to disseminate this kind of intelligence in wartime remains unclear.

NATO's information processing systems suffer from other serious shortcomings. The capabilities of the main CCIS system received mixed reviews from those experts intimate with its operation. Some described it as minimally effective and not user friendly while others criticized its outdated, failure-prone technology. According to one U.S. Air Force officer,

> Within the automated war headquarters, the WWMCCS-derived Honeywell based Automated Command and Control Information System (ACCIS) is the primary ADP resource available to the staff. Most of their terminals are off of that one system, meaning there is no backup capability should the machine be lost. Work is under way to internet several of these systems, which will provide limited backup to those interconnected nodes but virtually no connectivity to the other headquarters. Small computers are being introduced to handle specific functions such as message processing,

intelligence and weaponry. These systems are, for the most part, not connected to one another nor to the ACCIS host, meaning staff members must have their terminals off each of these machines if they want the most current information relative to their functional areas."[99]

Another serious problem is that the two central computer processors at Boerfink and Maastricht are not "dual homed." In other words, if either one ceases functioning for whatever reason, then the entire network cannot operate off the other one. Until the CENTAG-4ATAF headquarters at Ruppertsweiler receives its own host processor, AFCENT headquarters will be unable to exchange files with it in the same way it can with Maastricht.

Perhaps the most glaring deficiency of the CCIS system, however, is its lack of interoperability with the data processing systems used by adjacent NATO regional and even subordinate commands. Despite overlapping areas of interest and influence, AFCENT headquarters cannot exchange data automatically with counterparts in either the AFNORTH or AFSOUTH regions. Even more startling is that the primary NATO air command and control data processing network in the central region at the Allied Tactical Operational Centers and Sector Operations Centers (ATOC-SOC) level and below—a German system known as Eifel—cannot exchange information automatically with the CCIS system, which only extends down as far as the ATAF level. Instead data have to be exchanged by what are known as "swivel-chair" procedures by which operators manually download information from one system and then reenter it into the other. For obvious reasons such steps are time-consuming and prone to error. Though NATO is working to remedy the situation, it will be many years before a truly interoperable system is in place.[100] The operational consequences of this cumbersome arrangement, which one senior NATO air commander described as "nothing short of an international disgrace," is that key time-sensitive decisions on the

99. Capt. Stephen D. Shively, "A Local Area Network for NATO War Headquarters," *Signal*, vol. 38 (May 1984), pp. 137–52. The same person also observes that communications within some headquarters is so saturated that it is sometimes more effective to use runners.

100. An automatic interface device called Janus is being developed but is not expected to become operational until the SD & IC study project on common data processing standards has been completed. Several interim solutions are being considered, however, including extending the CCIS down to the SOC/ATOCs, extending Eifel up to the AFCENT PWHQ, as well as a procedure called "PC magic" whereby information from one system is downloaded onto floppy disks and then fed into the other. Interview.

apportionment and allocation of air power may have to be taken without the benefit of the latest status reports from the air bases. Ignorance of the effectiveness of a particular mission or the attrition suffered in the process could lead to unnecessary duplication of effort and, worse still, the continuation of an unproductive and costly strategy. As noted earlier, NATO doesn't have the air power to allow for too many wasteful or costly decisions.

The utility of these various data processing systems will ultimately depend on the survivability of the communications networks that serve as their carriers. Fortunately, the PTT networks, which can be considered among the more redundant forms of communication in the central region, seem to bear most of this burden. In the case of the Deutche Bundespost telephone system, a large share of what is reportedly in excess of 5,000 switches would have to be destroyed before a significant drop in service would occur.[101] The same cannot be said for NATO's military networks, however. The main CIP-67 system can be given a survivability rating similar to the one Ace High received earlier, which is very low. The majority of those experts interviewed believe the system would not last for more than a week in an intense conventional conflict. Although the rear portions of the CIP-67 grid, which have received some hardening, might remain operational for a longer period, the forwardly positioned radio towers are more exposed and also structurally fragile.[102] Moreover, not every tower would have to be destroyed to disable the system. A closer inspection of the network configuration in figure 5-6 shows the most fruitful targets for attack.

Added to this vulnerability is NATO's limited capacity to reconstitute damaged parts of the network following an attack. Spare antennas are apparently in very short supply since some of the emergency replacements have already been cannibalized to maintain peacetime operations. Furthermore, much of the manpower that would be needed to keep the system operating and provide back-up support in wartime comes from reserve units that would have to be mobilized and transported

101. Interviews. There is still the problem discussed earlier of the vulnerability of the cross-border links, which must be used by rear mobile headquarters.

102. One expert knowledgeable about the CIP-67 system declared that the stations classified as hardened refer only to the equipment in the associated control rooms and not to the antennas and waveguides. Furthermore, site protection against saboteurs is also rudimentary—a single fence in some cases. Another expert interviewed insisted that it would take only a hand grenade to disable some of the forward radio towers.

to the theater.[103] The ability of these reserves to work on allied communications equipment, which they are often unfamiliar with but will be expected to repair, has also been questioned.

The fragility of NATO military communications networks is not helped, furthermore, by the interoperability problem that exists. The national military networks that the CIP-67 system ties into often employ different signal encoding methods; some of them are analog, others are digital. The speed at which NATO and national communications equipment can pass data also varies, causing bottlenecks at key places. Some of these incompatibilities can be overcome through special NATO-developed "black box" connections (a common one being the 5040 device named after the NATO Standardization Agreement, or STANAG, that established it), but such connections are not the optimal solution. Besides being costly, they reduce communications flexibility and create vulnerable choke points.

Another widely acknowledged problem in NATO is the unsatisfactory quality and provision of secure communications equipment. Senior commanders frequently complained that NATO's secure voice equipment rendered speech unintelligible, especially when one of the speakers was not fluent in the language being spoken.[104] New equipment such as the U.S.-developed STU-III telephones would improve this problem, but they have not been made available to the United States' European allies for security reasons. This concern, besides depriving the alliance of a useful asset, compounds the already large NATO interoperability problem in encryption equipment.[105]

In fairness, NATO is endeavoring to rectify some of these serious shortcomings. The CIP-67 Step 2 program is intended to make the current network more redundant by increasing the number of connections to the PTT systems and national military networks. In wartime more rerouting opportunities to circumvent damaged or destroyed radio stations will, it is hoped, be available. The CIP-67, however, will still remain NATO's principal communications system for the next ten to fifteen years. Both

---

103. The central region Signal Group's reserve force is the British Eleventh Signal Brigade Territorial Army, based in the United Kingdom. Maintenance of the U.S. DCS is similarly dependent on reinforcements from the United States. See *Department of Defense Appropriations for 1985*, pt. 1, pp. 732–33.

104. Interviews. See also "British Army Experience with Ptarmigan and Wavell," p. 500.

105. See James B. Schultz, "STU-III: A Secure Phone Looking for a NATO Desk," *Armed Forces Journal International*, vol. 127 (August 1989), pp. 82–86.

the NORTHAG and CENTAG signal groups also expect to reduce their dependence on the currently small number of communications switching centers. Under the Joint Area Communications System (JACS) program additional mobile microwave towers and switches will be furnished to support headquarters operations.[106] Neither program will go into effect until the mid-1990s, however.[107]

At the tactical level of operations NATO's command and control arrangements are even more complex and diverse since they become primarily a national responsibility. While the alliance strives to harmonize the tactical doctrines and standard operating procedures of its members, the associated command systems vary considerably from country to country.

The Tactical Level: The Air Battle

The planning of NATO air operations begins with COMAAFCE issuing an air directive (AD) that lays out the overall apportionment and allotment of air power to specific missions and regions. This directive used to be issued on a daily basis but would in wartime be sent out when needed.[108] The ATAF commanders in turn translate this directive into a more detailed air battle plan for their specific areas of responsibility. Daily operations orders (DOOs) are then sent out to their subordinate ATOCS and SOCS for offensive and defensive missions respectively. These centers also receive a daily airspace control order (ACO) from ATAF headquarters, which delineates and reserves specific sectors or corridors of NATO's air space for certain operations at given times. This order is amended as the planning process proceeds.

Once it receives the daily operations order, the ATOC's Plans Division sets about organizing the following day's flying activities. Offensive

106. The NORTHAG plan is to increase the number of hubs to seven with three mobile alternates. The CENTAG modernization program will probably employ TRI-TAC Block III systems to raise the number of switches to six. Interviews.

107. "British Army Experience with Ptarmigan and Wavell," p. 500.

108. This section draws heavily on a description of NATO's air command and control system in Mitre Corp., USAF Eifel 1 Functional Description, Mitre Technical Report, MTR-8446 (Bedford, Mass., September 1981); and Maj. Thomas Buchanan, The Tactical Air Control System: Its Evolution and Its Need for Battle Managers, Research Report AU-ARI-87-1 (Maxwell Air Force Base, Ala.: Air University Press, 1987).

operations over enemy-controlled territory clearly require careful planning and coordination. On the basis of the latest information from the Intelligence Division, the targets have to be identified and the appropriate munitions and aircraft matched to them. Routes in and out of enemy air space also have to be mapped out. This procedure also requires alerting NATO's air defense forces to minimize the risk of mistaken identification and engagement. Fighters and tankers may also be needed to escort the attacking aircraft and refuel them at specific rendezvous points. Special arrangements will almost certainly have to be made to suppress enemy air defenses either by electronic countermeasures or by physical attack. In short, the actions of all these supporting units have to be meticulously planned and coordinated to achieve maximum effectiveness. Once the plans have been drawn up, an air tasking order (ATO), along with a revised air coordination order, is sent out to all the participating units. On the day of attack, oversight of the mission is handled by the ATOC's Current Operations Division. The take-off times, call signs, air control procedures, and time-on-target arrangements are prepared by this division and sent out in the form of air task messages (ATMs) to the Wing Operations Centers (WOCS).

The ATOCS also act as the main reception center for air support requests from the army corps. Attached to every corps headquarters in the central region is an Air Support Operations Center (ASOC) that forwards what are called air tasking requests (ATRS) for close air support, battlefield interdiction, and reconnaissance missions in their area. These requests are sent up the chain of command and balanced against the needs of the other corps for the next day's allocation of air support. There is, however, provision for meeting immediate requests for assistance that arise during the day. These are usually made directly from air force liaison units known as Tactical Air Control Parties (TACPS), which are attached to every division, brigade, and battalion headquarters. Forward detachments of these units, moreover, can guide aircraft to their targets in close support missions.

While the offensive air campaign is being orchestrated by the ATOCS, the Sector Operations Centers will be busy coordinating NATO's air defenses. Each of the SOCS has tactical control over the fighter interceptor squadrons and Hawk and Patriot surface-to-air (SAM) missile batteries assigned to defend its area. Also reporting to the SOCS are NATO's ground-based radars and air traffic controllers housed at mobile control and reporting posts (CRPS) and fixed Control and Reporting Centers (CRCS).

Smaller, more mobile forward air control posts (FACPs) may also be operating to fill in or extend radar coverage for certain areas. The West German low-level mobile radars, the U.S Tactical Air Control System, and the AWACS aircraft are controlled from the SOCs. To manage these various units the SOCs put out daily tasking orders (DTOs) that, among other things, allocate combat air patrol (CAP) sorties to certain control centers, assign surveillance duties to specific sensors, establish weapons engagement zones for given areas and times, and change the location of mobile radars and SAMs. The SOCs also issue air raid warnings to friendly units in their area and scramble aircraft in response. Furthermore, since most of NATO's air defense assets are under the control of the SOCs, army units request assistance through Air Defense Liaison Teams (ADOLTs) attached to every corps headquarters. And finally the SOCs report the results of the day's effort to their ATAF headquarters.

NATO's current air command and control organization is shown in figure 5-10.

Each ATAF in the central region has in general two ATOCs and two SOCs operating under its control. These are all located within fixed command posts, some of which share facilities with other units. Thus the main 2ATAF wartime headquarters at Maastricht is home to one of its ATOCs while the main AFCENT-AAFCE bunker at Boerfink also houses 4ATAF's main SOC, which functions, furthermore, as a CRC. The ATOC at Mestetten also operates as SOC IV. In general there are two CRCs linked to each SOC, which are all fixed facilities. The only mobile components of NATO's air command and control system—besides the German low-level radars and the U.S. TACS—are the CRPs and the ASOC-ADOLTs that move around with the corps. Figure 5-11 shows the main air command and control posts in the central region.

Though these command posts share common names and functions, there is a wide disparity in the quality of the technical equipment at each facility. For example, the U.S-operated ATOC at Sembach has undergone extensive modernization in recent years to handle both offensive and defensive air operations. It is widely considered the model for the combined air operations centers that are planned as part of the the Air Command and Control System (ACCS) program. The ATOC at Maastricht, however, a facility run jointly by the Dutch, British, and Belgians, is by comparison quite rudimentary and technically backward.[109] For

109. Interview. This particular facility is expected to move to a new location—possibly at Glons in Belgium—when "the cave" is vacated in the early 1990s.

Figure 5-10. *NATO Air Command and Control Organization*

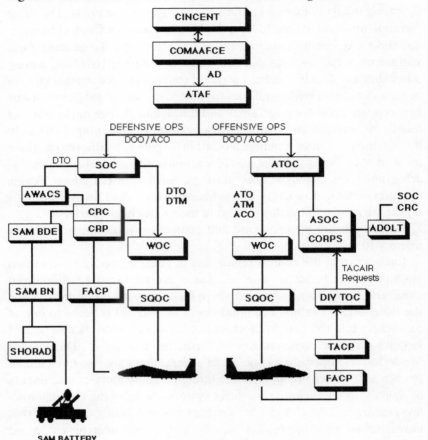

Sources: Maj. Thomas H. Buchanan, *The Tactical Air Control System: Its Evolution and Its Need for Battle Managers*, Report AU-ARI-87-1 (Maxwell Air Force Base, Ala.: Air University Press, 1987), p. 31; Conrad J. Rauch and Walter R. Edginton, "NATO Develops a Long-term Air Command and Control Plan," *Defense Systems Review*, vol. 2 (January 1984), p. 16; Ronald A. Enlow, "ACCS Architecture Evaluation—A Near-term Application of TACCSF," in *Information and Consultation: Keys to Peace*, pp. 36–41; and interviews.

exercising control over U.S. Air Force units assigned to the 2ATAF region, both of the ATOCs will be assisted by the U.S.-operated NATO Operations Support Cell (NOSC) at Kalkar in West Germany. This cell would receive intelligence directly from the Tactical Fusion Center and the Combat Intelligence Center.

The principal means by which NATO would effect the planning and coordination of air operations in the central region is by use of the Eifel automated data processing system. Eifel was originally developed for the German Air Force, but it now links every major NATO air command and control center and operating base. Thus the daily operations and air tasking orders are sent out over this system. The air situation assessments and postaction reports are also fed into it for evaluation by higher commanders. In other words Eifel is the central nervous system for NATO air operations at the tactical level.[110]

NATO's intelligence assets for fighting the air battle at the tactical level can be divided into those that are primarily supportive of air defense operations and those that are used for targeting purposes in offensive strikes. Although ground-based or airborne surveillance radars are not always categorized as intelligence assets, they provide information that NATO could not afford to be without when coordinating the air defense campaign. Some of NATO's main air defense radar systems have already been mentioned. In brief these include the network of fixed and mobile radars that make up the NATO Air Defense Ground Environment (NADGE) system, the West German mobile low-level radars positioned close to the border, the transportable U.S. Tactical Air Control System, which is being upgraded with modular control equipment (MCE), and miscellaneous British radars in the 2ATAF region.[111] The most important NATO air defense surveillance assets, however, are without doubt the fleet of E-3 AWACS aircraft. NATO operates eighteen of these and the United States, Great Britain, and France could also make some of their versions available to the alliance.[112]

110. For information on Eifel see Mitre Corp., USAF Eifel 1 Functional Description; "Air Force Modernizing Command, Control Units," Aviation Week and Space Technology, June 7, 1982, pp. 80–81; and William P. Schlitz, "C³ for the European Air War," Air Force Magazine, vol. 66 (June 1983), pp. 67–68.

111. For more information on these various radar systems see Ted Hooton, "NADGE Enhancements Lay Groundwork for ACCS," International Defense Review, vol. 21 (July 1988), pp. 781–84; Maj. Ron L. Erhardt and Lt. Col. Scott Pilkington, "NATO Air Defence in the Central Region," NATO's Sixteen Nations, vol. 33 (June 1988), pp. 37–38; and "NATO Air Defense Ground Environment," in C³I Handbook, pp. 124–27; and "Tactical Air Operations Central/Modular Control Equipment," in The C³I Handbook: Command, Control, Communications, Intelligence, 2d ed., prepared by the editors of Defense Electronics (Palo Alto, Calif.: EW Communications, 1987), pp. 124–27.

112. Seven British and four French AWACS are due to enter service in 1991. These airborne radar platforms can stay aloft unrefueled for around nine hours and are capable at their normal operating altitude (30,000 ft.) of detecting low-level targets 400 km away and higher-level targets at twice this distance. It is possible, therefore, to provide surveillance over an area spanning the Mediterranean to the Baltic with just three AWACS

Figure 5-11. *NATO Central Region Air Command and Control Posts*

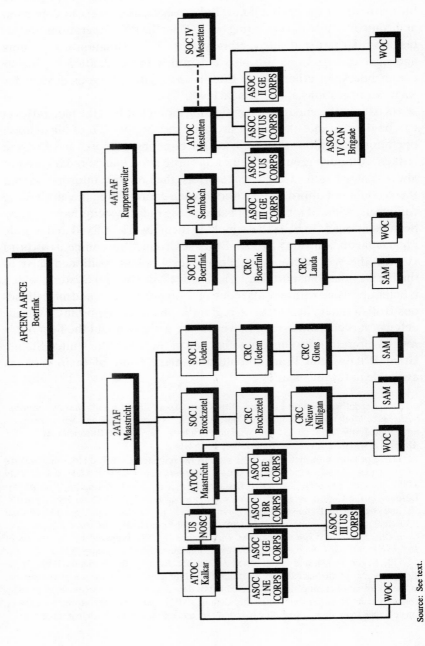

Source: See text.

The targeting information necessary for offensive air missions can be drawn from a variety of sources. Many of the long-range surveillance assets identified earlier would also be used to locate targets closer to the front. Their utility depends ultimately, however, on their respective "intelligence cycle" times. For some of these assets, the time taken to direct the platform, collect the data, and then distribute the product to the relevant users is too long to be useful for targeting certain types of enemy forces. It is unlikely, for example, that space-based sensors, despite their growing tactical applications, will be used for targeting mobile Pact forces in the immediate vicinity of the forward edge of the battle area. Most of the airborne sensors, however, especially the TR-1 and Tornado reconnaissance aircraft, will play a more active role in this respect. To augment these deep-looking assets, NATO's ground and air forces have a variety of shorter-range reconnaissance systems at their disposal (table 5-3).

The most important addition to NATO's shorter-range intelligence capabilities will be a new class of airborne battlefield surveillance platforms currently under development. In particular, the U.S. Joint Surveillance and Target Attack Radar System (JSTARS) promises to have the same impact on battlefield targeting as AWACS has had on air defense. Beginning in the mid-1990s, approximately twenty-two converted Boeing 707 aircraft designated as E-8AS are planned to be deployed by the U.S. Air Force. How many of these will operate in Europe is still unclear, however. Each will be equipped with a large multimode radar capable of being used either to detect and distinguish moving targets such as tanks and trucks over a wide area or, alternatively, for monitoring fixed targets with higher resolution. This information will then be fed either directly to ground attack aircraft for immediate targeting or to army-operated mobile ground support modules (GSMs) where it will be passed on to the appropriate artillery and missile units. Though the precise capabilities of JSTARS are classified, the radar reportedly can see targets at a distance of approximately 300 kilometers, but since it is likely that the aircraft will operate well back from the forward edge of the battle

---

aircraft flying well within West German airspace. At least five aircraft would be the preferred deployment in wartime, however. Interviews. See also Schlitz, "C³ for the European Air War," p. 63; Kennedy and others, *Intelligence Warfare*, pp. 140–41; and "E-3 AWACS: World Standard for Airborne C³," Boeing Aerospace Factsheet on E-3 AWACS, Seattle, Wash., Boeing Aerospace, 1988.

Table 5-3. *Central Region Short-Range Intelligence Assets*
Less than 150 kilometers

Platform	Name or designation	Sensor	Country and agency	Estimated number	Comments
Air based	RF-4C	Elint, IR, EO, SLAR	U.S.:USAF	18	To be replaced by RF-16C (ATARS)
	Jaguar GR-1	Imint	U.K.:RAF	24	Being phased out, replaced by Tornado
	Mirage 5BR	Imint	BE:BAF	19	. . .
Controlled by NATO air forces	RF-4E	IR, Photint	FRG:GAF	72	To be fitted with U.S. (ATARS)
	EGRETT, GROB G109	Sigint	FRG:GAF	8–10	55-km range
	RF-16A	n.a.	NE:RNAF	19	. . .
	Mirage IIIR/RD F-1CR	Imint, Elint	FR:FAF	44	. . .
	RC-12 D/K (Guardrail V)	Elint, Comint	U.S.:USA	19	. . .
	RU-21 (UTE)	Elint, Comint	U.S.:USA	n.a.	. . .
	RV-1D (Quicklook)	Elint	U.S.:USA	36	. . .
Controlled by NATO ground forces	OV-1D (Mohawk)	SLAR/Elint	U.S.:USA, USAF		. . .
	EH-60A (Quickfix)	Elint, Comint	U.S.:USA	77	. . .
	RPV CL-89	Imint	FRG/FR/U.K./CAN	n.a.	75-km range
	RPV CL-289	Imint	FRG/FR/CAN	n.a.	120-km range
	RPV Phoenix	Imint	U.K.:UKA		. . .
	RPV EPERVIER	Imint	BE:BA	n.a.	. . .
Ground based	Teampack (AN/MSQ-103)	Elint	U.S.:USA	n.a.	. . .
	Teammate (AN/TRQ-32(V))	Sigint	U.S.:USA	n.a.	. . .
	(AN/TRR-20)	Sigint	U.S.:USA	n.a.	. . .
	(AN/TRR-27)	Sigint	U.S.:USA	n.a.	. . .
	Trailblazer (AN/TSQ-114)	Elint	U.S.:USA	n.a.	. . .
	TACELIS (AN/TSQ-112)	Elint	U.S.:USA	n.a.	. . .
	REMBASS	Seismic, Acoustic, IR	U.S.:USA	n.a.	. . .
	Vampire, ACEWS	Sigint	U.K.:UKA	n.a.	With Fourteenth Signal Regiment
	Ceres	Comint	U.K.:UKA	n.a.	. . .
	Barbican, Setter	Sigint	U.K.:UDA	n.a.	. . .
	Spectra	Elint	NE:RNA	n.a.	. . .

Sources: International Institute for Strategic Studies, *The Military Balance, 1988–1989*; Bernard Blake, ed., *Jane's Weapons Systems* (London: Jane's Information Group, 1988); James W. Rawles, "U.S. Military Upgrades Its Battlefield Eyes and Ears," *Defense Electronics*, vol. 20 (February 1988), pp. 56–70; Martin Streetly, "US Airborne Elint Systems, pt. 5: The U.S. Army," *Jane's Defence Weekly*, April 27, 1985, pp. 726–28; and Mark Hewish and others, "Reconnaissance and Combat Drones," *International Defense Review*, vol. 20 (September 1987), pp. 1197–1203.
n.a. Not available.

area, though not as far as the AWACS aircraft, the depth of surveillance into enemy territory will probably be no more than 150 to 200 kilometers.[113]

Britain and France have also been developing airborne battlefield surveillance systems, though both nations rely on much less capable radars carried on small, low-altitude platforms. The British program known as ASTOR for Airborne Stand-Off Radar utilizes the small, low-flying Pilatus Britten Defender aircraft while the French ORCHIDEE system was to be fitted to special helicopters.[114] Besides using stand-off airborne radars, several alliance members are also developing long-range remotely piloted vehicles (RPVs) to collect intelligence.[115]

The fixed NATO air command and control centers in the central region are linked by various communications systems, many of which have already been described. The Ace High/CIP-67 network provides the primary link between the ATAF headquarters and their SOCS/ATOCs with the PTTs also carrying much of the traffic. Below this level such nationally operated military systems as the Defense Communications System, STARRNET, and the German air force communications network in combination with leased PTT circuits bear the burden. The U.S. air bases are also linked by their own satellite communications network.[116] As for the mobile parts of NATO's air command and control system, principally the CRPS, ASOCS/ADOLTS, FACPS, and TACPS, the main communications links are microwave, high-frequency radio and, if in range, very-high-frequency and ultrahigh-frequency radio. In an effort to facilitate the exchange of information at the tactical level, NATO has also established common data transmission and message-formatting standards for spe-

---

113. See Joachim Heyden, "Forewarned Is Forearmed—Different Reconnaissance, Surveillance and Target Acquisition Systems for FOFA," *NATO's Sixteen Nations*, vol. 32 (August 1987), p. 40; Stephen Broadbent, "Joint-STARS: Force Multiplier for Europe," *Jane's Defence Weekly*, April 18, 1987, pp. 730–32; and Ramon Lopez, "JSTARS Development Progresses," *International Defense Review*, vol. 20 (September 1987), pp. 1188–91.

114. ORCHIDEE stands for Observatoire Radar Coherent Heliporte d'Investigation des Elements Enemis. The system has now been canceled. See "French Army Approval for ORCHIDEE," *Jane's Defence Weekly*, March 1, 1988, p.353; "France Boosts EW Force," *Jane's Defence Weekly*, March 4, 1989, p. 352. Before the recent changes, the developers of these three systems were working on ways to make their associated ground stations interoperable in some way. It is not known whether this effort continues, at least between Britain and the United States.

115. See Mark Hewish, "Unmanned Aerial Vehicles, Part 1: European Programs," *International Defense Review*, vol. 22 (April 1989), pp. 449–57.

116. Under the NATO Air Base Satellite Communications program, U.S. airbases in the region have each been given their own SATCOM terminal.

cific communications links. For instance the standard data link for NATO's air defense network is Link 1 or Tactical Data Link A, in the U.S. nomenclature.

How would NATO's present air command and control system stand up to the stress and friction of wartime operations? Unfortunately, the outlook is not encouraging for three basic reasons. The first concerns the survivability of the main command posts and their supporting communications systems. While the ATOCs and SOCs are all housed in hardened facilities, they are not uniformly protected.[117] There is also little redundancy should any of them be put out of commission. NATO contingency plans stipulate that the SOCs and ATOCs be able to take over the responsibilities of each other in each ATAF region, but doubts exist over whether the centers could handle the additional work load.[118] The situation has improved, however, in the 4ATAF region with the modernization of ATOC Sembach and Mestetten to function as SOCs. The subordinate conduct reporting centers that are not colocated can reportedly also function as emergency SOCs, but most of these centers are situated within fixed semihardened facilities, which cannot be expected to escape destruction for very long in wartime.[119] If the CRCs are destroyed, then the mobile, more survivable CRPs will offer some back-up service, but they cannot fully substitute for the CRCs. Again the situation seems better in the 4ATAF region where there is also the U.S. TACS system with its new modular control equipment. Finally the AWACS aircraft will be of assistance although the NATO variants—unlike their U.S.-operated counterparts—are really only radar relay platforms with a limited capability to act as airborne command and control centers. Furthermore, they can only downlink this information to message processing centers and CRCs rather than directly to the Hawk and Patriot air defense units.

The fixed NATO radar sites with their exposed and radiating antennas are even more vulnerable than the command posts they serve.[120] They

117. Dan Boyle, "C³—The Essential Ingredient to Air Defense," *International Defense Review*, vol. 123 (June 1978), pp. 862–63.

118. Mitre Corp., USAF *Eifel 1 Functional Description*, p. 33; and interviews.

119. Hooton, "NADGE Enhancements Lay Groundwork for ACCS," p. 781. James L. Freeh, "Options for the European Theatre Air Command and Control System," *Signal*, vol. 38 (December 1983), p. 76; and interviews.

120. See Conrad J. Rauch and Walter R. Edgington, "NATO Develops a Long-Term Air Command and Control Plan," *Defense Systems Review*, vol. 2 (January 1984), pp. 12–17; and Freeh, "Options for the European Theatre, p. 75.

too are not expected to last very long in a conventional conflict. This will leave NATO relying on the mobile, low-level radars and, moreover, on its fleet of AWACS aircraft. Opinions differ, however, over the survivability of AWACS. Since the enemy can be expected to go to considerable lengths to jam or destroy these vital surveillance assets, some maintain that their prospects for survival are not good.[121] Others believe, however, that the AWACS aircraft will be able to operate out of harm's way over NATO's rear areas and still render effective service. They will almost certainly be given a fighter escort as well.[122] Also, if NATO's fleet of AWACS suffers heavy attrition, it can be augmented by the U.S. force. These forces train several times each year in the European theater.[123]

Similar doubts have been raised about the survivability of the JSTARS aircraft in wartime. They too will be obvious targets for the Warsaw Pact. Although supporters of JSTARS argue that these aircraft will be able to operate effectively under wartime conditions through a variety of countermeasures (fighter protection, antijam devices, and by operating well to the rear of the front), this assessment is not shared by all.[124] For example, an Office of Technology Assessment study concluded, "Even with such protection, Joint STARS would probably be vulnerable to fixed and mobile SAMs and to interceptor aircraft if operated, early in a war, at the setback range originally planned. If operated at a greater range from the FLOT [Forward Line of Troops], its vulnerability would decrease, but so would its coverage."[125] Others have questioned how useful JSTARS will be for NATO forces operating in areas adjacent to the U.S. corps sectors since the ground support modules used to downlink

121. See opinion of Tom Amlie in *The Independent*, October 5, 1987, referenced in the Defense Department's *Current News: Early Bird Edition*, October 7, 1987, p. 1.

122. One senior NATO officer interviewed stated that the AWACS aircraft could operate from as far back as the English Channel and still render valuable service for the air defense of the central region. Although at this distance the curvature of the earth would prevent radar observation of targets below 500 feet, it is apparently still possible to track aircraft above 1,000 feet. See also Schlitz, "C³ for the European Air War," p. 64.

123. See "USAF to Increase E-3A Effectiveness in Europe," *Aviation Week and Space Technology*, August 12, 1985, p. 57.

124. See *Department of Defense Appropriations for 1987*, Hearings before the Subcommittee on the Department of Defense of the House Committee on Appropriations, 99 Cong. 2 sess. (GPO, 1986), pp. 674–76; and Office of Technology Assessment, *New Technology for NATO*, p. 147.

125. Office of Technology Assessment, *New Technology for NATO*, p. 149.

the imagery will reportedly be furnished only to U.S. Army and Air Force units.[126]

Besides the vulnerability of the main command posts and surveillance systems, the supporting communications networks are also likely to suffer from direct and indirect attack. Two experts even go so far as to conclude, "The present linkage between sensors and command posts suffers from incompatibility, inflexibility, and *severe vulnerability.*"[127] More specific deficiencies have been identified: The links between the CRCs, for instance, are apparently "insecure both electronically and physically."[128] NATO's heavy reliance on the PTT network is also seen as a liability in wartime.[129] Furthermore, "NATO's primary tactical communications, Link 1, is non-secure."[130]

The implications of these communications vulnerabilities are difficult to judge without further information. While it appears as if 4ATAF has more redundant facilities at its disposal, 2ATAF is believed by some to be better able to adapt should command and control be disrupted or lost completely. The reason stems from an apparent doctrinal difference between the two tactical air forces over the employment of airpower. Whereas the U.S.-dominated 4ATAF evidently favors more centralized and continuous command and control to coordinate the many different supporting elements involved in penetrating enemy air space, 2ATAF evidently prefers smaller and more autonomous offensive operations in the belief that command and control cannot be taken for granted in wartime.[131] Although 2ATAF's approach can be seen to be making a virtue out of a necessity, it may prove to be more prudent.

126. "Joint STARS Interoperability with NATO Air Command and Control System Questioned," *Inside the Pentagon's Electronic Combat Report,* March 18, 1988, p. 6.

127. Rauch and Edgington, "NATO Develops a Long-Term Air Command and Control Plan," p. 14 (emphasis added).

128. Air Commodore Johannes A. Gijzen, "Operational Aspects and Broad Requirements for the NATO Air Command and Control System," in *NATO C³: The Challenges of the '80s,* NATO Symposium, 1981 (Brussels: Armed Forces Communications and Electronics Association, 1981), p. 5.

129. Rauch and Edgington, "NATO Develops a Long-Term Air Command and Control Plan," p. 12.

130. Quotation from Brig. Gen. Charles P. Winters, in Len Famiglietti, "AWACS under Threat by Improved Soviet Jamming," *Jane's Defence Weekly,* February 21, 1987, p. 256.

131. See Wing Commander Jeremy G. Saye, "Close Air Support in Modern Warfare," *Air University Review,* vol. 31 (January–February 1980), pp. 17–18; and Col. Rudolf F. Peksens, NATO Offensive Air Strategy in the Central Region: TWOATAF and

The second basic shortcoming of NATO's present air command and control system concerns its apparent tactical rigidity. Many experts believe that in an era of multirole aircraft, the separation of offensive and defensive air operations into two discrete planning and control organizations has outlived its usefulness. It is argued—particularly in U.S. Air Force circles—that as a consequence of this divided command arrangement, NATO can neither make optimum use of its air resources nor take advantage of the flexibility of some aircraft to switch missions on short notice.[132] Similar criticisms have also been leveled at the planning and execution of NATO's offensive air operations.[133] Once aircraft have been committed to a specific mission or set of targets, which is usually twenty-four hours in advance, there is evidently little latitude for change should a more pressing requirement arise. Advance planning is particularly difficult for close air support since specific mission needs are not always evident a day in advance. As a result, in exercises the corps commanders often request close air support for their specific area in anticipation of a requirement that may or may not materialize.[134]

NATO's inflexibility in this area is compounded by the unsatisfactory performance of the Eifel data processing system that underlies the whole air tasking process. In addition to its incompatibility with the CCIS network, Eifel is easily overloaded in exercises approximating wartime conditions, which causes long delays in the transmission of orders and the receipt of information. Even at the best of times Eifel's operators find it an "unfriendly" system to use.[135] A follow-on system known as Eifel II, which aims to expand the capacity of the mainframe computers and also rewrite some of the software, will, it is hoped, improve matters.

The third and arguably most grievous deficiency of NATO's air command and control system is the lack of an effective aircraft identifica-

---

FOURATAF *Contrasted,* Research Report, National War College (Washington: National Defense University, 1986).

132. Interviews. Air Commodore Johannes A. Gijzen and David A. Facey, "Planning for the Air Command and Control System: Views from SHAPE and NATO," *Signal,* vol. 36 (December 1981), p. 14.

133. See John P. Crecine, "C³I across the Seams of Military Organizations," in Merritt, Reed, and Weissinger-Baylon, *Crisis Decision Making,* p. 26-13.

134. Interviews. In fairness, some aircraft, notably the RAF Harriers, are reportedly very responsive to immediate requests for assistance.

135. These observations were made in several different interviews.

tion system. Currently NATO uses a variety of identification friend or foe (IFF) methods, all of which suffer from serious shortcomings. The most common is the cooperative method whereby aircraft are actively interrogated by electronic black boxes that then identify the aircraft by coded responses. The main NATO MK XII system for accomplishing this task is a 1950s vintage design that can easily be jammed and spoofed by an enemy. Its carrier frequencies and signal characteristics are also very similar to those used by air traffic controllers, leading to mutual interference. Moreover, not all of the allies have adopted the MK XII; some still rely on the even older MK X. As a result there are major interoperability problems among the different systems.[136] The other, noncooperative IFF methods rely on radar and other sensors to identify aircraft by their distinguishing characteristics. This is not a precise method since sensors are subject to environmental factors and operator error. In some cases the sensors depend on timely and secure communications links between the sensor platform, such as AWACS, and friendly air defense forces, which cannot be guaranteed. Thus, as a General Accounting Office study concluded in 1986, "The United States and NATO forces cannot identify aircraft at beyond visual ranges, at night, or in bad weather with a high degree of confidence."[137]

The operational consequence of the IFF problem is that NATO's air defenses must either limit their use to visual-range engagements only, which not only reduces their full potential but also risks being too late, or it can accept the danger that large numbers of friendly aircraft may be shot down by mistake. According to some NATO officials, who base their estimates on peacetime exercises, as many as 20 percent to 40 percent of NATO aircraft could be lost to this form of fratricide.[138] The

136. For current shortcomings see Harald Grammüller, "NATO Identification System (NIS)," *Signal,* vol. 36 (December 1981), p. 87; Michael Feazel, "IFF System Upgrade Will Improve Beyond-Visual Range Capabilities," *Aviation Week and Space Technology,* August 12, 1985, pp. 56–57; Melissa Healy, "Can NATO Fighter Pilots Distinguish Friend from Foe?" *Defense Week,* June 11, 1984, pp. 6–7; and Dan Boyle, "NIS: A New Identification System for NATO," *International Defense Review,* vol. 13 (March 1980), p. 352.

137. General Accounting Office, *Aircraft Identification—Improved Aircraft Identification Capabilities: A Critical Need,* GAO/NSIAD-86-181 (August 1986), p. 3.

138. Johannes Steinhoff, "Friend or Foe?" *NATO's Sixteen Nations,* vol. 29 (November–December 1984), p. 44; *Department of Defense Appropriations for 1988,* Hearings before the Subcommittee on the Department of Defense of the House Committee on Appropriations, 100 Cong. 1 sess. (GPO, 1987), pt. 6, p. 1133; After one REFORGER exercise prior to 1985 a NATO air commander reported that "friendly forces shot down all [his] aircraft in 5 days." See *Review of DOD's Combat Aircraft Identification Program,*

greatest danger comes from the growing proliferation of hand-held antiaircraft missiles on the battlefield. As recent conflicts, such as Afghanistan, have demonstrated, these missiles can be very potent against low-flying aircraft and helicopters. In wartime NATO intends to mitigate the risk of friendly aircraft being shot down from this source by designating air corridors known as low-level transit routes through which its aircraft can fly at certain times, with the knowledge that corresponding restrictions have also been placed on the use of ground-based air defenses.[139] While air space procedures are better than nothing, their effectiveness has been questioned nevertheless.[140] Some planners doubt whether they will be faithfully observed in the heat of battle or whether messages changing the status of certain zones will reach everyone in the field before operations begin. Air planners also find them restrictive in tying up portions of air space for long periods while the orders percolate down the army chain of command. Low-level transit routes, furthermore, may compromise the strike range of certain aircraft since they are likely to be routed around areas of heaviest fighting.

NATO is fully aware of these shortcomings and is on the verge of a massive modernization effort to upgrade and restructure virtually every component of its air command and control system. The present separation of offensive and defensive tasking by the ATOCs and SOCs is to be consolidated and carried out by Combined Air Operations Centers (CAOCs). By contrast the surveillance and control functions of the CRCs and CRPs are to be separated. In their place mobile sensor fusion posts will collect surveillance data from their reporting posts and in turn feed this information to recognized air picture production centers located within the new CAOCs. These centers, as their name suggests, will

Hearing before the Subcommittee on Legislation and National Security of the House Committee on Government Operations, 99 Cong. 1 sess. (GPO, 1985), p. 11. In another NATO exercise it was reported that 25 percent of all simulated missiles fired were accidentally aimed at friendly forces. See "NATO Fighters Shooting Friendlies," C^3I Report, November 3, 1986, p. 2.

139. These are broadcast as part of the daily air coordination order but can be changed every eight hours. See NATO, Military Agency for Standardization, *Doctrine and Procedures for Airspace Control in the Combat Zone,* ATP-40 (Washington: Department of the Air Force, January 1977).

140. *Review of DOD's Combat Aircraft Identification Program,* p. 22; and interviews. SACEUR Gen. Bernard W. Rogers described them as "cumbersome, nonresponsive procedures." See *Department of Defense Authorization for Appropriations for Fiscal Year 1986,* Hearings before the Senate Armed Services Committee, 99 Cong. 1 sess. (GPO, 1985), pt. 3, p. 1438.

correlate the incoming data to form a near real-time picture of the unfolding air battle that will then be distributed virtually simultaneously throughout the region. The control of air operations will in the future be handled by Air Control Centers (ACCS) and their subordinate air control units (ACUS). Finally, separate operations centers will be created to coordinate surface-to-air missile activities. Linking each of these elements will be a high-speed digitalized communications backbone system.[141]

Separate but related programs are also under way to improve NATO's air communications and replace the present IFF system. The first, known as the Multifunction Information Distribution System (MIDS), is the NATO version of the U.S. Joint Tactical Information Distribution System (JTIDS). Thousands of new radio terminals will be fitted to virtually every class of NATO aircraft so that they can automatically exchange position, navigation, and targeting information in a jam-proof fashion.[142] After much interallied wrangling the old MK XII IFF systems are also to be replaced under the planned NATO Identification System program. A new and, it is hoped, more secure and effective transponder system known as the MK XV will become standard equipment.[143]

Not everyone is convinced of the wisdom of some of the planned changes or pleased with the pace at which many of these modernization plans are expected to take effect. The MK XV IFF decision, for instance, amounts to a technical compromise among competing operating frequencies that, according to one senior NATO official, "has in fact emasculated the potential of the new equipment to overcome some of the deficiencies which beset the current MK 10A and MK 12 IFF systems."[144] Given that literally every NATO aircraft, radar, and surface-to-air missile system

141. For an excellent description of the ACCS program and its generic architecture see Ronald A. Enlow, "ACCS Architecture Evaluation—A Near-Term Application of TACCSF," in *Information and Consultation: Keys to Peace*, pp. 36–38. See also in the same edition Maj. Gen. R. Pelsmaeker, "Consultation Considerations in the ACCS Team," pp. 89–91.

142. See Glenn W. Goodman, Jr., "NATO Version of JTIDS Moves toward Full-Scale Development," *Armed Forces Journal International*, vol. 126 (December 1988); and Dan Boyle, "MIDS, Son of JTIDS: The Vital Link," *International Defense Review*, vol. 21 (October 1988), pp. 1325–28. This program is running into difficulties; see "Shrinking MIDS," *International Defense Review*, vol. 22 (August 1989), p. 1017.

143. See David Hughes, "USAF Selects Allied-Signal/Raytheon to Develop NATO-Compatible IFF," *Aviation Week and Space Technology*, December 5, 1988, p. 26.

144. Gabriel Ferenczy, "NATO Identification System," *NATO's Sixteen Nations*, vol. 33 (September 1988), p. 53.

will have to be fitted with a new IFF transponder, the modernization program will take the rest of this century to complete, during which time the interoperability problem will get worse. Similar problems reportedly threaten to compromise the full effectiveness of the long-heralded MIDS program. The new Class 2 communications terminals are evidently not compatible with the interim Class 1 equipment that has already been fitted to NATO's AWACS aircraft and its associated ground stations. Unless modifications are carried out, NATO aircraft using one system will be unable to communicate with those using the other.[145]

The Air Command and Control System plan to combine the Allied Tactical Operations Centers and Sector Operations Centers into four large Combined Air Operations Centers has been criticized for three reasons: first, the plan will make it easier for the Warsaw Pact to paralyze NATO's command system by reducing the number of targets it needs to attack; second, the versatility of multirole aircraft has been exaggerated since their crews are still trained for one mission; and third, the creation of the CAOCs will undermine the operational role of the ATAF headquarters and cause friction between the two echelons.[146]

With an estimated price tag of $25 billion, albeit to be spread over ten to fifteen years, the Air Command and Control System program had attracted a fair number of doubters even before the dramatic changes in European security took place. The ACCS program, as one senior NATO air force commander wrote, "will barely reach minimum standards, watered down far into the next century although it can clearly be seen that the rapid technological progress will confront us with even greater challenges before the year 2000."[147] Given what has occurred, the ACCS program is sure to be pared down considerably from its earlier plans.

The Tactical Level: The Ground Battle

The command and control challenges facing NATO's ground forces at the tactical level are in certain basic respects no different from those

145. Karen Walker, "NATO admits JTIDS Incompatibility Problem," *Jane's Defence Weekly,* March 28, 1987, p. 527. The frequency that MIDS will operate on—to be known as Link 16—apparently also overlaps the one used by civil air traffic controllers in Europe. Interview.

146. Interviews. This is disputed by some who argue that the ATAF will retain "operational command," while the CAOCs will have "operational control."

147. Maj. Gen. J. A. Bahnemann, "Extending Air Defence—A Test Case for the Western Alliance," *NATO's Sixteen Nations,* vol. 33 (September 1988), p. 48.

Table 5-4. *Areas of Interest and Influence for Different Levels of Command*

	Areas of interest			Areas of influence	
Level of command	Hours beyond FLOT[a]	Miles (km) beyond FLOT[a]	Level of command	Hours beyond FLOT[a]	Miles (km) beyond FLOT[a]
Battalion	0–12	9 (15)	Battalion	0–3	3 (5)
Brigade	0–24	43 (70)	Brigade	0–12	9 (15)
Division	0–72	93 (150)	Division	0–24	43 (70)
Corps	0–96	186 (300)	Corps	0–72	93 (150)
Echelon above corps	96+ hours	621+ (1,000+)	Echelon above corps	72+ hours	93+ (150+)

Source: Kennedy and others, *Intelligence Warfare*, p. 150.
a. FLOT, forward line of own troops.

described earlier for the operational level. The army corps and subordinate commanders must anticipate enemy actions in time to counter them effectively by maneuvering forces and applying firepower at key times and places on the battlefield. The main difference is that the command cycle time shortens as the size of the unit diminishes. While forces and firepower also become more flexible and responsive military instruments, this attibute applies to the offense as well as the defense, hence the compression in response time. The area of responsibility also contracts with smaller units, but so too does their area of influence. Although the operations of the corps are the primary focus of attention here, table 5-4 illustrates the diminishing operating horizons of subordinate tactical units.

Most discussions of corps operations divide their command responsibilities into three categories. The first consists of fighting the "deep battle," which means monitoring and, if possible, targeting enemy forces to approximately 150 kilometers beyond the forward edge of the battle area. It also means drawing up the appropriate plans and making the necessary adjustments to the corps military posture in anticipation of enemy activity several days hence. The second consists of fighting the immediate "close-in" battle at the front and responding to requests for fire support from assets under corps control. The third command responsibility is to maintain the security of the corps rear areas against attacks by covertly infiltrated forces and other threats, which is sometimes known as fighting the "rear battle."

Since command and control at the tactical level is essentially a national responsibility, one can argue that NATO faces less of a problem. The units that make up the national corps groupings regularly train together, using common equipment according to familiar operating procedures. Moving forces and directing firepower within corps boundaries therefore presents fewer challenges than the multinational coordination necessary at higher levels of command. Though likely to be true for some engagements, it is fundamentally wrong to believe—and NATO to its credit is beginning to accept this fact—that the individual corps arrayed along the central front can and would fight their own separate, self-contained battles. As General Nigel Bagnall, a former COMNORTHAG, has observed, "Soviet thrusts are not going to be obligingly directed at individual corps but will spill over into neighboring ones. In fact, even a cursory study of the map suggests that at least one major Soviet thrust would be directed along what is an inter-corps boundary."[148] NATO clearly cannot afford to fight as a loosely coupled collection of national armies. Close coordination is essential not only to harness the full military potential of new weapons systems that permit cross-corps targeting but also to prevent the seams among allied units from becoming a fatal defensive vulnerability.

Finally at the same time as the national corps must be tightly bound laterally, they must also be vertically integrated to pass information up to and commands down from NATO's operational commanders. The linkages between the tactical and operational levels are just as vital as those among the corps.

Whereas tactical air operations are almost solely directed from fixed command posts, NATO's smaller and corps-size ground forces are generally controlled from mobile headquarters that would disperse to the field. Though variations exist among and sometimes even within allied units, the organization of corps headquarters is basically the same among NATO allies. Besides an Air Support Operations Center and an Air Defense Liaison Team, each corps maintains in general a rear headquarters that handles, among other things, logistical and administrative support, a main command post responsible for planning and monitoring combat operations, and an alternate command post that is usually forwardly deployed and can substitute for the main headquarters if necessary. The British call the alternate a "step-up" command post, while the U.S. forces refer to it as the "tactical" command post.[149] While

148. Bagnall, "Concepts of Land/Air Operations: I," p. 62.
149. See Isby and Kamps, *Armies of NATO's Central Front,* p. 300; Headquarters, Department of the Army, *Combat Communications within the Corps,* FM 11-92 (Washing-

the rear headquarters remains relatively static, usually being located where there is some protection, the main corps command posts would probably move every twenty-four hours to avoid enemy targeting, although in some cases moving so frequently may simply be too disruptive to operations. Headquarters units are also not deployed in tightly clustered formations, as is the popular conception; they can be separated by many miles, albeit connected by land line or radio.

As table 5-3 indicates, the intelligence assets available to each NATO army corps vary considerably. The U.S. sectors are by far the most well equipped. The U.S. corps also receive the product of the vast national reconnaissance apparatus often simultaneously with the USAREUR intelligence center. Allied corps with access to fewer intelligence assets would, as a consequence, rely heavily on information provided by the army group headquarters or by adjacent corps. Each of the corps has transportable CCIS and LOCE terminals to receive information when deployed to the field.[150] Some of the corps—principally those that operate significant intelligence assets of their own—have fielded modern automated data systems to distribute battlefield intelligence among forces in their area. Artillery and rocket fire support has also been automated in most of the corps. The different systems are listed in table 5-5. Since the main corps communications networks that serve as the bearers of these systems are not directly interoperable, data cannot be passed automatically among the allied corps headquarters. With the appropriate connecting devices, such data transfers are possible, however.[151]

Army corps typically rely on a range of tactical communications nets for maintaining command and control within their area of responsibility.[152] The main command posts are usually linked by way of a network of multichannel FM-VHF radio relays mounted on trucks, although

ton, November 1978), p. 1–8; and U.S. Army Command and General Staff College, *Corps and Division Command and Control,* Field Circular, FC 101-55 (Ft. Leavenworth, Kans., February 1985), pp. 4-12–4-15.

150. The Bundeswehr also operates what is known as the Dedicated Intelligence Loop Circuit (DILC), which links the NORTHAG corps headquarters for the purpose of exchanging information. Interviews.

151. See Siegfried Seiffert, "Technical Interoperability of the Command, Control and Information System in the Central Region," *Military Technology,* vol. 11 (May 1987), pp. 92–95.

152. For good general descriptions of tactical communications see Maj. M. S. Wilson-Brown, "Tactical Communications Army," *NATO's Fifteen Nations,* vol. 25, Special Issue (February 1980), pp. 55–58; and Bill Bowen, "The Commander's Imperative—Communications in the Battle Area," *NATO's Sixteen Nations,* vol. 31 (October 1986), pp. 66–73.

tactical troposcatter radio is sometimes used for communications among relatively fixed sites. Mobile nodal switches located throughout the corps area control the flow and distribution of messages. High-frequency AM radio is also usually available though most commonly as a backup. For communications at the brigade level and below, single-channel (FM-VHF) combat net radio is the norm. At certain locations field telephone cable is also laid to supplement radio. Land lines, however, are more commonly found at the main command posts to tie together the covertly dispersed headquarters elements. Finally, some of the corps—notably the U.S. ones—also have tactical satellite links at their disposal, but they are generally used for rearward communications.

By the early 1990s NATO's ground forces deployed in Germany will all have either just completed or just begun a major overhaul of their battlefield communications equipment. The current and expected communications systems of each corps, including the French army, is listed in table 5-5. Unfortunately none of the communications systems fielded by the forces along the central front is directly interoperable with those of its neighboring corps. Only the French and Belgian forces equipped with RITA, and possibly the U.S corps when it takes delivery of its version of the same system, will be able to talk directly with each other.[153] To get around this problem, NATO countries have reached a series of standardization agreements (STANAGs) resulting in the development of special conversion devices or, black boxes, which can connect their incompatible communications systems together.

Under NATO's standing operating procedures, responsibility for establishing communications runs from the top downward and from left to right.[154] The army group headquarters, therefore, would establish the communications links down from their command posts to their subordinate corps, which in turn tie themselves together laterally from north to south along the front. Thus in practice the Dutch I Corps, in the northernmost sector of the central region, sends a Zodiac signal detachment to the German I Corps headquarters, which in turn runs an AUTOKO link to the neighboring British I Corps. The Belgian I Corps is likewise connected to the British by way of Ptarmigan and so on along the central

153. Even this situation might be problematic, however, since different encryption devices can, as noted, affect interoperability.

154. See STANAG 5048, referenced in NATO, Military Agency for Standardization, *Land Force Tactical Doctrine*, ATP-35(A) (Washington: Department of the Air Force, April 1987), p. 2-7.

Table 5-5. *NATO Central Region Corps Communications and
Data Processing Systems*

Country	Main corps communications system	Combat net radio system	Automated data processing system	Artillery fire support system
Netherlands	Zodiac	n.a.	n.a.	Verdac
Federal Republic of Germany	AUTOKO	SEM 70, 80, 90	Heros	Adler
United Kingdom	Ptarmigan	Clansman	Wavell	Bates
Belgium	RITA	Vera	n.a.	n.a.
United States	TRI-TAC, mobile subscriber equipment	SINCGARS	Maneuver control system	TACFIRE, AFATDS
Canada	TCCS	AN-VRC 12 GRC-106	n.a.	n.a.
France	RITA	TRC 920, 930, 950 TRPP 11, 13, TRVP 213, TRAP 111 (PR4G)	Sacra	Attila 2

Sources: William F. de Dufour, *Army Communications Interoperability with NATO Nations*, MTR-8016 (McLean, Va.: Mitre Corp., 1979); Giovanni de Briganti, "Dutch Army Orders New Automatic Communications System," *Defense News*, February 1, 1988, p. 6; John G. Roos, "Allies C³I Modernization Plans Rely upon Locally Produced Equipment," *Armed Forces Journal International*, vol. 125 (February 1988), pp. 54–56; Rupert Pengelley, "HEROS and Wavell: Battlefield ADP Enters a New Era," *International Defense Review*, vol. 19, no. 10 (1986), pp. 1459–63; Gerard Turbé, "From the TRC 900 to the PR4G: French Frequency-Hopping Combat Net Radios," *International Defense Review*, vol. 21, no. 9 (1988), p. 1183; Lt. Col. Hans-Peter Krause and Dieter Roth, "Tactical VHF Radio Communications in the German Army," *Signal*, vol. 37 (November 1982), pp. 27–32; and Mark Hewish, "Tactical Area Communications, Part 1: European Systems," *International Defense Review*, vol 23, no. 5 (1990), pp. 523–26.
    n.a. Not available.

front. In most cases the links are effected by the black-box devices just described. In wartime, the corps division and brigade commanders would also send liaison officers, equipped with radios, to the headquarters of adjoining units according to the same left-to-right principle.

NATO has made considerable progress in recent years improving its command and control arrangements at the tactical level. Arguably the most significant development has been a growing acceptance of the need for greater integration in the execution of allied operations. The widely accepted if not openly acknowledged conviction that each of the corps would fight its own battle in its assigned area with loose guidance from the army group commanders is now being replaced by a greater appreciation of the need for combined operations. This emphasis is particularly evident in the NORTHAG area of operations. NATO forces now regularly conduct exercises where division- and brigade-sized units are placed under the command of another unit. Multinational maneuvers that involve mutual reinforcement and fire support are also practiced.[155] To facilitate such joint operations NATO has revised and standardized many of its battlefield-coordinating procedures, notably those used for performing such difficult maneuvers as the passage of lines where the forces of one unit pass through or relieve the forces of another. These too have been practiced in recent REFORGER field exercises.

Although these signs are encouraging, considerable room remains for improvement in other key areas. As emphasized throughout this chapter, NATO can expect a significant part of a Warsaw Pact attack to be directed at disrupting and paralyzing its command system. At the tactical level, the corps command posts are the most obvious targets to attack and for this reason considerable effort is likely to be put into locating and destroying them.[156] In theory NATO plans to maintain the operation of its command posts through a combination of camouflage, frequent location changes, deceptive measures, and dispersed deployments. Yet in exercises there has been a marked reluctance—at least on the part of some corps—to implement these measures faithfully. For example, several U.S. Army officers interviewed noted a general resistance to moving corps command posts on a regular basis because of the effort and disruption involved.[157] Even frequent moves may not suffice since the latest intelligence sensors are making the task of hiding command posts increasingly difficult. One U.S. Army officer has declared, "Locating the huge electronic orgies that constitute our divisional and corps CPs is terrifyingly simple. It is unlikely that a single division or corps CP in a priority sector will survive the first 24-48 hours of war unless we immediately focus our efforts on wrecking the enemy's IEW [intelligence and electronic warfare] system."[158] If this statement is indeed a fair assessment of command post vulnerabilities, NATO exercises will have to emphasize simulating and adapting to command degradation much more than they do now.

155. See "Beyond the Corps Battle," p. 169; and interview with Gen. Glenn K. Otis, CENTAG Commander/Command U.S. Army Europe, Seventh Army, in *Field Artillery Journal*, vol. 55 (January–February 1987), p. 33.

156. See app. E, "NATO Command Posts under Attack," in Michael Sadykiewicz, *Soviet-Warsaw Pact Western Theater of Military Operations: Organization and Missions*, N-2596-AF (Santa Monica, Calif.: Rand Corp., August 1987).

157. One senior U.S. officer described the corps headquarters as having "feet of concrete."

158. Capt. Ralph Peters, "The Age of Fatal Visibility," *Military Review*, vol. 68 (August 1988), p. 56. See also Col. Richard M. Scott, Lt. Col. Julian M. Campbell, Jr.,

The management and distribution of intelligence at the tactical level in NATO is another area that warrants improvement. As indicated earlier, the provision of intelligence assets along the central front is quite uneven. At one end of the spectrum are the U.S. corps that directly control or have access to considerable intelligence resources while at the other end are the Belgian and Dutch corps that have almost nothing. The NORTHAG forces, in general, are not well catered to in this regard. Although the collection systems belonging to the U.S. III Corps would probably be called on for assistance, they are not expected to arrive in the theater until one to two weeks after mobilization. Their support is not axiomatic either, since they will still technically be under national control once they arrive.

The disparity in intelligence assets would not be so significant if NATO had a well-established system for laterally exchanging battlefield intelligence at the corps level and below. The most likely route for intelligence collected by one corps that could be of interest to another is for the intelligence to be passed up to the army group headquarters (perhaps first by way of a higher-level nationally run intelligence center), where it is reviewed and passed back down to the relevant corps. This arrangement is hardly conducive to timely exchanges of information. The current arrangement, as General E. B. Atkeson has remarked, "would appear to be a formula for catastrophic dysfunction."[159] Although some of the corps appear to have reached understandings with adjacent forces to share their intelligence more directly in wartime, ad hoc links are unlikely to function quickly or smoothly if they are not routinely exercised. For example, the ability of a non-U.S. corps to request and make use of U.S. intelligence offered to it is clearly limited if that corps is unfamiliar with the capabilities of the collection assets and unskilled in interpreting their product. As it is, the capacity of the current intercorps communications links to pass large quantities of intelligence data is suspect.[160] The differing communications security standards and encryption devices used by the allies complicate matters further. The BICES program, it is hoped, will redress this basic shortcom-

---

and Lt. Col. John R. Wallace, "Command Post Survivability," *Military Review*, vol. 62 (September 1982), pp. 12–20.

159. Atkeson, *Final Argument of Kings*, p. 207.

160. The DILC system, for example, has only a fifty-baud capacity that would be quickly overloaded in wartime.

ing but, as noted earlier, it will only be able to handle intelligence classified no higher than Secret.

Paradoxically, U.S. corps intelligence officers acknowledge that they are often swamped with more information than they can process and make use of. The capacity of their own communications systems to handle the streams of data from the latest sensors is of particular concern.[161] Correlating or fusing the collected data to furnish timely and comprehensive intelligence assessments is reportedly also becoming more difficult owing to the growing specialization of intelligence analysts. One U.S. officer has likened the situation to the medical profession in which general practitioners who can diagnose a range of ailments are being replaced by specialists who are knowledgeable only in their own field. Whether the creation of the All Source Analysis System (ASAS) at divisional and corps headquarters will remedy these problems remains to be seen.

Despite recent improvements, NATO communications at the tactical level still suffers from some grave deficiencies. The quality and paucity of secure voice communications are commonly heard complaints. The introduction of redundant and jam-resistant battlefield communications by the front line corps may have lessened their vulnerability to destruction and electronic countermeasures, but paradoxically it has exacerbated the interoperability problem. None of the allied combat net radios in or about to enter service, for example, can communicate with one another in a secure fashion.[162] This situation is particularly egregious in the U.S.-German case where the interoperability requirement is perhaps the least demanding. Yet the new U.S. SINCGARS tactical radio will not be able to talk to its German counterpart in the antijam mode.[163] This

161. There are contradictory reports over whether the new mobile subscriber equipment (MSE) will be able to handle the expected flow of intelligence. For more information see the exchange of letters in *Military Review,* vol. 68 (February 1988), pp. 88–89, and vol. 68 (September 1988), pp. 85–86.

162. Gen. John R. Galvin, "Foreword," *Signal,* vol. 43 (October 1988), pp. 27–28. And until some of the modernization programs are completed, there will be interoperability problems among units. For example U.S. Reserve and Guard forces will be the last to receive MSE equipment in the 1990s, yet these forces are a significant portion of the U.S. reinforcements to Europe. See *Department of Defense Appropriations for 1986,* Hearings before the Subcommittee on the Department of Defense of the House Committee on Appropriations, 99 Cong. 1 sess. (GPO, 1985), pt. 8, p. 184.

163. *Department of Defense Authorization for Appropriations for Fiscal Year 1987,* Hearings before the Senate Committee on Armed Services, 99 Cong. 2 sess. (GPO, 1986), pt 6, p.979.

example is not an aberration either. For example, adjacent U.S. and West German Hawk surface-to-air missile batteries cannot directly exchange information, even though in many cases they will be defending the same area. Although at higher levels the interoperability problem can be alleviated with the use of the NATO-procured conversion devices, this solution is not wholly satisfactory. Besides being expensive to buy and cumbersome to use, such devices slow down information flows and ultimately reduce operational flexibility.[164]

A different kind of interoperability problem is also inhibiting communications on the battlefield. The proliferation of radio users is making certain frequencies (especially the VHF bandwidth) so congested that mutual interference has become a common experience in recent field exercises.[165] Yet these exercises involve only a fraction of the radio users who can be anticipated in wartime (not forgetting the Warsaw Pact users). Nor do the exercises simulate the presence of friendly and enemy jamming, which will further crowd the usable parts of the electromagnetic spectrum. The corps communications officers have each established extremely complex planning documents to manage radio frequency use for their area of operations, but tremendous uncertainty surrounds these preparations. After lengthy planning, the U.S. III Corps, for example, has created elaborate communications and electronics operating instructions for its priority contingency in NORTHAG, but what if this situation should suddenly change? For the same reason, other corps signal officers may have to quickly amend their frequency management guidelines, owing to the unanticipated presence of allied forces in their area. Although senior NATO communications planners expect some relief when specific frequencies normally reserved for civilian purposes are freed for military use in wartime, they admit privately, however, that considerable uncertainty exists about the timing of their release. The situation is not likely to be helped, moreover, by the absence of an integrated information system to coordinate the allocation of frequencies among the various signal command authorities in the central region.

Another problem concerns the provision and training of liaison

164. Interviews. See also the testimony of Donald C. Latham, assistant secretary of defense, in *Department of Defense Appropriations for 1987,* Hearings before the Subcommittee on the Department of Defense of the House Committee on Appropriations, 99 Cong. 2 sess. (GPO, 1986), pt. 3, p. 486.

165. Interviews. See also "British Army Experience with Ptarmigan and Wavell," p. 499.

personnel who would play such a pivotal role in coordinating allied operations in wartime. Although there are commonly established procedures for carrying out liaison duties, the seriousness with which NATO countries take this responsibility is anything but uniform. The United States, to name one country, does not typically send its best personnel to fill liaison positions. These officers are also rotated more frequently than is the case with some European armies, which does not help to foster steady relationships among allied units. Furthermore, because of cost-cutting moves, there is currently no provision for liaison personnel and the necessary communications equipment in the U.S. divisional and brigade table of organization and equipment. In wartime, personnel would be culled from in-place forces or from the reinforcements. It seems highly likely, therefore, that in wartime personnel neither adequately trained nor familiar with their assigned units would end up performing liaison duties.

Finally language differences could also affect allied coordination in wartime, although this problem does not seem serious. English is now spoken so commonly in Europe that it has become the unofficial operational language of NATO. Difficulties are reportedly experienced only in exchanges involving precise technical details or when secure voice equipment is used. The biggest problem that NATO is likely to face concerns the participation of French forces, which evidently have relatively few English speakers.[166]

Conclusion

This chapter has exposed serious shortcomings in each of the main levels of NATO's wartime command structure. Taken together they raise important questions about the capacity of NATO to prosecute effectively a prolonged conventional campaign in central Europe of the type it has traditionally planned to fight. Unfortunately a significant and vital portion of NATO's command system is highly vulnerable to deliberate attack by conventional means. As a result, many of the alliance's key command

---

166. Interviews. Since French is one of the official languages of NATO, French forces participating in exercises have been known to insist on their mother tongue being used even though the French are not part of the integrated military command structure.

posts, surveillance systems, intelligence processing centers, and communications networks are unlikely to survive a large-scale, high-intensity conflict. Worse still, many of them have little in the way of survivable backups. The haphazard and, in many instances, unplanned deployment of command and control support systems by NATO members—notably in data processing and communications equipment—has also created serious interoperability problems that are likely to hamper operations and reduce the alliance's full military potential. Similarly, organizational problems, especially concerning intelligence collection management and product dissemination, significantly limit the usefulness of the information resources available to NATO's commanders. Their capacity to make informed decisions about the deployment of forces and the application of firepower is, therefore, in some doubt.

Few within NATO, it seems, have appreciated the full extent of these problems. The fragmentation of responsibilities and expertise has encouraged this oversight and neglect. NATO's regular field exercises, moreover, do little to raise the level of consciousness. Despite the care and attention that go into making exercises as realistic as possible, command and control is usually treated in a wholly artificial manner. Thus communications are almost never jammed or deliberately degraded to simulate their potential loss in wartime.[167] Major headquarters are also allowed to function as if there were no threat to their operation. Thus their potential incapacitation, be it temporary or permanent, is never simulated. Nor do many of the mobile command posts and communications centers practice the regular movements that wartime conditions will surely demand. And commanders can always take advantage of the intelligence assets at their disposal in peacetime without learning to adapt to their possible absence in war. Finally since many of the exercises are so heavily scripted, members of the command staff gain little experience in managing the uncertainty that is a common feature of war.

Those responsible for providing command and control in NATO have tried to make the exercises more realistic, but they have encountered strong resistance. Since there are only so many exercises each year (and only so many in a conscript's tour of duty), there is widespread reluctance to risk having them degenerate into chaotic and disorganized events by degrading command and control. Exercises are for the soldiers and

167. Signal officers interviewed at every level of command in NATO admitted this deficiency.

airmen to practice their combat drills, maneuver, and fire their weapons; they are not for wasting time by waiting for orders while communications are restored. Consequently, NATO has trained its forces in an unrealistic operational environment in which command and control is taken largely for granted.

CHAPTER SIX

Recommendations for the Future

FOLLOWING THE changes that swept through Eastern Europe in 1988–89, NATO no longer faces the threat of a massive Soviet-led Warsaw Pact attack. Few people believe, however, that the demise of the Warsaw Pact signals the moment to disband the North Atlantic alliance. Although a revival of cold war antagonisms is not considered likely, great uncertainty persists about the fate of the Soviet Union. Similar concerns apply to the political and economic future of Moscow's erstwhile client states in Eastern Europe. In contrast, NATO appears a bedrock of stability and its security guarantees a valuable and relatively cost-free hedge against the unpredictabilities of the future. Furthermore, although emerging pan-European structures like the Conference on Security and Cooperation in Europe or revitalized security organizations like the Western European Union (WEU) hold out promise for the long term, they cannot be considered workable alternatives to NATO for the time being. The CSCE is still in an embryonic stage and has yet to prove that it can function collectively to deal with security threats to its members. Hopes for a common European security policy and defense organization were also deflated by the differences of opinion that divided Europe during the Persian Gulf crisis. At the same time the leadership and commitment of the United States were a reminder of the value of its security guarantees to Europe, something that only NATO embodies. The alliance, therefore, will be viewed as the primary security organization for some time to come.

To its credit, NATO has recognized that it must adapt to the changed circumstances in Europe. At the conclusion of the London Summit conference in July 1990, NATO declared its intention to reduce force levels still further, lower their operational readiness, change the military doctrine, develop diplomatic links to former members of the Warsaw Pact, and emphasize the political nature of the alliance. It also stated its intention to further the process of military integration by creating multinational corps made up of national units.[1] However, if NATO is to serve its members' interests and play a constructive role in the creation of a stable security regime in Europe, it must also change the organizational ethos and orientation of the alliance away from the now-diminished threat of premeditated aggression.

This suggestion does not mean that NATO should ignore Soviet military capabilities or remain unconcerned about the course of political reform in the Soviet Union—quite the contrary. Soviet military power will remain formidable even after the anticipated reductions in conventional forces in Europe (CFE) take place. NATO must remain keenly watchful of unfolding events for any signs that may presage a basic reversal of policy. Nevertheless, even if the political complexion of the Soviet Union changes dramatically for the worse, it seems extremely unlikely it would seek to reestablish its hegemony over Eastern Europe and even more improbable that it would pursue aggressive designs against Western Europe. The Soviet Union, however, might use forces selectively to intervene in conflicts beyond its borders if it felt its security was threatened. And armed strife within the Soviet Union might conceivably spread outside its territory and affect NATO members that have contiguous borders.

Similarly, while the possibility of open conflict in Eastern and particularly southeastern Europe clearly exists, the likelihood that NATO members would become the object of deliberate attack is equally implausible. Alliance members, however, could suffer the indirect effects of conflict in these areas. Large influxes of refugees, for example, could cause serious economic and social disruption. NATO countries might also become directly involved should conflict spill over onto their territory. Furthermore, pressure could grow in some alliance countries to restore order or to intervene militarily in response to pleas for assistance. Direct intervention was unthinkable during the cold war because of the clear risk of direct confrontation with the Soviet Union,

---

1. "London Declaration on a Transformed North Atlantic Alliance," NATO press communiqué S-1 (90) 36, Brussels, July 6, 1990.

but in the future this danger may seem less apparent, reducing the inhibitions of the past. The Soviets, however, are sure to remain extremely sensitive about any foreign incursions into an area they still consider their security buffer zone. Any ambiguities about intervention could prove highly escalatory in a crisis.

Thus, while the threat of cold-blooded aggression against NATO has virtually disappeared, the danger that NATO countries might become embroiled in a conflict has not. For this reason, the alliance should dedicate itself to the mission of crisis management and conflict prevention. This goal entails more than reducing force levels, lowering combat readiness, and reforming the alliance's military doctrine; it requires a basic overhaul and reorientation of NATO's command system. Changes must be effected, moreover, in a way that supports and complements the long-term goal of creating more inclusive security structures in Europe dedicated to the same goal.

The Short Term: Reorienting NATO

Much of what constitutes NATO's existing command system remains relevant to the future task of crisis management and conflict prevention. The established communications links and consultative mechanisms can help the alliance coordinate diplomatic efforts to diffuse potential crises while the allied command channels can help control national forces and prevent accidental or unauthorized uses of force. For this reason many of the relevant shortcomings identified in previous chapters need to be rectified. Other parts or established practices of NATO's command system, however, require more fundamental reform. The most important changes are necessary in the following areas: intelligence and warning, crisis consultation and communications, and alerting. NATO, furthermore, must adapt its wartime command arrangements and support programs to the radically changed situation in Europe.

Intelligence and Warning

Intelligence gathering and warning has traditionally been a national responsibility in NATO. Information that bears on the security of the alliance is expected to be shared promptly to facilitate collective action. Doubts have always existed, however, about the timeliness and comprehensiveness of intelligence inputs into NATO channels because the principal suppliers are reluctant under normal circumstances to share their best intelligence in the belief that the sources and methods used would be compromised by wider distribution. NATO's capacity to receive and disseminate large amounts of high-grade intelligence that may be dumped on it at short notice has also been questioned, as well as its ability to reach timely consensus on the meaning of the events reported.

With the threat of short-warning attack no longer a plausible concern, the pressure on NATO's intelligence and warning apparatus would seem to have lessened. However, the need for an effective system for information gathering and sharing within the alliance remains just as important, if not more so. Besides providing support to the emerging arms control regime in Europe, the primary task of NATO's intelligence-gathering effort is to provide member nations with timely and accurate warning of potentially destabilizing events in neighboring countries. With these requirements in mind, a strong case can be made for NATO to develop and operate its own intelligence collection system for this purpose. A reconnaissance satellite system with the appropriate support personnel and imagery interpreters is the most obvious candidate. Although duplicative of some existing capabilities, a reconnaissance satellite system would lessen the problem of relying totally on national, and particularly U.S., intelligence.[2] A NATO reconnaissance satellite could also become the prototype for a more inclusive information network serving Europe's security needs. Similar multilateral arrangements, furthermore, might be established for other sensor systems, such as JSTARS and the TR-1.[3]

For the foreseeable future, however, national technical means will bear the burden of information collection in NATO. For this reason NATO should upgrade current facilities and procedures for requesting and handling intelligence from member nations. This improvement should include expanding the number of secure communications circuits that

2. Three NATO countries, France, Italy, and Spain, are developing a military version of the French civil reconnaissance satellite SPOT. See Alessandro Politi, "Italy Plans Military Satellite Network for Early Warning, Reconnaissance," *Defense News*, January 7, 1991, p. 3. The WEU has also proposed joint development of a reconnaissance satellite. See Giovanni de Briganti, "Europeans Waver on New Spy Satellites," *Defense News*, August 27, 1990, p. 1.

3. Theresa Hitchins and George Leopold, "U.S. Pushes Verification Role for JSTARS," *Defense News*, October 22, 1990, p. 1.

pass sensitive information, as well as increasing the number of staff members cleared to handle it. NATO should also upgrade the training of intelligence personnel with the help of realistic exercises that use more plausible scenarios to prepare them for making intelligence assessments under pressure in a real crisis. The miscellaneous NATO and national indications and warning centers designed to collate and display information on the readiness of Pact forces must also be radically modified if they haven't been already. Though the standard military-related indicators will be important for monitoring Soviet forces and the now-independent national defense organizations of Eastern Europe, political and economic indicators should receive greater prominence.

To help NATO intelligence analysts interpret events in a crisis, it would also be desirable for them to have access to information on what actions alliance members are taking, either collectively or independently. Special intelligence units, sometimes referred to as Red Teams, could be established to help understand how the responses of the alliance in a crisis might be perceived and interpreted by other parties. In particular, information about NATO's military-related activity would obviously be of great use to them.[4] Direct links could be established, furthermore, between the different national and NATO intelligence centers to share information and assessments. The new BICES intelligence data handling system could be configured for this purpose.[5] Finally the alliance should consider how it can directly support the monitoring and crisis management functions of new CSCE institutions like the Conflict Prevention Center that is to be set up in Vienna.[6]

Crisis Consultation and Communications

Without the bonding element of the Soviet threat, gaining consensus and maintaining cohesion are likely to become greater challenges to NATO in the future. As before, it needs all the organizational and technical support it can get to facilitate alliance consultation and communication.

4. Jeffrey Simon of the National Defense University made this suggestion.
5. See Neil Munro, "BICES Gains Importance as Allies Look to Future, Official Says," *Defense News,* January 7, 1991, p. 6; and Tony Le Hardy, "Europe's Changes Threaten North Atlantic Alliance," *Signal,* vol. 44 (May 1990), pp. 151–54.
6. Commission on Security and Cooperation in Europe, *Charter of Paris for a New Europe, Paris 1990* (Washington, 1990).

Unfortunately, NATO has neglected this part of its crisis management apparatus. As recent exercises have shown, NATO's communications links between the nations' capitals often become quickly overloaded, leading to long delays. The technical facilities at NATO's main headquarters are antiquated by modern business standards and certainly inadequate to handle the extra load that would be placed on them in a real crisis. The key committees at NATO headquarters are also apparently understaffed and would quickly become overwhelmed and exhausted by their workload. While NATO's exercises are useful for familiarizing personnel with crisis plans and procedures, they resemble carefully choreographed rehearsals that follow a predictable path for those who participate. They do not try to simulate the uncertainty or time-pressured conditions of a crisis. Neither do they practice crisis resolution tactics or deescalation since their object is to go through the complete menu of alert measures.

NATO can help prepare for future crises by making the following improvements. The capacity of its communications system should be expanded so that it can handle the anticipated surge in demand in a crisis. The message-processing facilities at NATO headquarters should be overhauled and expanded for the same reasons. Similarly the system for transmitting messages and data between the key committees and departments within the headquarters desperately needs modernization. Computational support for NATO staff must be updated and standardized. At the same time, more attention should be paid to training staff to use equipment and facilities appropriately in crises. This emphasis means fostering a greater knowledge of communications security procedures and an awareness of the importance of brevity when sending messages to reduce the strain on communications.

NATO, furthermore, should reconsider the way it formulates and runs the HILEX/WINTEX exercises. In place of the canonical contingency of Warsaw Pact aggression, new, more plausible, scenarios have to be employed. A reintroduction of Soviet forces into Poland, an armed clash between Hungarian and Romanian forces, civil war in the Balkans, and conflict on the Turkish-Bulgarian border are a few possibilities. This task will not be easy, however, since framing suitably realistic and universally acceptable alternatives has proved difficult in the past. Non-country-specific scenarios may be the most practicable route to take as a way to at least familiarize officials with procedures and the potential dilemmas of crisis management.[7] Moreover, emphasis should now be placed on crisis resolution techniques and deescalation rather than on practicing the process of escalation.[8]

Besides improving intra-alliance communications, NATO should consider extending direct communications links from its headquarters to the capitals of nonmember countries in Europe. Special hot lines could be established between the principal military command centers in Europe to exchange information and prevent misunderstandings from arising in a crisis.[9] Certainly while Soviet forces remain in eastern Germany and Poland, it would be useful for SHAPE to have direct links to its main headquarters. Such links are evidently to be established bilaterally between senior U.S. and Soviet military commanders in Europe as part of the Dangerous Military Activities Agreement signed by the superpowers on June 12, 1989.[10]

Alerting

NATO's contingency plans for alerting, mobilizing, and reinforcing forces that grew up in response to the threat of short-warning attack must similarly be reviewed and revised accordingly. Greater flexibility has to be built into these plans to allow for a variety of response options to new, more likely, contingencies. These must take account of varying expectations of warning time for each contingency and varying levels of readiness for different forces within the alliance. As the current CINCENT, Gen. Hans-Henning von Sandrart, has acknowledged, the changing situation calls for "graduated military options in the fields of readiness and mobilisation, and also for available, ready forces of high flexibility, and of a multinational character, to signal solidarity. This military element of crisis management has to become an important part of operational art, and should receive greater prominence within our revised NATO strategy. We should also keep in mind that the welcome development towards significantly longer warning time is only related

7. James A. Winnefeld, "Crisis De-Escalation: A Relevant Concern in the 'New Europe'?" N-3153-CC (Santa Monica, Calif.: Rand Corp., 1990), pp. 18–19.

8. Winnefeld, "Crisis De-Escalation."

9. For a useful discussion of direct communications links see Phil Williams, "A Hot Line For Europe?" unpublished paper, University of Pittsburgh, April 1990.

10. See Department of Defense, "Dangerous Military Activities Agreement," news release, Arlington, Va., June 12, 1989.

to the classical East-West scenario, while more limited conflicts, which could involve NATO or its member Nations, could spring up at very short notice."[11] As indicated earlier NATO should pay more attention to how it can contribute to the satisfactory deescalation and eventual resolution of a crisis. NATO's planning has been predicated largely on a forward or upward progression of tensions and military preparations, with apparently little thought given to reversing the process. Thus for each of the contingencies that NATO considers, deescalation should become an integral part of crisis planning.[12]

NATO should also pay more attention to the problem of monitoring and controlling its forces in a crisis. As chapter 4 argues, there is considerable risk of friction and contradiction between the national and NATO alert systems, which is exacerbated by the discretionary authority invested in local military commanders to implement measures as they see fit. Although this situation is difficult to overcome in an alliance of sovereign states, NATO's central authorities should at least be informed of national alerting activities to help their own evaluation of unfolding events and the motives of other parties in a crisis. Alliance members, however, are under no obligation to report their nationally authorized actions to NATO. Furthermore, the system of monitoring and reporting the implementation of NATO-authorized alerting activity is slow and antiquated.

As a first priority, NATO should review the discretionary authority that has evolved in response to the danger of short-warning attack. Tighter or more centralized operational controls can be reestablished here as well as for the rules of engagement at different levels of military alert. The alliance should also consider ways to increase the readiness of its forces in an unambiguously defensive or nonprovocative manner to minimize the danger of unintended military interactions being triggered by misperceptions and misunderstandings.[13] As NATO and its members revise their alert plans, they should strive to harmonize them whenever possible. Finally, NATO should establish appropriate procedures and mechanisms for reporting national alert activities to a central registry at

11. Gen. Hans-Henning von Sandrart, "Change in the Central Region," *RUSI Journal for Defence Studies,* vol. 135 (Winter 1990), p. 56.

12. For an excellent discussion of this topic see Winnefeld, "Crisis De-Escalation."

13. For some useful ideas on this in the context of confidence-building measures see Kurt Gottfried, ed., *Towards a Cooperative Security Regime in Europe,* Cornell University Peace Studies (Cornell University Press, August 1989), p.107.

its headquarters. The current system for reporting NATO alert measures must be modernized to facilitate rapid information exchange.

Wartime Command Structure and Support Facilities

The expected reduction in forces under the CFE and the unification of Germany have necessitated a complete review of NATO's wartime command structure and planned C^2 programs, especially in the central region of Europe. NATO has declared its intention to replace the current "layer cake" arrangement of national corps arrayed along the old inter-German border with the creation of multinational or binational corps groupings. These arrangements will not only allow the alliance to continue to field units of militarily meaningful size, but it will also help legitimize the presence of national forces on foreign soil, notably in Germany. Greater integration can improve coordination and control over national forces in a crisis. Although at the time of writing the constituent elements of the new formations had not been decided, it is expected that four or five multinational corps will be established, with each one having a dominant national contingent. The forces making up these formations are likely to be maintained at different levels of readiness, with some capable of rapid deployment at short notice to other areas within Allied Command Europe, while others will require a longer period of mobilization. The ACE Mobile Force might be enlarged or become part of a new rapid reaction force especially suited for emergency operations.[14]

NATO's command arrangements above the corps level should also be reviewed. The existing army group—ATAF arrangements were appropriate when Germany was still divided and when a clear need for an intermediate-command level between AFCENT and the more numerous national corps existed, but now this arrangement is open to question. The long-standing suggestion that a European officer be made SACEUR at least on a shared basis will probably also gain more support as the

14. For further discussion of the creation of multinational corps see Michael Evans, "NATO to Reshape Army Corps on Multinational Lines," *London Times,* October 15, 1990, p. 7; Gen. John R. Galvin, "Dramatic Events Spur Change in the Multinational Alliance," *Signal,* vol. 45 (October 1990), pp. 23–25; von Sandrart, "Change in the Central Region," pp. 53–58; Heinz Schulte, "Finding a New Role for NATO in a New Germany," *Jane's Defence Weekly,* January 26, 1991, p. 113; and Karl Lowe and Thomas-Durell Young, "Multinational Corps in NATO," *Survival,* vol. 33 (January–February 1991), pp. 66–78.

presence of U.S. forces and U.S. nuclear weapons diminishes on the continent. More generally, opportunities exist for NATO to consolidate major headquarters, streamline their size, and improve their efficiency.[15] In the process, NATO's wartime intelligence arrangements can be overhauled and current deficiencies addressed, particularly the problem of getting urgent information that has been collected and processed by nationally controlled systems and centers into the hands of operational-level commanders who must make the vital decisions about the allocation of reserves and air power.[16] A multinational fleet of TR-1 or JSTARS aircraft along the lines of the current AWACS force would help greatly in solving the problem.

Aside from NATO's organizational structure, numerous command and control improvement programs under way before the changes took effect have to be assessed for their continuing relevance. Certain theater-related projects, such as the mobile alternate command posts for NATO's senior officers, the new communications satellite program with transportable ground terminals, the NATO Terrestrial Transmission System, the NATO Identification System, and the various CCIS modernization programs, remain valid although their planned scale can be reduced. Programs like BICES and ACCS, however, will require rethinking and significant modification.[17] The part of the ACCS program devoted to supporting offensive air operations should be deemphasized in light of NATO's greater defensive orientation.[18] For the reasons just outlined, many programs designed to upgrade operational-level facilities in the central region, such as the new hardened command posts for 2ATAF, the replacement or major upgrade to the Eifel data processing system, the CIP-67 improvement program, the Joint Area Communications System, and certain intelligence "fusion centers," are now questionable, certainly in the configuration planned earlier. Savings in these areas can be reprogrammed to upgrade neglected parts of NATO's command system, especially on the flanks. Projects at the tactical level, in contrast, seem less affected since they are not so dependent on a certain scenario. Thus the planned upgrades to national tactical intelligence assets, battlefield

15. Lowe and Young, "Multinational Corps in NATO," pp. 71–72

16. The need to deal with this problem has been acknowledged by the current CINCENT. See von Sandrart, "Change in the Central Region," p. 58.

17. See "Allies Grapple with Structure as Central Threat Diminishes," *Signal,* vol. 45 (October 1990), pp. 30–33.

18. Theresa Hitchins, "Reduced Warsaw Threat Forces NATO to Revise Scope of ACCS," *Defense News,* October 22, 1990, p. 6.

data processing systems, and communications programs (including secure voice equipment) should continue. It is hoped that the rising cost of command and control systems and the creation of multinational units will promote greater levels of interoperability and better liaison arrangements.[19]

In the competition for scarce funds, which has already begun as a result of declining defense budgets, some danger exists that command system requirements will suffer when the new priorities are set. Although the military value of command performance remains just as difficult to demonstrate in comparison with the more obvious characteristics of weapons systems, several arguments can be made for its growing importance. As force levels decline, the need for greater military efficiency and flexibility increases. The margin for less than optimal decisions on the concentration and employment of military force narrows as the forces available to defend a given piece of territory become smaller. Forces, therefore, need to be highly perceptive in detecting and accurately characterizing threats in time to respond and make offsetting defensive adjustments so as to deny an attacker an overwhelming advantage in one particular area. The availability of long-range, rapidly targetable weaponry presents opportunities to concentrate firepower with devastating effect, but this benefit can be achieved only with accurate and timely targeting information. These forces and the commanders who control them, however, must be highly responsive to the opportunities such information can provide and more generally to the sudden and unexpected changes in the threat. The increasing tempo of warfare makes this awareness imperative. These forces, moreover, must be cohesive, coordinated, and synchronized to exploit fully the capabilities of their sophisticated weaponry and optimize the efficiency with which they are employed. This capability is particularly important and challenging for multinational forces.

These qualities depend greatly, as this book argues, on command performance. Improving NATO's command system, therefore, is one of the best ways for the alliance to lower peacetime military readiness and still remain prepared for unexpected contingencies. With the current desire to reduce the profile of military activities in Europe, command system improvements can be considered less provocative or politically controversial than many other defense programs. At the same time,

19. The same expectation applies to tactical procedures and battlefield doctrine.

emerging command and control technologies hold out the promise of becoming real "force multipliers" in the event that military power has to be used. New reconnaissance and surveillance sensors capable of accurately detecting military threats at long range, day or night, and in all types of weather can reduce dramatically the uncertainty about enemy intentions. The unprecedented speed and capacity of the latest data processing systems will also allow commanders to quickly evaluate intelligence information and choose the optimal response from among available options, while novel communications systems will enable them to control and direct the activities of their widely dispersed and more mobile forces.

The promise of new technology, however, requires careful exploitation. The proliferation of intelligence collection systems capable of generating vast amounts of data runs the risk of swamping communications channels and decisionmakers with more information than they can usefully assimilate. The concomitant development of intelligence fusion centers needed to correlate, filter, and distill the profusion of data will add to the already strong incentives to centralize decisionmaking, which the advent of reliable long-range communications has already encouraged. Besides the added risk of falling victim to decapitating-type attacks (since this goal becomes not only more attractive but also easier to execute as headquarters become larger and more difficult to hide), greater centralization may also deprive local commanders of their initiative, overwhelm higher echelons with superfluous information and unnecessary requests, and ultimately slow down their reaction to events.[20] The peacetime performance and support provided by the impressive new technical devices can be dangerously seductive. Forces could grow dependent on equipment that may prove either too fragile to withstand the rigors of battle or too vulnerable to deliberate attacks by an enemy. The consequences of suddenly losing the support of what was previously taken for granted in peacetime could be catastrophic in war. Furthermore, care must be taken to ensure that new equipment is mutually and functionally interoperable, or it will simply compound the problems of command and control. Finally, the benefits of new technology will be compromised if the appropriate organizational and

20. See Richard K. Betts, "Conventional Deterrence: Predictive Uncertainty and Policy Confidence," *World Politics,* vol. 37 (January 1985), p. 162.; and Elmar Dinter and Paddy Griffith, *Not Over by Christmas: NATO's Central Front in World War III* (Chichester, U.K.: Antony Bird; New York: Hippocrene Books, 1983), p. 65.

doctrinal adjustments are not made to exploit it fully. As an Israeli military analyst has observed, "The most sophisticated C^3 technology may be of no help or might even degrade combat effectiveness if it is superimposed over a command and control doctrine and structure that does not provide the organizational flexibility and adaptability to make effective use of the new C^3 capabilities."[21]

The Long Term: Transforming European Security

Over the long term, peace and stability in Europe rest on sustaining political cooperation and economic development through a shared commitment to democratic values and free-market mechanisms. Although the primacy of purely military determinants of security is likely to erode with time, the importance and sensitivity with which they are perceived should not be underestimated. The countries of Europe are sure to exercise their sovereign right to provide for national security by retaining some military capability, if only for territorial defense. Left unregulated, however, the presence of national forces could become the source of apprehension and insecurity to other countries, as it has so often in the past. Indeed, as the evolution of Western Europe over the last forty years attests, democracy and economic development can flourish in a benign security environment encouraged by strong military ties. As a result, Western Europe has become what some people label a true security community in which the use of military force to settle international disputes is now unthinkable.

The entrenched patterns of cooperation that developed in Western Europe must over the long term be extended to Eastern Europe. This process has already begun with the establishment of the Conference on Security and Cooperation in Europe. Its collective commitment to the inviolability of current European borders and the peaceful resolution of disputes, as well as its promotion of human rights and political self-determination, provides the solid foundation for a true pan-European

21. For a thorough review of this problem in historical context see Ranaan Gissin, "Command, Control, and Communications Technology: Changing Patterns of Leadership in Combat Organizations," Ph.D. dissertation, Syracuse University, New York, 1979, p. 85. In relation to NATO see John G. Hines and Phillip A. Petersen, "NATO and the Changing Soviet Concept of Control for Theater War," *Signal*, vol. 41 (May 1987), p. 138.

security regime. Progress in this direction will, it is hoped, receive impetus with the creation of a permanent secretariat and special agencies for conflict prevention and election monitoring. Eventually the CSCE may become a true instrument for collective security, as many hope, though, as noted earlier, doubts exist about its feasibility. The adoption of ceilings for national forces and confidence-building measures for the region bounded by the Atlantic to the Urals provide another indispensable component to the establishment of a stable security regime in Europe. Last but by no means least, the European Community will clearly become a major and, most probably, the primary contributor to stability in the region. Consideration is already being given to enlarging the community to include countries of Eastern Europe, which will almost certainly take place over the next ten to fifteen years.

The stability of Western Europe, however, was not just a product of shared democratic values and economic growth or of the protective umbrella of the United States. A vital factor was the process of military integration fostered and manifested by various cooperative security arrangements and, above all else, by NATO's international command system. Though established for the purpose of resisting Soviet aggression, it proved highly successful despite its shortcomings in promoting cooperation among the national defense establishments of Europe. The cooperation ranged from collective defense planning and collaborative weapons procurement to joint training and the adoption of common operational practices. As a result, the latitude for independent military initiative declined while confidence in the benign intentions of neighboring states increased. This outcome was not an unforeseen byproduct but a deliberately conceived attempt by the proponents of NATO's command structure to make the armed forces of Europe so integrated and interdependent as to preclude "nationalistic adventures."[22] The Warsaw Pact's command system, though constructed primarily as an instrument of Soviet control, contributed to stability in Eastern Europe.

Given the integrative benefits of command systems, long-term stability in Europe can be served if new, more inclusive, arrangements can be established that include nonmembers of NATO. Initially such an arrangement could be organized around special-purpose multinational

22. See Department of State, *Foreign Relations of the United States, 1952–1954, Vol. 5: Western European Security* (Washington, 1983), pt. 2, p. 1381. See also pp. 1281–82, 1294–1366, 1475.

units such as a European Emergency Reaction Force for the purpose of disaster relief or even a European Peacekeeping Force. The military air traffic control systems of Europe could likewise become integrated.[23] Eventually it will be desirable to transform and broaden the current military command arrangements in Europe as the necessary political structures are created and invested with the appropriate authority. A new regional command framework under the aegis of the Conference on Security and Cooperation in Europe is one possibility that would allow NATO's current arrangements to survive, but in a different guise. Similar arrangements would be established for other regions of Europe. Probably the Western European Union will progressively take over the functions of NATO, including its command system, and formally become the security arm of the European Community. As the WEU expands, so too will its command system. What is not desirable is that NATO and its integrated military command arrangements become moribund. European security, as a consequence, could become progressively "renationalized" as states make their own provisions for security, with potentially destabilizing consequences.[24] To prevent a fatal relapse of this kind, the importance of command systems and the value of command performance to European security must not go unrecognized as they have in the past.

23. I am grateful to John Steinbruner for this suggestion.
24. This term is attributed to James Eberle, "The Utility of Military Power," *RUSI Journal for Defence Studies*, vol. 135 (Winter 1990), p. 51.

The Soviet Countercommand and Control Threat

BY ALL ACCOUNTS, the Soviet Union has developed a multifaceted doctrine for destroying, disabling, and otherwise disrupting NATO's command and control system. Known as radioelectronic combat (*radioelektronaya bor'ba*), it evidently encompasses a much broader range of activities than the Western concept of electronic warfare with which it is sometimes erroneously equated. More emphasis, for example, is placed on coordinating intelligence collection—particularly Sigint—with the various physical and electronic forms of attack.[1] Integrated attacks against every echelon of the enemy's command structure from the theater down to the tactical level is also evidently a feature of Soviet radioelectronic doctrine.

Though difficult to evaluate with any precision, Soviet and until recently Warsaw Pact capabilities to carry out radioelectronic combat against NATO can be divided into three broad categories: physical attack, electronic countermeasures, and deception.

It is widely accepted that one of the highest priority targets for Soviet

---

1. For discussion of radioelectronic combat doctrine see James T. Westwood, "Soviet Electronic Warfare: Theory and Practice," E Systems, Falls Church, Va., January 1986; Floyd D. Kennedy, Jr., "The Radioelectronic Struggle: Soviet EW Doctrinal Development," *Signal*, vol. 39 (December 1984) pp. 59–63; Capt. Jerome V. Martin, "Electronic Warfare and Soviet Theater Warfare Capabilities," in Richard V. Hartman, ed., *The International Countermeasures Handbook*, 9th ed. (Palo Alto, Calif.: EW Communications, 1984), pp. 335–40; Gerald Green, "Soviet Electronic Warfare: Maskirovka and REC," *National Defense*, vol. 69 (April 1985), pp. 34–42; and U.S. Army Intelligence and Threat Analysis Center, *Soviet Army Operations* (Washington: Department of the Army, 1978), pp. 5-79–5-83.

Frontal Aviation at the outset of a war is the destruction of NATO's fixed command and control systems such as wartime headquarters, radar sites, and communications nodes.[2] Besides air-delivered munitions, conventionally armed short-range surface-to-surface missiles, such as the SCUD-B, FROG-7, and SS-21, are also available for use—range permitting—against fixed and, if located in time to be targeted, mobile command posts and communications systems in the rear. Artillery is the primary threat close to the forward edge of the battle.

Another often-cited threat facing NATO's fixed installations in the rear is predeployed saboteurs and covertly infiltrated special forces known as *spetsnaz* units. Their most likely targets consist of relatively isolated and unprotected sites such as communications towers and switching centers. Assassination of key officials and commanders is another mission for these forces.[3]

Finally, NATO's ground- and air-based intelligence-gathering systems, particularly those that must operate close to or over enemy-held territory, are also expected to suffer attrition from SAM missiles and antiaircraft fire as well as air defense aircraft. NATO reconnaissance aircraft will also be vulnerable to attack on the ground. Antisatellite attacks against U.S. and allied space reconnaissance systems also cannot be ruled out.[4]

Jamming is the other principal weapon for degrading NATO's communications and intelligence sensors. According to one source, the Soviet Union has more than 2,000 jamming systems of various types for use against the alliance.[5] Specific information on the capabilities of these systems is scarce.[6] As in any countercommand and control activities, jamming entails some discretion and coordination with friendly forces. More specifically, some communications links may provide a rich source of intelligence on NATO intentions and therefore are better left unmolested. Unjammed communications also provide the opportunity

2. For the definitive study of Frontal Aviation capacity to carry out the independent air operation see Joshua M. Epstein, *Measuring Military Power: The Soviet Air Threat to Europe* (Princeton University Press, 1984).

3. See Matthias Plügge, "Stay-behind Spetsnaz: Soviet Forces in Germany," *International Defense Review*, vol. 23 (November 1990), pp. 1216–17.

4. See Paul B. Stares, *Space and National Security* (Brookings, 1987), pp. 128–31.

5. Office of the Assistant Secretary of Defense for Program Analysis and Evaluation, NATO *Center Region Military Balance Study, 1978–1984*, declassified Secret Report (Department of Defense, 1979), app. B.

6. See David C. Isby, *Weapons and Tactics of the Soviet Army* (London: Jane's Publishing Company, 1988), pp. 480–91, 372–73, for more information.

to spread disinformation and employ other ruses. Furthermore, "barrage jamming," which is evidently favored by the Soviet Union, could interfere with communications among friendly forces. Even without the presence of jamming, there is likely to be a great deal of "electromagnetic fratricide" from the multitude of transmitters of various sorts on the battlefield.

Maskirovka, or deception, is related to if not subsumed within the doctrine of radioelectronic combat. This practice can take many forms, including the use of disinformation as well as various elaborate methods for spoofing enemy intelligence sensors.[7]

7. Graham Hall Turbiville, Jr., ed., *The Voroshilov Lectures: Materials from the Soviet General Staff Academy* (Washington: National Defense University Press, 1989), pp. 297–98, 360.

Location of Major NATO Command System Facilities

Table B-1. *U.S.-NATO Communications Switching Centers in Europe*

Country	Location (function)[a]	C² node[a]
Belgium	Casteau (SHAPE PWHQ)	TARE/IVSN switch
	Evere (NATO HQ)	TARE/IVSN switch
Denmark	Viborg (BALTAP PWHQ)	TARE/IVSN switch
Federal Republic of Germany	Baumholder (serving AFCENT/AAFCE PWHQ)	TARE switch (access to Pirmasens ASC)
	Boerfink (AFCENT/AAFCE PWHQ)	IVSN switch
	Heidelberg (CENTAG/USAREUR PHQ)	IVSN switch
	Rendsburg	IVSN switch
	Ruppertsweiler (CENTAG PWHQ)	IVSN switch
	Rheindahlen (NORTHAG PHQ)	IVSN switch
	Senden	TARE switch
	Pirmasens	ASC
	Feldberg	AUTOVON switch
	Langerkopf	AUTOVON switch
	Schoenfeld	AUTOVON switch
	Donnersberg	AUTOVON switch
Greece	Athens	TARE/IVSN switch
	Mt. Pateras	AUTOVON switch
Holland	Brunssum (AFCENT PHQ)	IVSN switch
	Maastricht (NORTHAG PWHQ)	TARE switch (access to Croughton ASC)
	Oegstgeest	IVSN switch
Italy	Naples (AFSOUTH PWHQ)	TARE/IVSN switch (access to Coltano ASC)
	Coltano	ASC AUTOVON switch
	Verona (LANDSOUTH PWHQ)	TARE/IVSN switch (access to Coltano ASC)
	Santa Rosa (MEDCENT PWHQ)	IVSN switch (serving Rome)
	Mt. Virgine	AUTOVON switch

Table B-1. *(continued)*

Country	Location (function)[a]	C² node[a]
Norway	Kolsaas (AFNORTH PWHQ)	TARE/IVSN switch (access to Croughton ASC)
	Reitan	TARE/IVSN switch
Portugal	Lisbon (IBERLANT PWHQ) Costa de Caparica	TARE switch
	Oeiras	IVSN switch
Spain	Humosa	AUTOVON switch
Turkey	Izmir (LANDSOUTHEAST PWHQ)	TARE/IVSN switch (access to Coltano ASC)
	Ankara	IVSN switch
	Gelintepe	TARE switch
United Kingdom	Northwood (ACCHAN PWHQ)	TARE/IVSN switch (access to Croughton ASC)
	Pitreavie (NORLANT/ NORECHAN PWHQ)	TARE/IVSN switch
	Croughton	ASC
	Hillingdon	AUTOVON switch
	Martlesham Heath	AUTOVON switch

Sources: Larry K. Wentz and Gope D. Hingorani, "NATO Communications in Transition," *IEEE Transactions on Communications*, vol. 28 (September 1980), p. 1530; U.S. Defense Communications Agency, *Defense Communications System/European Communication Systems: Interoperability Baseline* (Washington, 1981); and Erik Klippenberg and Farooq Hussain, "NATO's Southern Region, the Mediterranean, and the Persian Gulf: Problems of Command and Control," prepared for the European American Institute Workshop on NATO's Southern Flank, the Mediterranean, and the Persian Gulf, 1981, Naples, Italy.

a. ASC, AUTODIN switching center; IBERLANT, Iberian Atlantic Command; LANDSOUTHEAST, Allied Land Forces Southeastern Europe; MEDCENT, Central Mediterranean Area Command; NORECHAN, Northeast Channel Sub-area Command; NORLANT, North Atlantic Area Command; PHQ, peacetime headquarters; and PWHQ, primary wartime headquarters.

Table B-2. *U.S.-NICS Network Control Facilities*

Country	Location (function)	C^2 node[a]
Belgium	Casteau (SHAPE PWHQ)	NICS Central Operating Authority (NICSCOA)
		DCS TCF
Federal Republic of Germany	Bann	DCS TCF
	Baumholder	NICS SCC
	Berlin	DCS TCF
	Boerfink (AFCENT/AAFCE PWHQ)	DCS TCF
	Kriegsfeld	DCS facility
	Oberursel	DCS TCF
	Gablingen	DCS TCF
	Langerkopf	DCS TCF
	Muhl (serves AFCENT/AAFCE PWHQ)	DCS TCF
	Pirmasens	DCS primary TCF
	Pruem air station	DCS facility
	Senden	NICS SCC
	Vaihingen (EUCOM PHQ)	DCA EUR ACOC
		DCA satellite system control office
		EUCOM TCF
	Wiesbaden	DCS TCF
Greece	Mt. Pateras	DCS facility
	Mt. Vergine	DCS facility
Holland	Brunssum (AFCENT PHQ)	NICS RCC
Italy	Coltano	DCS TCF
	Sigonella	DCS TCF
	Naples (AFSOUTH PWHQ)	NICS RCC
Norway	Kolsaas (AFNORTH PWHQ)	NICS RCC
Spain	Rota	DCS TCF
Turkey	Incirlik	DCS TCF
United Kingdom	Croughton	DCS TCF
	RAF Uxbridge	DCS system control office
	London	DCS TCF
	Martlesham Heath	DCS TCF
	Mildenhall	DCS TCF
		Silk Purse control group
	Northwood (ACCHAN PWHQ)	NICS RCC

Sources: U.S. Defense Communications Agency, *Defense Communications System Global AUTOVON Telephone Directory* (Government Printing Office, January 1986), pp. 33–39; U.S. Defense Communications Agency, *Defense Communications System*; and Joachim M. Sochaczewski "The Role of Communications in NATO," *Military Technology*, vol. 8 (June 1984), p. 152.

a. ACOC, Airborne Combat Operations Center; EUCOM, European Command; TCF, technical control facility; RCC, regional control center; and SCC, sector control center.

Table B-3. *PTT Cross-Border Links in the European Central Region*

Town (from)[a]	Town, Country (to)[a]	Type[b]
Belgium		
Antwerp	Breda, Holland	M
Bastogne	Luxembourg	M
Dinant	Givet, France	M
Herentals	Tilburg, Holland	M
Liege-Herve	Aachen, FRG	M
Ronse	Lille, France	M
Verviers	Gressenigh, FRG	M
Antwerp	Roosendal, Holland (2 links)	R
Arlon	Luxembourg, Luxembourg	R
Bastogne	Neidhausen, Luxembourg	R
Liege	Aachen, FRG	R
Denmark		
Felsted	Hamburg, FRG	R
Roemoe	Westerland, FRG	R
Aabenraa	Flensburg, FRG (3 links)	M
Blaabjerg	Scarborough, United Kingdom (Filey)	S
Thisted (Klitmoellen)	Scarborough, United Kingdom (Cayton Bay)	S
Federal Republic of Germany		
Bremen	Stadskanaal, Holland	R
Burscheid	Liege, Belgium	R
Hamburg	Copenhagen, Denmark (2 links)	R
Huertgenwald	Liege, Belgium	R
Leer	Smilde, Holland	R
Welschbillig	Luxembourg, Luxembourg	R
Flensburg	Lundtofte, Denmark	M
Freienwill	Aabenraa, Denmark (2 links)	M
Konz	Luxembourg, Luxembourg	M
France		
Charleville (Mezieres-Givet)	Namur, Belgium	M
Lille	Oudenaarde, Belgium	M
Maubeuge	Mons, Belgium (2 links)	M
Metz (Forbach)	Saarbruecken, FRG (2 links)	M
Metz (Thionville)	Luxembourg, Luxembourg	M
Mulhouse	Freiburg, FRG	M
Paris (Bouvigny)	Tolsford Hill, United Kingdom	R
Saint Lo	Jersey, United Kingdom	R
Lille (Loos)	Courtrai, Belgium	R
Metz (Thionville)	Luxembourg, Luxembourg	R
Nancy (Dabo)	Bad Kreubenach, FRG	R
Nancy	Saarbruecken, FRG	R
Strasbourg	Willstatt, FRG	R
Boulogne	Dover, United Kingdom	R
Lille (Loos)	Tolsford Hill, United Kingdom	R
Courseulle	London, United Kingdom	S
S. Valery Caux	London, United Kingdom	S

Table B-3. *(continued)*

Town *(from)*[a]	Town, Country *(to)*[a]	Type[b]
Holland		
Domburg	Duesseldorf, FRG	R
Mierlo	Duesseldorf, FRG (2 links)	R
Terborg	Bruenen, FRG	M
Venlo	Duesseldorf, FRG	M
Winschoten	Leer, FRG	M
Alkmaar	London, United Kingdom (Lowestoft)	S
Leeuwarden	Roemoe, Denmark	S
Luxembourg		
Dudelange	Luttange, France	R
Luxembourg	Kell, FRG	R
Luxembourg	Angevillers, France	R
United Kingdom		
Archers (Court)	Boulogne, France	R
London (Tolsford Hill)	Fiennes, France (3 links)	R
London (Broadstairs)	Amsterdam, Rotterdam, Hague, Holland (Domburg)	S
London (Broadstairs)	Oostende, Belgium (Mariakerke)	S
London (Aldeburgh)	Amsterdam, Rotterdam, Hague, Holland (Domburg)	S
London (Aldeburgh)	Domburg, Holland (2 links)	S
London (Joss Bay)	Brussels, Belgium (Middlekerke)	S
London (Burwick)	Torshavn, Denmark (Hvidenaes)	S
London (South Margaret Bay)	Veurne, Belgium (S. Idesbald)	S
Winterton	Leer, FRG (Borkum) (2 links)	S
Winterton	Wilhelmshaven, FRG (Spiekeroog)	S
Jersey (Fliquet Bay)	Saint Lo, France (Pirou) (2 links)	S
Winterton	Roemoe, Denmark	S

Source: Plan Committee for Europe and the Mediterranean Basin, *General Plan for the Development of the Regional Network in the Region Europe and Mediterranean Basin, 1986-1988-1991* (Geneva: International Telecommunication Union, 1987), pt. 1.

a. The location in parentheses is the landfall or connecting site.

b. M, metallic lines; R, radio-relay system; and S, submarine telephone cable.

Table B-4. *Major NATO-U.S. Fixed Satellite Ground Terminals in Europe*

NATO Terminals[a]

Kester, Belgium (master control center); Oakhanger, United Kingdom (alternate control center); Euskirchen, Federal Republic of Germany; Ankara, Turkey; Civitavecchia, Italy; Schoonhoven, Netherlands; Lundebakke, Denmark, Atlanti, Greece; Costa de Caparica, Portugal; Izmir, Turkey; Verona, Italy; Keflavik, Iceland; Bjerkvik, Norway; Catania, Italy; Hoenefoss, Norway; Perth, United Kingdom; Schmalenberg, Federal Republic of Germany

U.S. Defense Communications System Terminals

Croughton, United Kingdom[b]; Landstuhl, Federal Republic of Germany

Sources: Larry K. Wentz and Gope D. Hingorani, "Outlook for NATO Communications," *Signal*, vol. 37 (December 1982), pp. 53–59; William M. Arkin and Richard W. Fieldhouse, *Nuclear Battlefields: Global Links in the Arms Race* (Ballinger, 1985); Joint Tactical Command, Control, and Communications Agency, *Joint Connectivity Handbook* (Washington: U.S. Defense Communications Agency, 1988), pp. 6-19–6-23; and Maj. Gen. Giovanni Battista Pesci, "NATO Communications Systems in Support of Consultation and Military Command/Control," in *Information and Consultation: Keys to Peace*, proceedings of the Eighth AFCEA Europe Symposium, held in Brussels, 1987 (Brussels: AFCEA Europe, 1988), pp. 78–85.

a. North American– and Atlantic-based terminals for this system are located at Chesapeake, U.S.A.; Carp, Canada, and the Azores Islands. Lists excludes a mobile satellite ground terminal at SHAPE.

b. This terminal, along with Pirmasens, is a Defense Communications System high-frequency ground entry point.

Index